DREAM

Also by Mirin Fader

Giannis: The Improbable Rise of an NBA Champion

DREAM

THE LIFE AND LEGACY OF
HAKEEM OLAJUWON

MIRIN FADER

New York

Hachette Books
Hachette Book Group
1290 Avenue of the Americas
New York, NY 10104
HachetteBooks.com
Twitter.com/HachetteBooks
Instagram.com/HachetteBooks

First Edition: October 2024

Published by Hachette Books, an imprint of Hachette Book Group, Inc. The Hachette Books name and logo is a trademark of the Hachette Book Group.

The Hachette Speakers Bureau provides a wide range of authors for speaking events. To find out more, go to hachettespeakersbureau.com or email HachetteSpeakers@hbgusa.com.

Books by Hachette Books may be purchased in bulk for business, educational, or promotional use. For information, please contact your local bookseller or Hachette Book Group Special Markets Department at: special.markets@hbgusa.com.

The publisher is not responsible for websites (or their content) that are not owned by the publisher.

Print book interior design by Amy Quinn.

Library of Congress Cataloging-in-Publication Data

Names: Fader, Mirin, author.
Title: Dream: the life and legacy of Hakeem Olajuwon / Mirin Fader.
Description: First edition. | New York, N.Y.: Hachette Books, 2024. |
    Includes bibliographical references and index.
Identifiers: LCCN 2024021530 | ISBN 9780306831188 (hardcover) | ISBN
    9780306831201 (ebook)
Subjects: LCSH: Olajuwon, Hakeem, 1963– | Basketball players—United
    States—Biography. | Nigerian Americans—Biography.
Classification: LCC GV884.O43 F34 2024 | DDC 796.323/092
    [B]—dc23/eng/20240515
LC record available at https://lccn.loc.gov/2024021530

ISBNs: 978-0-306-83118-8 (hardcover), 978-0-306-83120-1 (ebook)

Printed in Canada

MRQ

Printing 1, 2024

For my family

You may happen upon it without realizing that this is the work through which your whole life will sing. We should always be ready. We should always be humble. Creativity should always be a form of prayer.

—Ben Okri, *A Way of Being Free*

CONTENTS

CHAPTER 22   Toronto   301
CHAPTER 23   Ambassador   311
CHAPTER 24   Mentor   325

              Epilogue   *333*
              Acknowledgments   *341*
              Notes   *345*
              Bibliography   *373*
              Index   *377*

DREAM

PROLOGUE

LeBron James arrived early to the gym, eager to learn from the legend known as *Dream*. By the time Hakeem Olajuwon walked in at 10 a.m., James had already worked up a sweat.

It was summer 2011, and memories of the prior couple of months still tugged at James. His Miami Heat had lost in the NBA Finals against the Mavericks, 4–2, and James had struggled to score inside the paint, avoiding the area almost completely. *The Chosen One*, as James was called, seemed . . . mortal.

Walking back into the tunnel at American Airlines Arena in Miami, he knew his game needed to change. Reggie Berry, now an NBA agent with AMR Agency but also friends with many in James's camp at the time, thought: *'Bron needs to see Dream.* Berry had grown up in Houston and knew one of Olajuwon's close friends, Frank Rutherford. He brought the idea of seeing Olajuwon to both Rutherford and James's team, and they all agreed: Olajuwon was just what James needed. To win a championship and to ease the sting of failure, James had to master the paint. And who better to teach him than the center who shimmied and shook opponents into oblivion with his signature move, the Dream Shake?

"I feel like at the end of the day, for me to become a complete player, I'm ready to get down there and be more of an efficient player in the post," James told Olajuwon on a group call. "I'm ready to make the change in my game."

That summer, James and his team drove to Olajuwon's gym, about forty-five minutes west of Houston in the small city of Simonton. The group soon realized this was no ordinary gym. Down a secluded, narrow dirt road lined with pine and oak trees, past a cracked driveway and miles of grassy land, lay the destination: Olajuwon's four-hundred-acre ranch. The Rockets Hall of Fame center had converted a former livestock barn into his own state-of-the-art basketball gym. His number, 34, was painted at half-court above the word *DREAM*.

This is where a number of players had come to learn from Olajuwon, including the late Kobe Bryant just a few years before. That even *perimeter players* sought out Olajuwon was a testament to how unique he was as a big man. He was nearly seven feet tall but operated like a guard, using his quickness, creativity, and mobility to outsmart taller opponents. Whereas most centers were slow and flat-footed, Olajuwon was nimble and graceful.

And he was still in immaculate shape at forty-eight years old when James joined him on the court that day. Wearing a bright orange tank, Olajuwon demonstrated catching the ball above the right block, then spinning toward the middle. Next, Olajuwon showed faking one way, spinning the other way, and finishing with a silky, fallaway baseline jumper. Over and over, Olajuwon completed the move, and then James attempted to copy it. There was no music, no fanfare; one could hear only sneakers squeaking and Olajuwon's command: "Again."

"LeBron spent three days there, but he struggled with it," says Ibrahim Arch, a close friend of Olajuwon's, who was present. "The moves are absolutely complex. They're simple, but they're complex, because it's all footwork." As James tried to find his footing,

Olajuwon realized how much pressure James had put on himself to win a title. "He was so determined," Olajuwon later said. "That pushes me, when somebody wants it so much and is so eager."

Olajuwon worked just as hard as James, sweating through his shirt. He didn't know how to teach any other way. The joy, for him, was in the *doing*. He stopped James between each move because no detail was too insignificant to tweak: ducking the shoulder, looking off a defender. Each spin, each fake, needed to be crisp. "It was like a masterclass in the nuances of basketball," Berry says. At one point Olajuwon and James paused, catching their breath, a smile emerging on each face. It was beautiful. Teacher and student, past and present, standing side by side.

James was finally mastering the moves. And by the next season, his game had evolved significantly. He had become comfortable—dominant, even—in the post. It was gratifying for Olajuwon to watch James win his first championship, over the Thunder in 2012. Olajuwon loved mentoring others as many had for him, including former Rockets star Moses Malone.

Today, Olajuwon's footprints are all over the NBA; he embodied *positionless basketball* before the term was commonly used. He played forcefully yet elegantly. He considered himself an artist, and his moves resembled ballet as much as basketball. "He was doing something different [that] no one could do, and no one could teach it except him," said Jerry West, who gave an interview for this book before he died in June 2024 at eighty-four.

Bill Russell changed the game with his defense. Wilt Chamberlain overpowered opponents with his strength and athleticism. Kareem Abdul-Jabbar redefined the position with his skill, talent, and sheer authority with the sky hook. But Olajuwon brought a different kind of dominance on both ends of the floor with his versatility. Olajuwon is the only player to win a championship, the MVP award, and

Defensive Player of the Year in the same season, and is one of just four players to ever record a quadruple-double. He remains not just first all-time in career blocks in NBA history but is also in the top ten for *steals*, a remarkable feat for a center.

"Let me tell you this: there ain't going to be another Dream ever in life," says Gary Payton, former Sonics All-Star guard.

Since retiring in 2002, Olajuwon has kept himself out of the limelight. Some hoops pundits seem to have forgotten about him, leaving him out of all-time-best-player discussions. "I don't think he gets the recognition he deserves," says Rudy Tomjanovich, his former Rockets coach.

Olajuwon, though, has never cared for nor sought recognition. And although he may be one of the most underappreciated modern superstars, younger players have long admired him. "The future generations, you look at when everyone was just struggling at one time how to score. Kobe, LeBron. They all went to him. They went to *him*," says Kenny Smith, Olajuwon's former Rockets point guard. "For me, that's the ultimate compliment, when the greatest players in the game said: '*You're* the greatest in the game.'"

• • • •

A BIG, BOOMING VOICE FILLED THE LIVING ROOM; HIS LAUGH WARMED the entire home. It belonged to Olajuwon, who was visiting his close friend Henri de Ybarrondo one night in December 2022. Olajuwon regularly visited Ybarrondo here in Houston. Ybarrondo, eighty-nine, was his former lawyer and financial adviser, but the two maintained a more personal bond, for Ybarrondo considered himself a father figure to Olajuwon. I happened to be there at the time, interviewing Ybarrondo for this book. Ybarrondo passed away in March 2024.

During his interview, Ybarrondo had sometimes struggled to speak: he had Parkinson's disease. But when discussing Olajuwon, the joy, the pride, in his voice was clear. He had a profound impact on Olajuwon when Hakeem stood at a spiritual and professional crossroads in the late 1980s. Olajuwon was materially successful, emerging as one of the best young stars in the NBA. But he was, by his own admission, untethered. Lonely, empty. Far from the serene, patient, sixty-one-year-old man of today, Olajuwon was getting ejected from games for fighting, unable to cool his temper, which spilled over off the court as well.

Ybarrondo recalled the concern he felt for Olajuwon, who was not even thirty at the time. "He was alone," Ybarrondo said. "Hakeem was a kid who came over from Nigeria. He had no one to guide him." Week after week, Olajuwon came to this very home, sitting in the living room, staring at the religious art and modern paintings on the walls, as Ybarrondo asked him layered questions:

"What do you value?"

"What does it mean to be successful?"

Olajuwon began to realize that Islam, the religion he was raised in, had mostly disappeared from his life. Since immigrating to America, starring for the University of Houston from 1981 to 1984, and then being drafted number one overall by the Rockets in 1984, he was no longer as observant. But after a period of soul-searching, and once he rededicated himself to Islam in the early nineties, he had found an anchor and an inner peace.

His game flourished, too; he became a two-time NBA champion and the 1993–1994 MVP. "He was an unbelievable competitor," West said, adding later: "I don't think I would have wanted to play against him and get embarrassed." Shaquille O'Neal saw that first-hand as Olajuwon and the Rockets swept O'Neal's Magic, 4–0, to win the 1994–1995 championship. "He was probably the only player I couldn't intimidate," O'Neal says. "He played the game the right way." That series shaped his view regarding his list of the all-time greatest centers. "A lot of people look at championship criteria, a lot of people look at stats, but because he beat me, I always have him before me," O'Neal says. "It'd probably be Bill [Russell], Kareem [Abdul-Jabbar], Hakeem, and then me."

In December 2022, when Olajuwon visited Ybarrondo's home, the two caught up with each other as they often do. Ybarrondo also had a few friends over, and they asked Olajuwon about the NBA recently renaming the Defensive Player of the Year award the Hakeem Olajuwon Trophy. Olajuwon just smiled and shrugged, deflecting praise, as he always does. Sometimes when he's at an event and a host is announcing his career accomplishments, he thinks the host is talking about somebody else. "He could never have imagined that [his career] would have [gone] that way," says Arch, also the former vice president of Olajuwon's off-court venture, DR34M. "He himself is surprised."

Olajuwon gave much to basketball but was never defined by it. Basketball was part of his life, but it was never his *life*. He had little to say about the award or the magnitude of the honor.

But before heading toward the door to leave Ybarrondo's home, Olajuwon asked about something he valued much more. He wanted to know one thing from me: "Did you go to the mosque? What did you think?"

• • • •

THE ISLAMIC DA'WAH CENTER, THE MOSQUE OLAJUWON FOUNDED and restored in the mid-nineties, lies in the heart of downtown Houston. Formerly a bank, the imposing space features elaborately painted decorative ceilings. The library on the third floor houses thousands of Islamic texts. Much of the place is finished in teak, Olajuwon's choice. He has a passion for architecture and design, and he is just as creative off the floor as he was on it. A platinum ball from the 1996 Olympics signed by Olajuwon, alongside the gold medal he helped Team USA win, sits in a nearby glass case. "He still comes here to study all the time," says Ameer Abuhalimeh, director of the center.

Olajuwon has been studying Arabic for years so he can read the Qur'an in its most original form. "Hakeem is a very, very competitive person," Abuhalimeh says. "I think that's part of his nature, to be competitive, and not only that, but he strives for excellence." He continues: "Hakeem is not [just] practicing Islam; he tries to practice it to the fullest."

Olajuwon is beloved by Muslims all over the world. Many fondly recall watching him regularly drop forty points while fasting during Ramadan, which commemorates the month of renewed spirituality for Muslims and the period in which the first verses of the Qur'an were revealed to the Prophet Muhammad (peace be upon him). During Ramadan, Muslims, health permitting, abstain from food and drink from dawn to sunset. While facing some of the most elite centers in the NBA, Olajuwon refused to take even a sip of water during Ramadan.

After those feats, Olajuwon would speak to the press about Islam openly, lovingly, raising awareness with non-Muslim audiences. Olajuwon's accessibility made him unique. He attended different US mosques on Rockets road trips, never missing the Friday *Jumu'ah* prayer. He was, and still is, deeply involved in the Houston Islamic community. "He walks in with humility," says Majid Syed, Houston native and Rockets fan. "Sometimes you can get caught up in the hoopla and say [to him], 'What do you think about this?' And then he goes, 'Brother, I'm here to pray just like you. Let's leave worldly things outside of the mosque.'"

Aman Ali, a producer and comedian, was raised Muslim in Houston in the nineties. His mother asked him to begin fasting during

Ramadan when he was ten. *Waking up at 5 a.m.? No juice boxes? No, I'm not doing that,* he thought. Then he saw Olajuwon on TV. A broadcaster noted that Olajuwon "wakes up an hour before sunrise, only has juice and oatmeal, and then has no water or anything else before sundown!" before dominating a game. So Ali began fasting.

Years later, Ali finally met Olajuwon and told him what it meant to see that interview when he was a child. Ali recalls Olajuwon telling him: "You have no idea how many people have come up to me and said, as kids, they saw that story, too, and that's what got them more into Islam and more into basketball. That, to me, is a greater blessing than any championship, and any trophy I've ever won."

Olajuwon has devoted much of his life to philanthropic work in mosques around the world, but those acts are not much heard about because he refuses to promote them. It is, he notes, against his religious beliefs to seek praise, for those deeds are between him and Allah. "He's trying to say, 'Look, it's not about me. I humble myself. I'm a servant,'" says Lynden Rose, his close friend and college teammate. "He cares about letting his life journey be his legacy, his story."

Olajuwon's example as the NBA's first African superstar continues to shape the next generation, helping usher in a much more internationally diverse hoops era. Recent MVP winners include Giannis Antetokounmpo (Nigeria and Greece), Joel Embiid (Cameroon), and Nikola Jokić (Serbia). And in September 2023, Antetokounmpo worked out with Olajuwon in Houston, the latest NBA star to seek the legend's wisdom.

Seven players of African or first-generation descent were selected in the 2023 NBA draft, including the number-one overall pick, seven-foot-four Victor Wembanyama from France, with ties to the Democratic Republic of Congo. Wembanyama is a generational talent, one who could reshape the NBA for years to come. In 2023–2024 there were fifteen players born in Africa on opening-night rosters.

Those numbers are expected to increase. "Hakeem opened the door," says Alphonse Bilé, president of FIBA Africa. "We call him the miracle. He was the pioneer."

Olajuwon's story has been framed as a *dream*like fairy tale and he himself almost as a mythical figure. Of course, he is neither otherworldly nor a saint. But his story, a powerful meditation on transformation and growth, has been less discussed as time has passed, as another generation has come of age. Unlike his contemporaries, many of whom have transitioned into TV broadcasting or coaching, building their brands on social media, Olajuwon continues his work quietly but meaningfully. He remains one of "the hidden ones," says Imam Suhaib Webb, former resident scholar at the Islamic Center at NYU (ICNYU) who now runs an online religious school that trains imams and religious educators. Webb is referring to a certain *hadith*, the compiled record of the Prophet Muhammad's (PBUH) life, words, and guidance: "Indeed, Allah loves the righteous, the pious, the concealed ones, those who, when absent, are not missed, and when present, are not recognized. Their hearts are lamps of guidance; they emerge from every obscurity into the darkness" (Al-Hakim, Al-Mustadrak, 3:270).

There is much to learn from Olajuwon, a hidden one who continues to guide.

CHAPTER 1

KING

HAKEEM OLAJUWON YEARNED TO DUNK. FOR WEEKS, THE SIXTEEN-year-old had been memorizing the proper footwork to gather himself, leap up, and throw the ball down.

But no matter how many times he practiced the steps at the nearby outdoor court at Rowe Park in Lagos, he couldn't pull it off. Sometimes he'd get nervous, rising to the rim but unable to jam the ball through at the last second. Other times, while focusing so hard on his footwork, he wouldn't elevate as high as he needed and would land flat-footed, deflated.

It was 1979. He was still very green. The late bloomer had been playing basketball for only about six months, picking up the sport much later than his peers. He was playing for Lagos State, a state team comprised of high school players from various Lagos club teams. "He couldn't dribble," says Dominique Ojehonmon, one of his former Lagos State teammates. "He couldn't do anything."

But Olajuwon, who has said his last name translates to "being on top" in Yoruba, the language of his family's background, had a gift that his teammates didn't: he was six feet eight, taller than anyone else in his school, in his neighborhood.

It was a gift that up to this point he had not come to fully embrace. Strangers stopped and gawked at the teenage Olajuwon as he walked down the street. The attention made him uncomfortable, so he tried to shorten his frame by slouching to the height of his teammates. "Bending, bending, bending," says Ganiyu Otenigbade, Olajuwon's former Lagos State coach. Otenigbade, now seventy-seven, laughs, remembering how Olajuwon tried to hide: "Hakeem [was] the shyest kind of person."

But on the court, Hakeem soon learned he couldn't afford to be shy. He couldn't shrink. He was too busy playing catch-up. What he lacked in experience he made up for with heart; Olajuwon didn't quit on plays, especially when struggling to master a move, in this case the dunk.

During one basketball practice with Lagos State, Olajuwon and his teammates huddled under the hoop as Coach Otenigbade explained a concept. The team then briefly took a break. But Olajuwon, clutching a ball, seemed to have other thoughts. He eyed the rim as if by staring hard enough he might one day dominate it. Suddenly something in Olajuwon spurred him to . . . *go*. He bounced the ball hard, then rose to the basket, thundering in his first dunk, clean and commanding.

The gym fell quiet. His teammates looked at one another. *Did . . . he . . . just . . . ?* A chorus broke out: "Hakeem dunked! Hakeem dunked!" Olajuwon was thrilled. "From that day onward," says Gbade Olatona, another former teammate, "almost any ball that Hakeem [got] was a dunk."

Soon Olajuwon looked as if he had been dunking for years. His body seemed pulled by some instinct, some power that had lain dormant, bottled, and waiting to be unsealed. Otenigbade smiled, watching Olajuwon learn to harness that power, day after day. This is what he had envisioned back when he had spent months trying to convince Olajuwon to quit handball, an emerging sport in Nigeria that he had taken to, and give basketball a try. Each time, Olajuwon politely resisted.

Olajuwon simply had no interest in hoops.

But after he dunked that ball and eventually committed to the sport, his life would take on a surreal quality. The novice who only reluctantly started playing at sixteen would somehow become one of the greatest basketball players *ever*? It was a . . . *dream.*

"He's destined to be where he is today," Otenigbade says. Growing up, Olajuwon never thought about playing in the NBA. For him, basketball was not a vehicle to *get somewhere. Be somebody.* All he knew was that unbridled joy coursed through him when he hammered home the ball with such force that Rowe Park's metal-chained nets would rattle for several seconds after each blast.

· · · ·

As a child, Olajuwon played every sport *EXCEPT* basketball: football (soccer), handball, field hockey, track, volleyball, table tennis. Anytime there was a competition, Olajuwon was there. Many boys like him began playing football almost as soon as they could walk, as natural as one's first breath. It had long been the dominant sport of the African continent.

Olajuwon and his classmates would watch weekly telecasts of British football—and sometimes clips of Brazilian legend Pelé. In 1977 they witnessed one of the most upsetting defeats in Nigerian football history, a 1–0 loss to Tunisia in Lagos. Had the team tied, Nigeria would likely have made the 1978 World Cup. Shock permeated Olajuwon's entire neighborhood. Many internalized the loss. Olajuwon realized that football was more than a sport; it was part of the pride of the country.

Although Nigeria played basketball in regional competitions, it didn't play at the national level until approximately 1964, four years after becoming independent from Great Britain. Back then, soldiers from Nigeria's army largely represented the country at the national level, playing pickup games in the quarters of the Dodan Barracks, the official military seat where Olajuwon would later find himself playing against some of Nigeria's most talented players.

But back when Otenigbade first spotted Olajuwon, a high school junior walking by the basketball courts to get to handball practice one afternoon in 1978, he didn't know if the young man had any basketball skill: "I fell in love with his height." Otenigbade, who in addition to coaching Lagos State, served as the basketball coach at Olajuwon's high school, Muslim Teachers College, so named because it offered additional curriculum for aspiring teachers. He had previously played point guard for Nigeria's national team from the late sixties to the mid-seventies. He then coached various teams in Lagos, including assisting with the University of Lagos program.

When Otenigbade first caught a glimpse of Olajuwon, he asked some of his players who he was. "That is Hakeem," they said, "the one we've been talking about."

Olajuwon seemed reserved as Otenigbade introduced himself: "Stay and come have a workout with me." Olajuwon, respectful in the way that his parents, Salam and Abike, had raised him to be, turned him down. Otenigbade wasn't about to give up, but he knew that Olajuwon, like many of the boys he coached, was more focused on his studies. Olajuwon often had to sneak out to play football (soccer) in the street because his parents didn't approve. "Hakeem's parents were the same as most parents at that time," says Oliver B. Johnson, another coach who tried to steer Olajuwon to the basketball court. Johnson, now eighty-three, is considered the god-father of Nigerian basketball. "Coach OBJ," as he is affectionately known, served as Nigeria's first full-time paid national team coach, from 1971 to 1986: "They always thought that doing sports was for those who didn't really want to study. They were called *wayward people*."

Education was seen as the key to success; sports was viewed more as an extracurricular activity, one that could not interfere with one's academic pursuits. Many of Olajuwon's classmates dreamed of studying at a university abroad and returning home to a well-compensated job. Salam and Abike wanted that for Hakeem and his siblings, who included one sister, Kudirat, and three younger brothers: Akinola, Tajudeen, and Abdul Afis. He also had an older brother, Yemi Kaka, fourteen years his senior. The siblings were not competitive with one another because they were in different schools, studying at different grade levels, but Hakeem's older siblings provided an example of success. Kudirat in particular was "very, very studious," Hakeem later recalled. She ended up studying at American University in Cairo.

Salam and Abike, devout Muslims, instilled a sense of discipline and commitment. "In that house," Otenigbade says, "they put God first."

• • • •

OLAJUWON WAS BORN IN 1963, ALMOST THREE YEARS AFTER NIGEria gained independence from Britain. Salam and Abike raised the family in a bright-red, concrete, one-story, three-bedroom home behind a modest, fenced-in courtyard. They lived at 19 Bank Olemoh Street in Surulere, a middle-class, suburban neighborhood. It was a quiet, idyllic enclave inside the bustling, vibrant, cosmopolitan city of Lagos. Lagos was a hub of innovation, of culture. Of joy. Of honking cars. Of the traffic jams known as *go slows*, where drivers were helplessly trying to will the traffic to move. Everyone seemed to be going *somewhere.*

His neighborhood was a melting pot. Olajuwon and his family spoke Yoruba at home, but he was surrounded by many other cultures, languages, religions, and ethnicities: Igbo and Hausa,

Muslims and Christians, Europeans and Asians. He was proud to be Yoruba, enmeshed in the culture, especially when it came to fashion.

Teenage Olajuwon *loved* fashion, thoughtfully piecing together outfits. In a kind of game, he and his friends would try to dress in something so bold they'd be considered trendsetters. They enjoyed going to a popular spot called Keyside, along the marina in Lagos Island, where some of the world's trendiest styles could be found. "Growing up in Lagos," says former teammate Oritsejolomi J. Isebor, one "must be a good dresser."

Olajuwon and his friends also often spent hours plucking fruit for fun from trees behind the last row of houses in his neighborhood. Fresh mangos hung low, ripe enough to eat straight from the tree. Across the street was a makeshift, sandy football field surrounded by scrubby trees and a homemade goal that was made of two skinny poles leaning to one side. Olajuwon, a goalie, loved playing pickup games with anyone who dared to try to scoot one past him. It was easy for him, with his long, lanky body, to stretch one leg out and stop a ball. He also had the quickness to dribble faster than anyone, surprising defenders that someone so tall could move so fluidly.

The field was, in a sense, the center of the neighborhood. Parents could watch their kids playing through their windows. They were close enough to come out if any fights erupted. It was a small, tight-knit community, where everyone knew one another.

A short walk from Olajuwon's home was the National Stadium, home of the Super Eagles, the national football team. The modern multisport facility, where Olajuwon also trained, had indoor and outdoor basketball courts. It was a concert venue as well, which, from January 15, 1977, to February 12, 1977, hosted FESTAC '77, the Second World Black and African Festival of Arts and Culture. More than fifteen thousand Black artists, intellectuals, and performers from more than fifty African nations gathered in Lagos for the event.

Olajuwon and his neighbors lived so close they could hear echoes of Miriam Makeba and Stevie Wonder and feel the warmth of the community—of a hundred thousand people marching and dancing at the opening ceremony. *Ebony* magazine captured the scene in its May 1977 issue: "For the first time since the Slave Trade, *for the first time in 500 years*, the black family was together again, was whole again, was one again." It was the "peak of Pan-Africanist expression," wrote Marilyn Nance, the photographer for the US contingent of the North American delegation, in her collection of photographs from the event, *Last Day in Lagos*. "For me, it was all about imaging joy." FESTAC '77 symbolized the sense of unity that many felt in the country, the culture.

Years later, when Olajuwon attended college in Houston, Texas, and when predominantly white American sportswriters asked him uninformed questions that assumed Nigeria was nothing more than a war-torn, poverty-stricken nation, he was quick to explain the beauty of Lagos: the culture, the food, the fashion, the wealth, the music, the dance.

Fela Anikulapo-Kuti, creator of Afrobeat in the early seventies and a political activist, lived in the neighborhood. Late into the night from their bedrooms, some of Olajuwon's teammates could hear Fela practicing with his band, Egypt 80, singing songs about the stain of colonialism, maintaining Pan-African identity, and standing up to government oppression. From an early age, Olajuwon learned his country's history, the shadow of colonization. *Things Fall Apart*, by acclaimed Nigerian writer Chinua Achebe, was his favorite book.

Lagos, an international port city, pulsed with the steady rhythm of shipments being loaded in and out of the busy wharves. The port was so active that in the mid-seventies it was not uncommon for five

hundred ships to sit in the harbor, waiting to be unloaded. Olajuwon's parents worked nearby in their cement business. Salam and
Abike would buy bags of cement from foreign shippers, then resell
them to a wide range of customers.

Abike monitored the ships docking at Apapa Wharf, one of the
busiest ports. She'd hand out business cards to clients that read
"Mrs. S. O. Olajuwon and Sons, Dealers in All Kinds of Cement."
Both the cement and oil businesses were booming. *Time* magazine
declared at the time that "Nigerians can revel in their emergence as
black Africa's richest and most powerful nation—and a rising economic force on the world scene."

Olajuwon and his family lived in comfortable circumstances.
There was always a warm meal, likely featuring some of Hakeem's
favorite dishes, including *fufu*, a traditional African staple he'd
have with soup, and *dodo*, fried, sweet plantains. His family traveled often. Olajuwon would go to Europe, visiting his older brother,
Yemi, who studied abroad at Oxford. Olajuwon also had friends
in Italy. But the family wasn't particularly affluent. Things weren't
always easy when Olajuwon was younger. "We struggled like most
families, with modest financial resources," Olajuwon's father, Salam,
later said. "But we have always been a closely knit and contented
family."

One photograph in the family's home featured Salam's father
seated on a horse, wearing traditional Nigerian clothing (Olajuwon's parents also wore *aso okes* and *filas*, the traditional gowns
and caps of the Yoruba). Hakeem, who, for the most part, preferred to dress in what he considered Westernized attire, would
look at this picture often, marveling at his grandfather: how tall he
sat, how regal he looked.

Early on, Olajuwon had a skewed view of his parents' finances,
thinking they were rich because every evening after work, he and his

siblings would see them counting money by hand. He didn't realize their palms contained their entire life savings, stuffing each day's profits under the mattress, as he'd later recount in his 1996 memoir, *Living the Dream*.

But Salam would teach his kids about what truly mattered in life. "Our wealth is not material wealth," Salam later said. "Our wealth is born from the fact that every member of this family is his brother's keeper." That was especially true for Yemi. He always looked out for Hakeem, reminding him of three family tenets: "Face your studies squarely. Keep away from bad friends. Stay calm, collected." Yemi was educated, successful, and financially independent. Hakeem knew that he needed a similar work ethic to match his brother's success, but he wasn't as focused yet. Like any kid, he just wanted to play in the street. Olajuwon would later recall his parents telling him: "You're not serious. People who are going somewhere, who are successful, they work. There must be balance."

• • • •

As comfortable as his home was, political instability outside never seemed too far away. Three years after Olajuwon was born, two military coups in 1966 temporarily incapacitated the civilian administration and resulted in the death of prominent political leaders, including Prime Minister Abubakar Tafawa Balewa and the head of the northern region, Ahmadu Bello. The coups planted the seeds for Nigeria's deadly civil war, the Biafra War, from 1967 to 1970, between the federal government and the army of the breakaway would-be nation of Biafra.

By 1968, some historians estimate that more than a thousand Biafrans were perishing each day. The war would ultimately kill up to one million people and lead to the militarization of federal politics, ensuring that the army would continue to have a prominent role in civic life. As a result, with the exception of a period of short civilian rule under Shehu Shagari from 1979 to 1983, the military ruled Nigeria continuously from 1966 to 1999.

Olajuwon came of age as power continued to shift. In 1975, when he was just twelve, Nigeria had its third coup in under ten years. A year later, General Murtala Ramat Muhammed, the Nigerian head of state at the time, was assassinated in a failed coup attempt. Olajuwon later recalled being fearful: "They were killing people at the top of the government on their way to work. If you were going to work, you might mistakenly get hurt. So everybody went back home."

In some ways, the country seemed far from the optimistic views that prevailed prior to independence. "The possibilities for us were endless, at least so it seemed at the time," Achebe wrote in his memoir, referring to earlier days.

Olajuwon poured his energy into his studies. He attended boarding school, a vestige of British colonization. In secondary school his teachers barred students from speaking any other language but English, the national language of Nigeria. Olajuwon saw a big sign that said: "Speaking vernacular is totally prohibited." That's when Olajuwon realized Yoruba wasn't welcome. Students were charged the equivalent of a dime each time they spoke Nigerian languages in class.

The language, however, was welcome at home. "He was a child that was properly brought up," says Tari O. Preh, a former teammate who currently serves as financial secretary/treasurer of the Basketball Coaches Association of Nigeria (BCAN). When Preh went to Olajuwon's home, he noticed that "the discipline is there." Olajuwon's family "didn't go out, and stay nights out."

Olajuwon's parents sought to teach him Islamic values, including sincerity, honesty, humility, confidence, respect, selflessness, and compassion. They also taught him that "prayer is the answer," recalls Otenigbade, Olajuwon's former coach. They didn't "enforce Islam" on him and his siblings, as Olajuwon later recalled, but he learned Islamic culture and ethics from a young age.

As a boy, Hakeem noticed people preparing to perform *hajj*, the annual pilgrimage to Mecca that Muslims are obligated to make once in their lifetime if they are physically and financially able (Salam and Abike were both able to make the pilgrimage). Olajuwon attended the local mosque with his parents but wasn't yet as devout as they were. Sometimes he'd wake up before sunrise and find his mother kneeling on her prayer mat. No matter how long the previous day had been, she didn't let the sun beat her. Even on weekends, she knelt; she prayed. He was amazed at her commitment. *What kind of religion is that?* he'd wonder, knowing he didn't yet have such patience.

His parents fasted during Ramadan. Olajuwon and some of his young friends tried their hardest to fast, viewing it as a challenge, but ultimately couldn't last until sunset. Abike would allow them to break their fast early, acknowledging their efforts in lasting through the morning. The family would have a big celebration for Eid al-Fitr, commemorating the end of Ramadan. They dressed in their best traditional attire, boasting bright colors and patterns.

On Fridays, when Olajuwon would walk to school in the morning, he could hear radios outside blasting the recitation of the Qur'an, melodically reciting the verses in Arabic. He most loved hearing the Call to Prayer, or *Adhan*. As Olajuwon would later recount in his memoir, he was so moved by the sound that he'd stop and wait to hear it in its entirety, relishing the way the caller would extend his voice, making each note linger. The rhythms comforted him and those around him. He would see people just as entranced, a beautiful and powerful mass of worshippers allowing themselves a brief respite from the hustle of the day.

• • • •

BUT MANY TIMES, OLAJUWON FELT ANYTHING BUT COMFORTED. He just wanted to fit in, to look like the students around him, but that was nearly impossible; the teenager was already much taller than even most adults. "When he is walking on the street, it's like a show. 'Hey, who is this man up there walking on the street?' It was surprising," says Peter Nelson, a former teammate who currently serves as director of the Nigeria Federal Ministry of Youth and Sports Development. It seemed natural that he would be tall—his father was six feet three, and his mother was six feet even—but that was no consolation.

Hakeem felt so embarrassed in class he'd slink to his seat, not standing up until class ended. He dreaded lining up for prayer before school because everyone noticed a steady line of heads and then . . . Olajuwon, two, three heads above everyone else. It was humiliating, but he couldn't skip school; everyone would notice that, too.

As Coach Otenigbade observed early on, Olajuwon was painfully shy. That was evident in the classroom, too. He'd get nervous when teachers called on him to read a passage and more so when they'd ask him to stand and read. The kids were merciless, calling him "dongo," a slur that he said means "freak." He felt he had to defend himself and would constantly get in fights. He was known as a bit of a troublemaker, but he was just trying to hold his own.

Sometimes when he was alone, he'd plant himself under the shade of a tree and cry. *Why am I such a freak?* he'd think. *Why can't I be like everyone else?* "I was so out of place," Olajuwon said later in life. "Sometimes, I would be ashamed of being so tall."

Once, his parents found him slouching near the doorway of their home so no one would see that he was taller than the frame. Salam, sensing his discomfort, reminded him where he came from. *Who* he came from. "Stand tall in the Nigerian culture," Salam said, explaining that the traditional clothes he and his siblings wore to the mosque looked just right on a man of his stature. Such a man, his father reassured him, was unique. Born to be a leader. Such a man should be proud of his gifts, not ashamed.

"When robes hang from such a man," Salam said, "he looks like a king, and is treated with respect."

CHAPTER 2

CENTER

A GROWING NUMBER OF COACHES KEPT NUDGING OLAJUWON TO play basketball. Coach Otenigbade, from Lagos State and Muslim Teachers College, wasn't the only one who saw Olajuwon's potential. Coach OBJ, the national team coach, would notice Olajuwon walking to school each day because he happened to live nearby. He, too, was captivated by Olajuwon's height.

Coach OBJ was focused on finding talent and on spreading hoops throughout Nigeria. He'd drive to neighborhoods in his VW Beetle painted green, white, green, Nigeria's national flag colors, stopping kids on the street and asking if they'd want to try out basketball. "Sometimes they responded, sometimes they didn't," he recalls.

He finally approached Olajuwon to see if he wanted to start training with him, with the hopes of eventually having Olajuwon join the national team system. The teen brushed him off and did so again and again as Johnson kept trying. It felt like a losing battle. "The focus was on studying," Coach OBJ says.

Another local coach, Agboola Pinheiro, made his own attempt with Olajuwon. Pinheiro hoped Olajuwon might join his top-tier team, the Leventis Buffaloes. Like Lagos State, the Buffaloes played other competitive teams throughout Nigeria.

Pinheiro, a former elite player on Nigeria's national team himself, first spotted Olajuwon at the National Stadium on his way to handball practice. "Please, can you come closer to me?" Pinheiro, now seventy-two, recalls saying, "How tall are you?" Olajuwon told him he was somewhere between six feet eight and six feet nine. Pinheiro was only six feet four but had played as a center.

"Would you like to play basketball?" Pinheiro asked.

"No. Basketball is too tough and rough," Pinheiro remembers Olajuwon saying.

At the time, Olajuwon was more interested in handball. And his family was a bit wary of allowing him to play any sport. Yemi, Hakeem's older brother, was also concerned about the coaches' motives. "They just want to use you," he'd tell Hakeem.

Olajuwon wasn't as concerned. He just wanted to *compete*. He had just started playing handball more seriously. The game, which involved basketball-like movements of dribbling, passing, and shooting, seemed tailored to his strengths. His long arms and big hands allowed him to throw the ball far above his opponents' heads. His quick feet helped him twist and turn around the court as if he were dancing.

Players could hold on to the ball for only three seconds, so he learned to be decisive with his targets and sharp with his cuts. He could fake and juke defenders, scoring whenever a seam opened. "We called him 'Hot Shot,'" says Gbade Olatona, his former teammate. "Nobody could stop him. When Hakeem held that handball in his hand, nobody could get near to where he held the ball."

But even though Yemi was initially skeptical, he wondered if Hakeem might have potential for hoops. Coaches had approached him in regard to Hakeem as well, and his view was changing, so much so that he eventually helped convince their parents to let Hakeem play. Yemi assured them that hoops wouldn't interfere with his studies, which would remain the priority. Coach OBJ, who had gotten to know Hakeem's father, Salam, because he lived close to the family's neighborhood, also put in a good word. "His parents were disciplinarians to the hilt," Coach OBJ says. "[Hakeem] knew himself, if he didn't get his studies, that basketball and everything else would be a mirage for him."

Salam was dubious, but he and Abike finally let Hakeem attend his first basketball practice. "I had no choice but to cool down," Salam said later, "and pray for him."

• • • •

COACH OTENIGBADE HAD TO FIND A DELICATE WAY OF STEALING Olajuwon away from handball. He knew the handball coach personally and had to be diplomatic: "I [didn't] want it to look as if I'm trying to lure Hakeem to my side. So, I gave Hakeem all the freedom to go and play [handball]. I didn't mean to kind of force him to come. I wanted him to get interested because when you are interested in the sport, you'll *want* to be a part of it."

Otenigbade was a renowned coach in Nigeria and was dedicated to helping grow the game throughout the country. "Coach Ganiyu [Otenigbade] had an eye for picking talents," says Ayodeji Omotoyinbo, a Nigerian sports journalist who has covered hoops for more than thirty years. "He knew how to develop talent." Otenigbade also seemed effortlessly *cool*. He wore Chuck Taylor Converse All-Stars and T-shirts from American colleges.

Otenigbade's steadfastness paid off: Olajuwon found him one day and said he was ready to give hoops a try, but he would also continue playing handball. Under normal circumstances, Otenigbade wouldn't automatically add Olajuwon to the Muslim Teachers College school team because he was a beginner and hadn't yet earned his keep, to say the least. The season was also already well under way. "But in order not to trample his interest," Otenigbade says, "I said, 'OK. I'll give you room to go to Sokoto with me as a kind of exposure.'"

A tournament in Sokoto State called the All-Nigeria Teachers Sports Festival awaited in northwestern Nigeria. Otenigbade didn't have much time to tutor Olajuwon, but he demonstrated some basics. He walked inside the key, explaining the three-second rule. He showed him how to catch the ball in the post and hold it high. "Whenever they give you the ball," he said, "take the ball *up* because guards will not be able to get there with you."

Olajuwon wasn't exactly a natural. During his first game in Sokoto State, when the ball came to him in the final seconds, he didn't know how to properly shoot or dunk yet, so he simply tried to chuck the ball in. It rolled around before sputtering out. He was frustrated with himself. *I give up. I don't want to play this game anymore*, he thought.

But there was also a stubborn part of him that didn't want to quit, especially because Otenigbade kept reminding him of his potential. Olajuwon didn't play very much as the tournament wore on. His teammates weren't impressed by his talent but welcomed him anyway. "Everybody knew that, look, this one is an asset," says Olatona, the former teammate, "because he stood much more higher than every one of us." He also towered above the competition among other elite teams across Nigeria. (Each of Nigeria's nineteen states at the time had its own team.)

However, Olajuwon was astonished by his teammates. He watched them dribble, crossing the ball over between their legs, behind their back, without once looking down. It seemed pure sorcery to Olajuwon. *How can they do that?* he thought.

In the coming months, Otenigbade taught him the fundamentals of the game. Nothing flashy. "Perfect the basics" was the coach's motto. Otenigbade taught him that the center position is the sun around which everyone orbits. The paint was *his* to own. The center defends, scores, and, if he works hard enough, dominates. He could always control his intensity on defense. Otenigbade told him, "You cannot let anyone score." He also showed Olajuwon how to box out: how to put his body on someone and how to swing out his elbows if anyone tried to slap the ball away. It was as if he were saying *You have the right to take up space. You have the right to be tall.*

Olajuwon had spent so many years trying to slouch that being affirmed in this way was a bit shocking. Someone was praising him for what others had mocked. "This is an American game," Otenigbade told Olajuwon. "There are a lot of tall people there."

"Taller than me?" Maybe he didn't have to hide anymore. Maybe he could be . . . powerful.

Sometimes during practice, Otenigbade would break into a big smile. He saw beyond this moment, those airballs. He saw someone who ran harder than any person his height should be able to. But it was the intangibles that made Otenigbade "fall in love with him." It was the way Olajuwon listened. The way he respected his elders. "He's quick to learning," Otenigbade says.

But Otenigbade stressed that improvement would take time and that he would have to be patient. Olajuwon struggled, kept mixing up the footwork for a layup. He also lacked proper shooting form. And he was so skinny that he couldn't hold his own on the block. "I'm gonna just tell you straight up: I wasn't impressed," says Akin Akin-Otiko, a former teammate, looking back on Hakeem's early days. "But he caught on like wildfire."

• • • •

ALTHOUGH BASKETBALL WAS NEW TO OLAJUWON, THERE HAD already been a rich history of hoops across the African continent. Football wasn't the only sport.

Basketball was initially more popular in northern Africa, in Africa's predominantly Arab countries, as well as those once occupied by France, because of their proximity to Europe, where basketball was already blossoming. Egypt was particularly dominant in hoops, participating in the 1936 Olympics, the first time basketball was an official competition in that event. Between 1937 and 1953, Egypt claimed two medals at the FIBA EuroBasket, including one bronze in 1947 and one gold in 1949. And Cairo is believed to have hosted the first international basketball competition within Africa, in 1949.

Africa's predominantly English-speaking countries, such as Nigeria, began to play basketball much later, after independence in the early 1960s. Although the first-ever formal basketball game played on the continent is not recorded, missionaries and/or French, English, and Italian schoolteachers introduced the sport, according to Sal "Red" Verderame, an American coach from Connecticut who coached around that time in Sudan, Ethiopia, Ghana, Kenya, Nigeria, Côte d'Ivoire, and Senegal.

Verderame served as basketball coach for the then–United Arab Republic at the 1964 Olympic Games in Tokyo and helped the UAR team win gold at the Pan-Arab Games in Cairo in 1965. He was one of the first US coaches to come to Africa on behalf of the State Department, writing in his 1967 book *Basketball in Africa*: "The future of basketball in Africa is very promising. . . . There is no doubt that African teams soon will be among the best teams in international competition."

Basketball began to take off in the Central African Republic, Côte d'Ivoire, Senegal, and later in Angola, which would become a dominant power for decades to come. Once Nigeria's National Stadium was built in 1972 to host the second-annual All-Africa Games, a sort of Olympics, hoops began to spread in the country.

A crowd of fifty thousand roared as more than three thousand athletes from forty African nations marched in a torch-lighting ceremony to open the All-Africa Games. It was at that point the largest gathering of African athletes in recorded history. Throbbing drums and a marching band boomed in the distance as dancers flipped and cartwheeled across the pristine eight-lane, all-weather track. A twenty-one-gun salute echoed in the night air, and a thousand pigeons were released into the orange-and-red sunset sky. About a month before, Nigeria's military ruler, General Yakubu Gowon, had declared that the stadium was an "essential product of our development efforts and a symbol of our aspirations in the field of sports."

In the 1960s and 1970s, great Nigerian players emerged, such as Emmanuel Chagu, who is believed to be the first Nigerian to shoot from above his head (previously, players launched shots from their chest). Alabi Adelanwa, another one of Olajuwon's early coaches, was the first modern-day big man to play with his back to the basket. The late general Joseph N. Garba, a shooting guard for the Scorpions from 1964 to 1970 on Nigeria's army team, was also instrumental in growing the game.

Coach OBJ was another crucial voice. He was born in Washington, DC, but found his way to Nigeria in 1969 after serving in the US military and then the Peace Corps in Kenya. As an African American, he had long wanted to travel throughout the continent. He settled in Lagos and began to scour the neighborhoods for talent or, truthfully, for anyone taller than he was at six feet. "I was one of the tallest people in Nigerian basketball," Coach OBJ says.

"I knew the job was bigger than just me. All I was trying to do is set the infrastructure." Coach OBJ estimates that when he started his work in the early 1970s, there might have been fewer than five hundred kids actively playing basketball in all of Nigeria, which then had twelve states. (Today, there are twenty-five thousand active players, OBJ estimates.) He's still teaching the game throughout the country. "OBJ has been so important to all of us," says Masai Ujiri, president of the Toronto Raptors, who was one of those dreamers, growing up in Zaria, Nigeria. Ujiri had become the first African general manager in major US professional sports when he joined the Denver Nuggets in his previous post.

Coach OBJ constantly fed Ujiri stories about Olajuwon. "He was my first coach," Ujiri says. "He really identified with the youth and basketball players. All he wanted to do was develop the game in the continent."

But back then? "We weren't competitive at all," Coach OBJ says. "Very few facilities existed when I came in." Among other innovations, Coach OBJ introduced the importance of keeping stats among coaches in the area.

Many international coaches had an impact on the game in those early years, too, including Vladislav "Lale" Lučić, a former Serbian coach and player who began coaching the Nigerian national team in 1976. "At that moment, basketball was not that known and popular," Lučić says. "There were many talented players at the time I arrived, but the national team had no success in international competitions." Prior to his arrival, Nigeria's team would often fall to its fellow West African countries: Togo, Benin, Mali, Côte d'Ivoire, and Senegal.

There were other international coaches in Nigeria contributing to many different sports. American coaches had also been traveling to Nigeria and to other African countries since the 1950s and 1960s, on behalf of the State Department and as members of the Peace Corps. Jim McGregor, an American from Oregon, coached the Moroccan national team and the Central African Republic national team while also conducting clinics in Gabon, Senegal, and Nigeria. Mal

Whitfield, the three-time Olympic gold-medal–winning runner, was a foundational figure in sports diplomacy across the continent. The Hall of Famer worked abroad for four decades. YMCA missionaries also played a key role.

The Harlem Globetrotters also came to Africa, dazzling with their high-flying tricks and moves. Prevented at times from playing in professional leagues in the States, and treated as second-class citizens in the Jim Crow era, they became, as *Esquire* put it in 1948, "the game's most indefatigable travelers." According to Dave Zinkoff, the team's traveling secretary, the Globetrotters' appearance in Casablanca inspired "the most enthusiastic crowd ever to cheer the Globetrotters," which had played on nearly every continent.

Celtics Hall of Fame coach Red Auerbach and point guard Bob Cousy also traveled to Africa on behalf of the State Department in the early 1950s and 1960s, visiting Rabat, Tangier, Marrakesh, Dakar, Casablanca, Port Etienne, and more. Cousy left with an appreciation for the passion and intensity of the players. "Their interest level for the game . . . ," says Cousy, now ninety-six, "they were so committed to it. It was impressive."

Cousy and Auerbach were there for diplomatic reasons. "The State Department was interested in making friends," Cousy says. "I remember them telling us: 'We give them money, but they don't love us. But when we send the people from the arts or sports, it seems to make a stronger bond.' And basketball was just getting started." The State Department began sending prominent Black athletes such as Whitfield, the Globetrotters, and Celtics star Bill Russell, promoting a skewed image of how Black people were treated in the United States. The State Department encouraged them to reinforce an image of egalitarianism abroad, an image that didn't correspond with the reality in America, where Black people often faced discrimination, segregation, and violence.

Russell visited various African countries, including Liberia. "I found a place I was welcome because I was Black instead of in spite of being Black," Russell said in 1963. He eventually started a fifty-thousand-acre rubber plantation in Liberia because of his desire to live in "an America without discrimination." Visiting a class in Liberia, he was particularly moved when a student asked him why he was there: "I came here because I believe that somewhere in Africa is my ancestral home." He wept.

Kareem Abdul-Jabbar visited Nigeria on behalf of the NBA in summer 1971, when Olajuwon was just eight. It was the first time the NBA had been on African soil, planting seeds to germinate in decades to come. Abdul-Jabbar, then on the Milwaukee Bucks, traveled to Africa with teammate Oscar Robertson and their coach, Larry Costello, after winning the 1971 NBA championship. The twenty-five-day State Department–sponsored tour began in Algeria, then continued in Senegal, Mali, Nigeria, Tanzania, and Somalia. The visitors conducted coaching clinics and shooting exhibitions, and met with players and coaches.

Ahead of the trip, the *New York Times* wrote: "Basketball is the fastest growing sport in each of the countries on their itinerary." The United Press International (UPI) quoted Costello as saying how "enthusiastic" Nigerians were about basketball.

Abdul-Jabbar stressed to reporters that the tour shouldn't be interpreted as his being an ambassador for American policies and that he "opposed U.S. policies on Indochina and on racial matters." He also said he would decline an invitation to visit South Africa, given the nation's apartheid regime. It was a deeply meaningful experience for him and would shape his politics for years to come.

Many did not realize that the trip to Africa precipitated his insistence on being called by his new name: he had changed his name from Lew Alcindor to Kareem Abdul-Jabbar in 1969. Days before departure, he said to reporters: "Now that I am going overseas to represent my country, I would appreciate that courtesy." He corrected journalists who called him "Lew" or "Mr. Alcindor." "I have been kind of quiet about it until now," he said. "But now since I am representing my country as Kareem Abdul-Jabbar, I would like to get that respect from you, from my countrymen."

He felt pulled to Africa, viewing the tour as a "return to the fountainhead," telling reporters that he had studied African history at UCLA and long wanted to travel to Africa: "My grandfather was from the West Indies, but he spoke Yoruba and I think he came from Nigeria. . . . In a lot of ways, going to Africa is like going home." He also felt this trip was a pivotal step in his ongoing commitment to "the betterment of Black people," said his father, Ferdinand Alcindor, also interviewed before the trip.

Abdul-Jabbar and Robertson played in front of big crowds on the trip, including seven thousand in Senegal who "roared every time Jabbar or Robertson moved," according to State Department cables. As the Senegalese daily paper *Le Soleil* wrote, "It is very lucky and encouraging for us that the visit of the celebrities of American basketball gives us the chance to learn more, and to persuade ourselves that to reach the top we still need to work and persevere."

Coach OBJ spent time with the visitors, showing them traditional Nigerian food. They originally told him that they couldn't play actual games, given NBA stipulations. But on their last day they had a change of heart. OBJ made sure that Abdul-Jabbar and Robertson were on opposite teams. It was *supposed* to be a light scrimmage. "Kareem put on a *show*," OBJ says. Part of that might have been a result of a Nigerian player scoring on him. The crowd was ecstatic.

Olajuwon wasn't present, of course, and had no memory of the trip. But he would later learn about Abdul-Jabbar from his coaches and teammates. "We had access to television and NBA programming all the time," says former teammate Akin Akin-Otiko. And, fast-forward, one day Olajuwon would compete against Abdul-Jabbar and even be hailed as his successor as the next great NBA big man.

. . . .

TEENAGE OLAJUWON CONTINUED TO PRACTICE WITH OTENIGBADE, despite some early struggles. On occasion he would notice people on the sideline laughing at him, saying things like "Look at the big guy miss!" At times, Olajuwon felt ashamed, but he would tune out the noise and sprint back on defense. He would rise up, swat his hand high, and smack the ball down with such force that the ball would fly out of bounds.

Having finally pulled off his first dunk at practice, leaving his teammates awestruck, he started dunking whenever he could. The moves now came easier to him. Although he was still thin as a twig, easy to bump around, he brimmed with promise. He was naturally gifted, not just in terms of athleticism but also in his hoops IQ. He anticipated the exact time to rotate over to block a shot from the weak side. He had remarkable coordination and agility from playing football (soccer) as a child, as well as handball. "He was probably the best handball player in Lagos," says former teammate Dominique Ojehonmon, also on the handball team. "He was a workaholic."

That work ethic fueled him on the basketball court, too. During one hoops tournament in Akure, the capital of Ondo State, in early 1979, only a few months after he had begun playing, Olajuwon scored with ease, looking far more polished than he had in Sokoto State. "He was a different kind of player," Otenigbade says. The tournament's final game was physical. Opponents were fouling him, clobbering him every which way, ripping his jersey. Olajuwon's team had lost, and he was so furious with the referees that he asked

Otenigbade to talk to them. "Why can't you go to them and talk to them, to stop them from the way they are officiating?" Otenigbade recalls Olajuwon saying.

Otenigbade laughs at the memory: this young, inexperienced player, who could barely make a layup, wanted the referees to show *him* a little more respect? But it was clear to Otenigbade: Olajuwon was passionate, determined. He cared about basketball more than he let on.

At the same time, he was still practicing as hard, if not harder, for the handball team. His basketball teammates tried to convince him to leave handball and focus solely on hoops. "We had to try as much as possible to talk to him, to woo him to come assist us," says Peter Nelson. Nelson was the point guard, the one who'd most regularly pass to Olajuwon in the post, so he made it his personal mission to foster Olajuwon's commitment to basketball. He let him know that he cared about his progress, continuing to pass the ball to him in the post day after day. It wasn't because Nelson saw incredible potential, though. "We didn't see him as he was going to be a great basketball player," Nelson says. "But we wanted his height."

Playing both handball and basketball had its complexities. On road games, Olajuwon represented his school in both sports and therefore was toggling between what seemed like two worlds. Players slept in the school's dorms, so he had two rooms: one in the handball players' dorms and one in the basketball players' dorms. Often, when basketball teammates came looking for him, he was gone. "We were already resigning our hope to the fact that handball had him primarily," says Lagos State teammate Gbade Olatona. "We had to be patient."

That was evident at the 4th National Sports Festival in Oluyole in 1979, held in Ibadan. Olajuwon represented Lagos State in both sports. He'd play one game and then hop into a vehicle that would transport him to the other sport's game. He was often late because one game would end when the other began. "Hakeem was working like a superhuman being," Olatona says. "We'd be looking for him, thinking, 'I hope they bring this man on time.'"

Sometimes he even had to switch sports *mid-game*. "Both coaches wanted Hakeem, but they could not reach an agreement," says Colonel Sam Ahmedu (retired), who played for the Nigerian Universities team at the World University Games in Romania in 1981. He now serves as president of FIBA Africa's Zone 3, which includes Nigeria and a range of neighboring countries. "They [eventually] agreed: Hakeem would play five minutes of basketball. He will leave the basketball court and go and play five minutes of handball."

As fatigued as Olajuwon might have been, he never showed it. In a game against the Kano Pillars, one of the premier clubs in Nigeria in the 1970s and 1980s, Coach Otenigbade had a conflict and couldn't attend, so the late Sunday Osagiede, another one of Olajuwon's coaches, known as "Papa Jam," took over. With Hakeem's help, the team pulled out a gritty 64–63 victory. Local Nigerian papers printed a photo of Olajuwon and his teammates jumping, screaming, lifting Osagiede on their shoulders.

Olajuwon's mother, Abike, once reluctant to let him play, was beaming when he got home from defeating the Pillars. She could hardly believe it. She kept newspaper clippings about him, including a picture of him with his gold medal hanging from his neck. He had also won gold in handball at the same tournament. *Punch*, a Nigerian newspaper, took a particular interest in covering Olajuwon: one of its journalists, the late Ayo Ositelu, lived in the Surulere neighborhood. Ositelu followed Olajuwon's rise with pride, once writing that he was "our golden boy."

Opponents started realizing that Olajuwon was talented. He intimidated on defense, making guards think twice about entering the lane. He started toying with them, almost *letting* them blow by him, and when the ball handler thought he was safe, Olajuwon would come out of nowhere and pin the ball on the glass. He *loved* that feeling. His teammates saw how quickly he was improving. "He didn't come with the intention to come and play basketball," Nelson says. "[But] eventually he discovered that this was where he really belongs."

As his focus shifted from handball to basketball, Olajuwon began to play for several teams simultaneously. Now he couldn't seem to get enough of hoops. And his coaches from these various teams worked on reinforcing this newfound enthusiasm. Otenigbade, Coach OBJ, Pinheiro, Osagiede, and Adelanwa spent hours with him, working closely with Olajuwon so he would want to stay for good.

One afternoon after a training session, Pinheiro remembered Olajuwon coming up to him, asking: "Coach, have I done well?" It warmed Pinheiro's heart—how sincere, how earnest the teenager was. Olajuwon was humble around veteran players, too, such as Tari O. Preh, who had a strong, wide body that could challenge Olajuwon in ways his peers couldn't. "I was his sparring partner," Preh says. Olajuwon respected him, sometimes even carrying Preh's gym bag. There was still a shyness to him. "I just saw him as a kid brother that needed protection and guidance."

But Olajuwon wouldn't back down on the court. Another side of him emerged when the two would battle one-on-one. They'd play to ten, with Preh giving him an eight-point running start. Olajuwon would almost always lose. But as he became more confident, he would say, "Give me six this time." Then, a few months later, "Give me four this time."

Once, Olajuwon attempted to block Preh's shot, but with such uncontrolled force that he clipped Preh's hand, eventually leaving a scar. "The scar is still there, in the middle of my four fingers,"

Preh says. The future basketball star learned something valuable that day: blocking shots is as much about anticipation and finesse as it is about power; it's a dominant yet delicate act.

Looking back, one can wonder if Olajuwon would have stuck with basketball without the dogged encouragement and protective care of his coaches and teammates. "It was a community effort," says Akin Akin-Otiko, his former teammate, "because we believe that if one of us makes it, we all can make it. And that was the hope."

CHAPTER 3

YOMMY

MOST DAYS, OLAJUWON PLAYED AT ROWE PARK, AN OUTDOOR asphalt court in Yaba, Lagos. A modest scoreboard stood near one basket. Kids would hang on the metal bars supporting the backboard, watching their favorite local players. Adults would watch, too, huddled on the sidelines. It was *the* place to play both pickup and official games. To measure oneself against the best. "If you don't play at Rowe Park as a basketball player in Lagos State, you don't know how to play," says former teammate Dominique Ojehonmon.

It is still thriving today. "It's like Rucker Park in the US. It's where legends are built," says Oluwafemi Adefeso, a prominent African sports journalist living in Lagos and founder of Balls Activating Literacy Leadership (BALL) Africa, a nonprofit organization focused on promoting education using sports to teach life skills and advocacy. He also served as a project manager for NBA Africa and Nigeria developmental programs, as well as the Africa Court Refurbishment Program (ACRP).

Even rain couldn't keep Olajuwon and his friends from playing at Rowe Park. The only time they'd leave was to get food at *bukas* (small casual restaurants). Olajuwon began to emerge from his shell a bit and came to be known for his unexpected and quick sense of humor—a quality he carries to this day.

But there was a quiet focus to him, too. The now seventeen-year-old started to study NBA players. "All he dreamed was 'One day, I will play with Kareem Abdul-Jabbar,'" Nelson says. Olajuwon found himself slouching less at doorways, thinking less of shrinking. Thinking more of dominating.

• • • •

ONE AFTERNOON, ANOTHER COACH, RICHARD MILLS, SPOTTED OLA-juwon playing pickup. He was impressed with Olajuwon's coordination, even if he was still clearly a novice. Mills kept his eye on him.

The two eventually played one-on-one. Like Coach OBJ, Mills was an American, from San Diego. He had played basketball for Cal Poly Pomona in 1969–1970. Mills roughed Olajuwon up, but Olajuwon started holding his own. "Hakeem, you've earned your basketball," Mills said to him, giving him a brand-new ball in a carry sack. He believed that Olajuwon had enough promise to train with the national team for Coach OBJ, the primary national team coach.

The next day at practice, warming up in the gym before his first national team workout, Olajuwon was taken aback. Players were so big, so athletic. So experienced. So . . . unlike him. He had sprouted to six feet ten, but he was still a toothpick. His game was still limited to dunking and blocking shots. But these players could *shoot*. Score at will.

The national team players outplayed Olajuwon during practice. Sometimes they'd jump into him, Olajuwon's frail body simply bouncing off them and crumpling onto the floor as they scored. Olajuwon could no longer block shots with ease as he had done at the high school and club level. These players were far more seasoned, knowing they could get him in the air for a foul because he was so determined to block shots. But when Olajuwon fell to the ground, he didn't sulk. He'd pop right back up, ready for the next play.

Yommy Sangodeyi, known as "Yommy Basket" and considered Nigeria's best center, mesmerized Olajuwon. His jump shot was so pure that people were almost surprised when he missed. Every time Sangodeyi drained a shot, everyone would scream "YOMMMYYYYY BASKET!!!" Sangodeyi, six feet nine and 230 pounds, and about three years older than Olajuwon, was skilled with his back to the basket but was also strong and athletic. "Besides being a great athlete, he had a fantastic sense for the game," says Vladislav "Lale" Lučić, who had coached Sangodeyi early on in his time with the national team. "His best quality was his ability to constantly improve."

Sangodeyi, who was named to the FIBA Hall of Fame before his death in October 2020, was everything Olajuwon wanted to be: powerful, smooth, creative. Sangodeyi was extroverted and charismatic as well. That first practice, the introverted and shy Olajuwon was so nervous he couldn't get out the words to greet Sangodeyi. "To me," Olajuwon later recalled, "he was a legend."

Olajuwon would watch and study Sangodeyi, who also played for a team called Ogun Rocks. Sangodeyi told Olajuwon that he had patterned his game after Rockets center Moses Malone. Sangodeyi was an avid NBA fan, and as one of Nigeria's premier players, he had traveled much more than his younger teammates, learning more about the NBA and its best teams and players. "[Sangodeyi] was a good role model for Hakeem to study," says Gbade Olatona, a former teammate. "Hakeem knew that, 'Look, I have to borrow from this guy.'"

Sangodeyi took Olajuwon under his wing, helping him finally master the footwork for layups. "Yommy, of blessed memory, was the one who trained [Hakeem]," says Buffaloes coach Agboola Pinheiro. The two became inseparable, developing a friendship off the court, too. "They were almost like twin brothers," says Sangodeyi's wife, Delphine. "Yommy likes to always give back. If he can help somebody, he will. That was his personality."

Olajuwon became tougher, stronger. And he realized why these older players were so difficult to compete against. They weren't just basketball players; they were soldiers in the Nigerian Army as well. He'd watch them put on their military uniforms after practice, for many sessions were held at Dodan Barracks, the official seat of the military.

General Joseph N. Garba had turned the military base into a sort of basketball paradise in the late 1960s. Before then, the court was just a patch of sand surrounded by banana leaves. Around 1968, concrete replaced the sand, and outdoor lights were installed. Games ran until two in the morning. "You are driving your car on the road and you say, 'What is that light?'" says Colonel Sam Ahmedu (retired), the former Nigerian player. "People that never knew basketball, that never cared about the game, they would come out of curiosity to look at what lights are this, and they'd see people playing."

The competition was fierce. During one game, players shoved and elbowed Olajuwon to the point where he just walked off the court. Coach Pinheiro ran after him, setting him straight, telling him he couldn't let anyone get under his skin.

In another game, a tight contest in which Olajuwon's team narrowly held the lead with little time remaining, instead of slowing down and running out the clock—standard procedure when you're ahead—Olajuwon rose up strong for a dunk.

And missed.

Although Olajuwon's team won, he almost cost them the game. One of his older teammates chastised him afterward. Coach Pinheiro recalls him saying: "Why are you trying to show off? Is it because you're on the national team now?" Olajuwon let the words seep in. A few days later, he apologized. "Don't worry," the teammate said. "You're growing. You'll grow."

. . . .

OLAJUWON FINALLY QUIT HANDBALL FOR GOOD DURING HIS FINAL year of high school, dedicating himself to basketball. His coaches kept pushing him, laboring on the basics: grab the rebound, outlet the ball to a teammate. Don't put the ball on the ground. But Olajuwon kept asking for more advanced drills. "He was very ambitious," Coach OBJ remembers.

He also continued to play with Lagos State. The team was supposed to travel to Minna, in Niger State, for a championship. But the trip was canceled the day of their departure because they weren't able to raise enough money to cover their expenses. Olajuwon and his teammates gathered at teammate Gbade Olatona's home to brainstorm ways of traveling on their own. But hours later, everyone chickened out, picturing their parents' disapproval. "Every other state enjoyed the fact that we were not present," Olatona says, envisioning their relief, "because of Hakeem."

His reputation was growing. Instead of *him* backing down, *he* was now feared. Lagos State structured its offense around Olajuwon, allowing him to roam the key and score where he pleased. He became part of a pair with Peter Nelson, the point guard. They had natural chemistry. "They were like, how will I call it? Magic Johnson and Jabbar. Karl Malone and [John] Stockton," Olatona says.

But Olajuwon would soon face another challenge when Coach OBJ called him up to the senior national team for the All-Africa Games in Rabat, Morocco, in March 1980. The coach saw him as a project, someone to develop. He wasn't necessarily going to play much, but he would get valuable experience. It was a controversial decision, adding him to the team after he had been playing for only about four months altogether. It was practically unheard of. And he had also taken another player's spot, a player who was much more skilled and experienced. Olajuwon was the youngest on the team.

"I was not good enough to make the national team," Olajuwon later admitted. "I was lucky."

Olajuwon was nonetheless excited. *His first international tournament!* He tried to play it cool, though, knowing he was playing behind Sangodeyi as well as Pinheiro, who took a brief break from coaching to suit up for this tournament.

In the team picture for the tournament guide, Olajuwon stood in the back-left corner in his green-and-white team tracksuit. Although the suit was a bit worn, Olajuwon cherished it. "The sleeves were short," says former teammate Akin Akin-Otiko. "The legs were short. They just got us what they could get us." He adds that "we were proud to represent our country."

Olajuwon didn't play in the first game. But in the second game, for the first time in his life, playing against much older men, Olajuwon looked small. Some opposing teams had seven-footers. His confidence evaporated. About midway through the first half, Coach OBJ looked at his bench: "Hakeem! Go get Yommy!" Sangodeyi was in foul trouble. Olajuwon couldn't believe it. Deep down, he was afraid. Shocked. He didn't feel ready to play. His muscles were cold. He managed to score once and grab a couple of rebounds in his debut. But mostly, whenever he subbed in, he looked out of place. Despite Nigeria's win, Olajuwon was disappointed in himself. As the tournament wore on, his playing time dwindled. Still, opponents began whispering about the big man on Nigeria's bench who hadn't even been playing for a full year.

Alphonse Bilé, currently the FIBA Africa president, was then a star and captain for Côte d'Ivoire and was also playing in the tournament. He had never heard of Olajuwon but remembers looking the kid up and down and asking his teammates: "Who is that tall guy? Who is this *boy*?" He didn't look as if he could hold his own. Though tall, "when you pushed him," Bilé recalls, "you think that he's going to fall down. He was not the Hakeem we have come to know. Nobody can recognize him at this moment. Impossible. We were surprised that they put him on the courts because he was not a good player."

Olajuwon learned a great deal from the tournament. "We took him along to get experience," says Tari O. Preh, his former teammate. But Olajuwon didn't just want to come along for the ride; he ached to become great.

When he returned home from the tournament, the Muslim Teachers College principal called him to the morning assembly, introduced him to students, and told everyone how proud he was that Olajuwon had represented the country. Olajuwon was the first from the school to play for the men's national team.

Over the coming weeks, Olajuwon continued to study Sangodeyi as the two began dreaming of playing on the same NBA team one day. He saw how Sangodeyi played with his back to the basket and then gave the defender a certain *shake* that would lose him completely. Sangodeyi's feet seemed to move so quickly, spinning left, spinning right, before the defender even knew what was happening. Teammates called the move "gba-bi-ma-gba-be" in Yoruba, which they say translates to "to go this way, not the other."

It was magic. Music. A melody that Olajuwon would memorize and come back to in years to come.

* * * *

OLAJUWON CHALLENGED HIMSELF AGAINST PLAYERS OUTSIDE OF Lagos, joining the Ogun State team. They often faced ASOPT, the Central African Republic's U18 team, which featured three stars: Anicet Lavodrama, Fred Goporo, and Bruno Kongawoin. Against Olajuwon, the trio knew immediately they couldn't just run into the lane. Olajuwon, who belonged to a select group of Lagos State players called "Dan Blockers" because of their shot-blocking abilities, would swat the attempt away.

"After our first game, we feared him," Kongawoin says. "We said, 'Oh man, we're going to play against *this* player again? No way are we gonna shoot the ball!' Because anything that went up . . . went back to you. We felt like we were playing against three guys at the same time, but it's just one guy."

Goporo, about five feet nine, had never seen anyone as tall as Olajuwon. "He wasn't that advanced," Goporo says, but he noticed that Olajuwon had great balance. But he still lacked fundamentals. *The key to stopping him was to make him shoot*, he thought.

Off the court, Goporo appreciated Olajuwon's kindness. "Even when he became Hakeem the Dream that we all know, he was very nice," Goporo says. "Very sweet." Olajuwon became friends with ASOPT's U18 players, even joining their team bus and serving as an impromptu tour guide around Lagos whenever there was a tournament in town. Lavodrama remembers Olajuwon's generosity: he would sit near the front of the bus, pointing out each sight, the places that were meaningful to him. "It was awesome," Lavodrama says. "The way he was there for us—we didn't ask him to; he just wanted to be with us, for no reason. That was extraordinary. He wanted us to feel welcome in Nigeria."

Local colleges started to notice Olajuwon. Coach OBJ had moved north to Zaria, Nigeria, taking over as coach of Ahmadu Bello University (ABU) Zaria. He offered Olajuwon a scholarship, as did the University of Lagos. Olajuwon visited the University of Lagos, where he stayed with a former teammate, Oritsejolomi J. Isebor, who had begun to play for the university. "Without any doubt, he was going to be an outstanding college player in Nigeria," Isebor says. "Visiting my college dorm was like an inspirational move. He looked forward to attending the university."

But Olajuwon was also thinking about the United States for his education. That had been his dream since he was a boy, as it was for many in Nigeria. "They say if you don't come over here [America] and go to school, you'll never make anything of yourself in life," Olajuwon later said. "But if you come to America, you'll be a big success."

One afternoon, Olajuwon came upon a copy of *Ebony* magazine, the May 1980 issue, with Lena Horne, the singer, actress, and activist, gracing the cover in a radiant purple jeweled blouse. Flipping through the pages, he found an article about Abdul-Jabbar and Magic Johnson. They had just won the 1979–1980 championship for the Lakers. He knew of Abdul-Jabbar, but this was his first time seeing Johnson, then a rookie. In one photo, Johnson held the ball, looking to pass, wearing an expression that said to his defender "I dare you." The article mentioned how Johnson had a $30,000 Mercedes Benz and earned additional money from TV commercials. Johnson talked about having turned down a $1.5 million deal from the Kansas City Kings (now the Sacramento Kings) to stay in college.

The article was eye-opening to the fledgling Olajuwon. He hadn't thought much about basketball as a career. The world of turning pro, TV commercials, and big-time contracts seemed far from his. He simply loved the feeling of clutching the ball, backing a defender down, and dunking.

. . . .

A FEW MONTHS LATER, THE STILL VERY GREEN OLAJUWON WAS selected to represent Nigeria's junior national team in Luanda, Angola, at the prestigious September 1980 U18 Afrobasket tournament, also known as the African Junior Men's Basketball Championship. He and his teammates were excited for the chance to compete in the biggest tournament of their lives. Olajuwon also looked forward to finally competing in his age group; he would no longer have to hold his own against grown men as he had in the All-Africa Games in Morocco earlier that year.

Nigeria pummeled its first two opponents, Libya, 82–46, and Togo, 119–64. Every time Olajuwon caught the ball, people shouted: "Hakeem! Hakeem! Hakeem!" It was said in later media guides and articles during Olajuwon's college years that Olajuwon had a whopping sixty points against Togo. Although this can't be confirmed because there aren't any statistics available from the tournament or from FIBA Africa, Silva Candembo, a prominent Angolan sports journalist and author, was present at the tournament. He notes that given his caliber of play at the tournament, it's possible Olajuwon *did* score sixty against Togo. "Hakeem, to me, was essentially a scoring machine," Candembo says, adding later: "That Nigeria team was practically Hakeem plus four."

Angolan newspaper *Jornal de Angola* included in its coverage photos of Olajuwon jumping higher than everyone around him; one even showed him tapping the top of the backboard. He seemed to score at will in Angola. "It was like another spirit entered him," says Dominique Ojehonmon, his former teammate.

Nigeria then battled Team Angola, the toughest competition Olajuwon had yet faced; the Angolan team was just beginning to rise as a powerhouse. Angola's national team had been started by a legendary coach named Victorino Cunha, a white Angolan of Portuguese descent. The country gained independence from Portugal in 1975 but descended into civil war from 1975 to 2002. Many Angolan basketball players and coaches left the country, but Cunha stayed and rebuilt the team from scratch.

The team represented hope and refuge during the civil war that killed as many as one million people and forced nearly a third of the population of thirteen million to flee their homes. In the cataclysm of the Angolan civil war, basketball was religion.

Coached by Mario Palma, Angola defeated Nigeria 87–77 behind the poised shooting of José Carlos Guimarães, considered one of the best all-time Angolan players. Angola eventually won the tournament, defeating the Central African Republic team in overtime, to claim the first hoops title in Angolan history. "The emotion was unleashed, infecting an entire country," Candembo says. The 1980 Afrobasket was a "transcendental event for Angola."

But it was also Olajuwon's coming-out party. Nelson Ferreira, then the captain of Angola's team, was struck by Olajuwon's fluidity in the post. "He already moved with elegance," says Ferreira, who remembers Coach Palma telling the Angolan players, "We are the champions, but the future belongs clearly to number seven of Nigeria," referring to Olajuwon. "Although more than forty years have passed," Ferreira says, "I still maintain relationships with colleagues who remember Hakeem's [performance]. . . . The talent and potential were clear."

Olajuwon and Nigeria lost, 107–87, in the semifinals to the Central African Republic team, which included Lavodrama, Goporo, and Kongawoin. Lavodrama guarded Olajuwon tightly, proving to be the more seasoned player. They keep in touch to this day: Lavodrama recently sent Olajuwon a grainy clip from that 1980 game. Olajuwon had gotten Lavodrama in the air with a fake. "Good memories," Olajuwon wrote back. "Why you going for the pump fake?!" with a crying-laughing emoji.

Olajuwon helped propel Nigeria to a bronze medal, Nigeria junior team's first-ever medal in international hoops competition, defeating Mozambique, 95–90. At seventeen years old and just over a year into hoops, Olajuwon was named MVP, a stunning feat for a non-championship player. As Angola's minister of education, Ambrósio Lukoki, handed him the MVP trophy, Olajuwon smiled. Basketball was still so new to him, and he was already winning MVP awards?

Even *he* seemed surprised. The Nigerian magazine *Quality* captured the larger significance of the tournament for Olajuwon: "This was [his] break into limelight."

But life was about to change even more dramatically, in ways Olajuwon could not have fathomed. Central African Republic's coach, a white American named Christopher Pond, kept his eye on Olajuwon all through the tournament, and even before that. He had first spotted Olajuwon months before, when Lagos State traveled to Bangui, the capital of the Central African Republic, to play ASOPT U18's team in a club game. Pond was the technical adviser to the country's basketball federation and constantly scouted talent. Olajuwon intrigued him. He wondered how long the teen had been playing and if he aspired to play at the collegiate level.

Somehow, some way, Pond recalled, he had to find a way to speak to Olajuwon. After the tournament, he made his way to the hotel where Team Nigeria stayed, according to his own recollection as well as Olajuwon's. But the story of what they discussed that night in the hotel lobby and how Pond eventually helped him move to the United States would morph into urban legend in the coming decades, blurring the line between fact and fiction. And like the childhood game of telephone, as one person told the story to another, the story kept changing, slightly and then more dramatically, until the original version was almost lost altogether.

This part of Olajuwon's story—how he came to America and to the University of Houston—is central to his *dream*like portrayal. Yet to this day, the question of exactly how the previously unknown Olajuwon came to play for the University of Houston is shrouded in contradictions and competing narratives.

CHAPTER 4

TICKET

THE TALE BEGINS: ONE NIGHT IN ANGOLA, SEPTEMBER 1980, AT the AfroBasket tournament, Christopher Pond met Olajuwon at his hotel and explained that in addition to coaching the Central African Republic team, he was an American scout and coach working in various countries to teach the game of basketball for the US State Department. He had connections all over Africa, he explained, because he had worked in Liberia while in the Peace Corps. He thought Olajuwon had a great deal of potential, and he could help land Olajuwon a basketball scholarship at an American university. If Olajuwon's parents could pay for the airfare, Pond could do the rest.

A short while later, Pond gave Olajuwon a list of American universities, including St. John's, Houston, Providence, and Georgia, and told him he had arranged visits for him to see those schools. He gave him numbers for those coaches. Pond then took him to the US embassy in Angola, the story goes, and Olajuwon received his visa upon somehow proving to an embassy official that an American university was considering granting him a scholarship. He then went to the Nigerian embassy to get the official paperwork needed.

The tale continues: nearly a month later, October 1980, Olajuwon arrived in New York ready to visit the schools, beginning with St. John's. One problem: it was cold, very cold. According to the story, Olajuwon thought it was too cold and didn't think he could go to school there. He asked an attendant at the airport which city had weather similar to Lagos. The attendant said Houston, so Olajuwon just continued on to Houston two days earlier than he had planned.

From the airport in Houston, Olajuwon then took a cab to the University of Houston because Cougars coach Guy V. Lewis hadn't bothered to send anyone to pick him up. Olajuwon wasn't viewed as a prized recruit; in fact, no one had heard of him. Nonetheless, Olajuwon was able to essentially try out for the team and join soon thereafter, enrolling in the university and miraculously morphing into a superstar over the next three years, catapulting Houston to national prominence.

It sounded like a fairy tale, the personification of the *American Dream*. The press ate it up.

"Akeem is the dream in Houston," wrote the *Philadelphia Inquirer*, using the misstated name that Olajuwon failed to correct until well into his NBA career (more on that later).

"It was October 10, 1980, when this Cinderella-like story began," wrote *Ebony*.

"Olajuwon's life has been compared to a Horatio Alger story, only better," wrote *Texas Monthly*.

The *New York Times* wrote that Olajuwon had "poked his head seven feet high into the nippy fall air" in New York, feeling so cold that he *had* to adjust his airplane ticket to Houston: "Once again, climate has helped determine history."

Throughout his college tenure, details of Olajuwon's journey to America kept changing. More schools were added to Pond's original list. Then there was a cab driver who almost took him to the University of Texas at Austin because in Olajuwon's Nigerian accent, his pronunciation of "Houston" sounded like "Austin." The story became more convoluted by the month, and no one bothered, at least publicly, to question it. Part of the reason was that Pond, interviewed numerous times over the years by local and national press, told his side of the story a little differently each time. And Olajuwon, simply relaying information Pond had told him while in Angola, never fully addressed the contradictions.

Pond was an enigma, a complicated man who helped an extraordinary number of people before his death in 2008. Among others, he helped Lavodrama, Goporo, and Kongawoin, the stars of the Central African Republic team, secure scholarships to play for Houston Baptist University. To this day they have nothing but love and gratitude for Pond. They saw him as loyal, caring, and selfless, an international hoops scout ahead of his time. He preached dedication: players had to wake up at 5 a.m. and run twenty-five laps on the track before practicing. They say he changed their lives for the better. "I wanted to be able to sit with Chris and say, 'Thank you,'" Lavodrama says. Goporo agrees: "Chris made a huge difference in our career. I think he deserves a lot of credit."

Rob Evans, who later coached against Olajuwon as an assistant coach at Texas Tech, spoke with Pond a few times as he tried to recommend players. "His deal was not getting kids over here to make money off of them," Evans says. "He was in it for the kids, for the families."

But as Olajuwon became more famous, especially as he reached peak success in the NBA, Pond gave several interviews insisting on his role in Olajuwon's rise. He continued to introduce himself over the next few decades as the person who "discovered Hakeem Olajuwon." At the height of Olajuwon's collegiate fame in 1983, Pond boasted to the United Press International that "I had all these kids like Akeem lined up to come over there. I had a pipeline."

• • • •

DURING OLAJUWON'S COLLEGE CAREER, POND WAS DESCRIBED IN both local and national papers as a US State Department "employee" or someone who "works with the US State Department." The *New York Times*, as well as the *Baltimore Sun*, more boldly identified him as a "State Department official."

But a Freedom of Information Act (FOIA) request in August 2022 for this book revealed that none of those characterizations were accurate: "No responsive records subject to the FOIA were located." When asked for clarification—if no documents found meant that Pond had *not* worked for the State Department—the liaison handling the FOIA request responded: "A review of records in our office and the National Personnel Records Center, fails to reveal a record of federal employment or pay history for Christopher Pond. He may have been a Contractor, and our office does not maintain information on Contract Employees."

It's an intriguing admission, one that begins to cast doubt on Pond's account of his interactions with Olajuwon. Still, although Pond may not have been an *employee* of the State Department, that doesn't necessarily negate the possibility that he had connections within the department or within African basketball circles. "There are a lot of different people that work with or on the periphery of a US embassy or a diplomatic mission abroad that can loosely be described either as 'working for' or 'with' the State Department," according to a veteran US diplomat with experience in Africa. "Pond did not work for the US government, specifically for the Department of State, but that doesn't mean that he wasn't necessarily associated with the embassy. He could have been a contractor or a grant recipient."

The Peace Corps confirmed that Pond had served in Liberia in 1976–1977. And before his stint with the Central African Republic, Pond coached in Liberia, confirmed by one of his former players,

David Chieh, who played for the University of Liberia from 1977 to 1980. Chieh enjoyed playing for Pond. "He brought the best out of you," Chieh says, noting Pond's "fiery, competitive spirit."

But there were other oddities in Pond's narrative, most notably the list of colleges he gave to Olajuwon. To this day, articles surface every few years about the "St. John's weather story" with headlines such as "Did St. John's Miss Out on Hakeem Olajuwon?" It was even mentioned in ESPN's "30 for 30" documentary, *Phi Slama Jama*, the nickname for Houston's team that went to three straight Final Fours during Olajuwon's tenure. "Hakeem lands at JFK in New York, and St. John's is supposed to meet him. No one's there," one Cougars player said in the documentary. Olajuwon also mentioned in his own memoir that he was supposed to visit St. John's, recalling the information that Pond had given him all those years ago. He said that Pond had given him the St. John's coach's number to call when he arrived in New York.

This story has been widely embraced as fact, but the truth appears to be that St. John's never recruited Olajuwon, let alone planned to pick him up at a New York airport. Olajuwon never visited the university, either. "No one at St. John's University ever had any contact with Hakeem or Mr. Pond about Hakeem attending SJU," says former St. John's Hall of Fame head coach Lou Carnesecca, now ninety-nine, via his former assistant coach Carmine Calzonetti. Carnesecca adds: "I have been denying the story for years. We never recruited Olajuwon. None of that was true. Nobody at St. John's has any recollection of ever receiving a phone call—there weren't emails at that time—that Olajuwon was visiting St. John's."

Surviving coaches from the other schools on Pond's list made similar statements in interviews for this book. In many articles, Louisville was also on the list. In an interview before he died in May 2023, Denny Crum, the former Louisville and Hall of Fame coach, couldn't recall having any contact with Pond or Olajuwon. "University of Louisville did not recruit Olajuwon," Crum said. Gary Walters, Providence's coach from 1979 to 1981, says he didn't have any contact with Pond, either. And Hugh Durham, Georgia coach from 1978 to 1995, who is now eighty-six, says he had never heard of Pond and can't recall speaking to him.

Adding to the mystery, other schools began appearing on Pond's list as Olajuwon's star rose in college: Georgia Tech, Oregon State, and then Illinois State. Later, Pond added yet another school to his narrative, telling reporters he "thought about sending" Olajuwon to North Carolina State, where his brother, Nick Pond, had played from 1954 to 1957. And years later, Pond added that while he and Olajuwon waited at the US embassy in Angola, he had flipped a coin to determine whether he should first call NC State or the University of Houston. (He called Houston's Lewis, he said, and Olajuwon would later remember Pond telling Lewis over the phone that day that he "wanted to send him to America" and that Olajuwon "would dominate college basketball.") Still, Pond hung onto the NC State narrative, claiming he would have liked Olajuwon to play there, and the young prospect might have if not for the result of the coin flip. Of course, a United Press International headline followed: "Pack just missed Akeem."

Further complicating matters, Olajuwon *himself* later recalled the coin flip and remembered Pond telling him "You will like Houston." Or even bolder, Olajuwon claimed in a separate interview that Pond had told him that "Houston was where I belonged." But why would Pond say either of those things if he had arranged visits to other schools and flights to other cities? Was Houston the plan all along? (Olajuwon has said that he had plane tickets for not just New York but also Louisville, Houston, and Providence.)

It appears Pond could be an enigma even to his own family, according to Pond's lone surviving sibling, Jennifer Neis. "Whatever

Chris said, you had to take it kind of with a grain of salt," Neis says. "I don't know how much of it truly was real."

• • • •

SOMEWHERE ALONG THE WAY, POND HAD MET HOUSTON COACH Guy V. Lewis, who died in 2015. One article stated that Pond was an "old Army buddy." (Lewis had served as a pilot in the US Air Force.) Another article called the two "close friends." Vern Lewis, Lewis's son, who also played for the Cougars from 1966 to 1968, isn't sure where Lewis met Pond: "As far as I can remember, [Lewis] was doing overseas coaching clinics, and he met this gentleman in one of those overseas clinics."

More details kept changing: Pond later claimed that while he and Olajuwon were at the US embassy in Angola, Pond used a pay phone in the street to call Coach Lewis and had Olajuwon "running in and out of the embassy, cashing traveler's checks and we're pumping money into the phone."

Why did Olajuwon trust this man who he barely knew? "I didn't know [Pond]. I didn't know his connections, his contacts," Olajuwon later recalled. "So, I'm just hoping he can deliver." Olajuwon's parents weren't sure if Pond's offers were too good to be true, but went along.

One question bloomed into two. Two into three. But most reporters at the time didn't seem to investigate them. "Houston *loved* this at the time—that there was this mythical, dreamy thing about it all," says Brad Buchholz, who covered the team for the *Austin American-Statesman*. "That was way more fun to feed the writers than get to the heart of what happened. There was a certain clumsiness to that whole thing."

It became a frenzy. "Hakeem stories have lives of their own. It was hard to keep up with them," says Jay Goldberg, Houston's former sports information director. "Everyone wanted a scoop, *the* story."

Coaches within the conference did, too. "We thought, 'Man, who is this guy?' Everybody was suspicious of how he ended up there," says Rob Evans, former Texas Tech assistant coach.

Only one reporter, Remer Tyson of the *Detroit Free Press*, who eventually traveled to Lagos to profile Olajuwon in 1984, seemed to suggest some level of suspicion: "Just how Akeem got to Houston is open for dispute."

What *is* certain is the emotion that Olajuwon's coaches in Lagos felt when he left for America. Coach OBJ had thought he had a real shot at bringing Olajuwon to ABU Zaria, having spoken with Olajuwon's parents about the opportunity before the 1980 AfroBasket: "Two or three weeks later, I'm reading in the paper that Hakeem is in Houston."

Everything happened so fast. Olajuwon had just started to play basketball; now he was on a plane to play collegiately in America? Coach OBJ says that perhaps Olajuwon didn't tell him because he didn't want to seem ungrateful, abandoning someone who cared for him. The coach never felt that way. "It's not an issue," he says. He was proud of Olajuwon. So was Coach Otenigbade, seeing how much work Olajuwon had put into his game and how much he had grown. "Hakeem had acquired a perfect base [of] fundamentals before he left the shore of Nigeria," Otenigbade says.

Otenigbade, who currently lives in the suburbs of Lagos, about an hour's drive from the Lagos mainland, has a framed and signed Olajuwon Rockets jersey. Another wall boasts a photo of Olajuwon rising for a dunk. Otenigbade has kept old, black-and-white record books, ones that show a skinny, reticent, teenage Olajuwon.

Even though Olajuwon is now sixty-one, Otenigbade still refers to him as *young man*: "I'm very proud of the young man. Players go and play basketball and fall by the wayside. I'm proud of him because he *went* for it," says Otenigbade.

Coach Pinheiro was also full of emotion as Olajuwon prepared to leave for America: "My joy was very high. Hakeem was very, very excited."

Olajuwon was also a little nervous, a little scared. He remembered the emotion of his family and friends who came with him to the airport. They were happy for him, but they were unsure of what was to happen next. They were crying. He was crying. His parents gave him some last words of advice: Don't get caught up in bad company. Be a leader, not a follower. Stick with your principles.

He was moving to another country without knowing anyone. How could he trust an opportunity from Pond, a man he hardly knew—someone who, many of his former coaches to this day, *still* don't know much about? Perhaps his desire to study in America, to have that college experience, outweighed any lingering doubts. He had the proper documentation to travel, and that was all he needed.

Before he left, Pinheiro sensed Olajuwon's hesitation in informing him of his decision. "Coach, I've been given a visa," Olajuwon finally told him, stopping by his home. "I'm going to America. I have to leave."

The two held each other's gaze, neither letting the other reveal too much emotion.

"May God be with you," Pinheiro said. "I know you're going to make it."

CHAPTER 5

AKEEM

Donnie Schverak, a former Houston assistant coach, remembers sitting in the basketball office at Hofheinz Pavilion as Head Coach Guy V. Lewis kept glancing at the clock. "God, I hope he gets here soon," Lewis said. "I gotta go to lunch."

"Who is that?" Schverak asked.

"That kid from Africa," Lewis replied.

This was the first time Schverak had heard of "Akeem." Schverak offered to pick Olajuwon up at the airport, but Lewis said not to bother; Olajuwon would catch a cab. "He's probably only six six," Lewis said. Several international players had tried out for Lewis's team over the years, claiming to be six feet ten or thereabouts, only to show up at six feet one and with a mediocre game. Lewis assumed that would be the case with Olajuwon. "I never dreamed the guy would be able to play," Lewis later said. "I had never heard of anyone from Africa being able to play."

Lewis actually hadn't sent a cab because he wasn't expecting Olajuwon for two more days, according to Olajuwon, because Olajuwon was supposed to spend his first visit at St. John's. It has become part of the folklore, of how Olajuwon's tenure at Houston began, that Lewis didn't pick him up at the airport because he wasn't good enough or well-known enough to merit a ride. But according to this narrative, neither may have been true. It may have been simply that no one came to pick him up because no one expected him for a few more days.

Yet when Lewis, still inside the basketball office, peered out the window and saw Olajuwon step out of the cab in front of the building, his eyes widened. He couldn't believe how tall Olajuwon appeared. Olajuwon's elegant white dashiki and white pants elongated his frame even more. "I swear to God," Schverak says, "[Hakeem] just kept getting out [of the cab], kept getting out. It looked like somebody unfurled him like a flag."

"Donnie!" Lewis said, grinning. "Get your ass out there and get those bags!"

• • • •

As soon as Olajuwon saw Schverak, he bent forward slightly as a sign of respect. "No, no, no," Schverak told him. "We don't do that here." Olajuwon then rushed to the door to open it for his new coach. Lewis, who had come outside to get a closer look, called over Ralph Adams, a student manager: "Go get Akeem some running shoes."

Adams took Olajuwon to the locker room. "What size do you wear?" Adams said.

"I wear a size 13."

Adams looked down at Olajuwon's feet, confused. "No, you don't wear a 13."

"That was the biggest size that they had in Nigeria."

Adams handed him a 15, but even those turned out to be uncomfortably snug. Adams then gave him a 16. Olajuwon smiled. They fit perfectly. Adams gave him two pairs: a tan one for the track, a white one with a red Nike logo for the basketball court. "I don't know if I've ever seen that kind of relief on someone's face in quite some time," Adams says. "He was so excited about having a pair of shoes that fit him."

Adams took him to the field where his new teammates were running. They would soon scrimmage. Olajuwon sized them up, trying to imagine how he would compete against them. This was, in essence, almost like a tryout for Olajuwon. His place on the team wasn't necessarily secure; he still hadn't technically enrolled in school. A scholarship was still in question. Besides, the coaches didn't know what to make of him as a basketball player and how he might fit into the team. The players weren't sure either. Aside from his size, all they saw was the fact that he was painfully skinny. He didn't look as if he could physically compete. "No idea how he could play," remembers Larry Micheaux, the team's starting power forward.

"He could scratch his knee without bending his waist," recalls center David Bunce, who also stood six feet ten. Olajuwon was quiet, unassuming, bending forward once more to his teammates, this time tilting his head only slightly. Schverak came over again: "You don't need to do that. You're in the United States now. You're in Texas. You just gotta learn how to say *howdy*!"

Olajuwon didn't know much about Texas. He had expected to see people wearing cowboy boots and cowboy hats. He didn't have much time to contemplate the scene because an informal scrimmage broke out. When Olajuwon subbed in, he looked awkward. Some teammates remember him not knowing the basic rules. After the ball was inbounded to him, he caught the ball and took off running without dribbling.

Still, it was clear he had something special one couldn't teach. "His athleticism was very noticeable," says Michael Young, a star forward on that 1980–1981 team. Young observed how easily Olajuwon ran up and down the court, one second blocking a shot, the next beating everyone down the court for a layup. "A lot of God-given talent."

Olajuwon just didn't know how to harness it yet. He'd swat a shot away, only to be called for goaltending. Or he'd miss shots poorly because he didn't yet have a jumper. "He wasn't a real good basketball player when he first got there," Schverak says. Olajuwon brimmed with potential, but in the eyes of his coaches he was still a project. "I don't care how you slice it," Lewis later said. "He flat out didn't know how to play."

But after that initial scrimmage, Lewis began daydreaming about what Olajuwon could become. He saw athleticism that one couldn't teach, as well as an inner drive, a hustle, that not every player possessed. It isn't that he knew Olajuwon could become a star, but he knew Olajuwon had the work ethic to potentially become a really good player. Lewis ran up the stairs to see Sports Information Director Jay Goldberg. "That's probably the happiest I ever saw Guy," Goldberg says.

However, the players weren't sure if Olajuwon could handle the game's physicality, especially given his tendency to bend forward in respect; they didn't want opponents to mistake the gesture for softness. "The reason we didn't want him to do that is because there would be someone who would take advantage of that," says guard Eric Davis, a team captain. Dave Rose, another guard, echoed the sentiment. "I thought it was going to be kind of a stretch for him to be an actual contributor to our team. I just felt like to play with the kind of confidence and swagger that you'd need to, that his shyness was going to be tough to break through," says Rose, who went on to become the second-winningest coach in Brigham Young University men's hoops history.

Olajuwon felt a bit like an outsider. "All I knew is I could play in Nigeria. I was dominating," Olajuwon later said. "But I did not know if I could play in America." He had an inner self-assurance, though. When Houston's athletic department handed out a questionnaire to every player that day, asking about their goals, Olajuwon made a bold projection: "I guarantee nine or eight blocked shots a game." His teammates and coaches laughed, but Olajuwon did not.

. . . .

THE FIRST FEW WEEKS OF PRACTICE WEREN'T EASY FOR OLAJUWON, especially during Lewis's two-on-one drill. Two offensive players would attack Olajuwon as he stood under the basket attempting to defend against them. "Man, everybody was flying in there, dunking on Hakeem," Young says. "*Slamming* on him."

Lewis would stop play, hollering at Olajuwon: "Akeem! Go get that ball!" Olajuwon had been worried about goaltending, but Lewis told him, "I *want* you to goaltend on their first couple shots early in the game, because they're going to remember that."

So next time when Young and high-flying guard Clyde Drexler charged full speed ahead against Olajuwon, he was ready. Young went up for the dunk, but Olajuwon jumped high enough to force him to dish to Drexler. Olajuwon, who had stumbled to the ground, somehow popped up in time not only to *meet* Drexler at the rim but also to swat his shot down with authority. "Clyde was stunned," Young says. So was everyone else, especially Lewis, who yelled *"That's what I'm talking about!"*

Olajuwon was unlike any other prospect Lewis had ever seen— and he had coached phenomenal big men before, including Hall of Fame center Elvin Hayes. Sure, Olajuwon had been playing for only about a year and change—he'd foul excessively and turn the ball over. But then he'd grab a rebound, dribble the length of the court, and finish with a dunk. Centers of that era just didn't do *that*. They were never supposed to leave the paint. But Olajuwon didn't want to be contained.

On one play, he caught the ball at the free-throw line and attempted a jump hook. But he was so long, and covered so much ground, that he appeared to change his mind midair, nearly dunking the ball before softly dropping it in.

"If he can do that," Lewis said, turning to his assistants, "I can teach him the rest."

· · · ·

LEWIS HAD BEEN THE COACH AT THE UNIVERSITY FOR NEARLY thirty years when Olajuwon arrived. He was one of the first coaches in the American South to recruit Black players, spearheading the integration of Houston's team, and he was the mastermind behind the "Game of the Century" between Houston and UCLA on January 20, 1968, the first nationally broadcast regular-season game in college hoops history. Houston, in front of a crowd of 52,693 fans at the Astrodome, snapped UCLA's and then–Lew Alcindor's forty-seven-game win streak.

By the time Olajuwon arrived, Lewis had also introduced an up-tempo style of play that resembles much of today's NBA game. Some possessions, he'd tell players the ball couldn't touch the floor more than three times. On defense, he used a full-court press.

Although he would eventually be inducted into the Hall of Fame with five Final Four appearances, two Associated Press College Coach of the Year awards, and a 592–279 lifetime record, Lewis didn't always receive his due while actively coaching. His critics claimed he simply "rolled the balls out," meaning he wasn't a true "X's and O's coach," succeeding only because of his talented, athletic players. It wasn't true. Lewis prided himself on preparation and fundamentals. He'd fill notebooks with practice plans. There was always skill work, too. "He had a philosophy. He really was a defensive coach," says Don Chaney, who starred for Houston from 1965 to 1968. "I learned a lot from him on the defensive end."

He had a keen sense of humor, cracking players up with his East Texas accent (he grew up in the town of Arp): "Dunk the day-um bawyl!" He clutched a lucky red polka-dotted towel each game. He once took some of his worst free-throw shooters to see a hypnotist before the game (Houston later won, hitting its free throws). Once, before playing Rice (a sort-of rival because Lewis was not too fond of the university after it denied him a basketball scholarship after World War II), Lewis burst through the locker-room door, looking ready to fight someone. "Rice is like a big ole rattlesnake!" he said. "You know what that rattlesnake will do if you sit there and try to jack with that rattlesnake?" He pretended to slit his neck: "That rattlesnake will get you right in the throat! That's who we're playing tonight!"

Lewis loved his players and loved Cougar basketball, building the program from scratch, at one point in the early days bringing his own practice gear for players. "[Lewis] always told me, 'My goal is to build up basketball in the state of Texas,' and he did," says Jim Perry, former Cougar cocaptain and later graduate assistant coach. "Because there was football, and then there was spring football. There was no such thing as basketball."

Olajuwon quickly realized that Lewis demanded a certain level of intensity, which made him raise his level of play. Lewis hardly ever called fouls. "I don't care if somebody knocked you out in mid-air, [Lewis] would just turn his back to it," Young says. "It was very physical play, but that really helped develop all of us."

Lewis taught Olajuwon one move that first year: the power step. Again and again, the coach would demonstrate posting up, pivoting, and powering the ball up to the hoop without dribbling. But it was difficult. Olajuwon feared he was traveling. His coaches were constantly in his ear: "Akeem! Don't put the ball on the floor!"

Day after day, he caught the ball in the post, laboring on his pivots, trying to keep the ball high above his head. He didn't want to disappoint his coaches.

• • • •

WORD SPREAD THAT HOUSTON HAD A *SEVEN-FOOT RECRUIT FROM Africa*, as Olajuwon was often described. That was because Lewis insisted he be listed on the roster at seven feet despite the fact that he was six feet ten—*maybe* a half-inch more. "Just to add to the mystique," says Goldberg.

Olajuwon was an unknown: "Nobody knew how good he was," says Gerald Myers, former Texas Tech coach, now eighty-seven. People didn't know how to spell his name, either. The United Press International first spelled Olajuwon's name as "Akeem Abdul Olajuowa." Another writer said his name was a "train of syllables" that was "thrown in for spelling practice."

Olajuwon didn't correct anyone for spelling or pronouncing his first name with an "A." *Akeem*. It appears the team's basketball secretary at the time couldn't decipher Hakeem's signature and incorrectly wrote "Akeem" on his initial documents. Besides, that was how his name sounded to Houston's coaches, too, with a silent "H." Throughout his college career, his full name also appeared on rosters as "Akeem Abdul Olajuwon." (Abdul was dropped once he turned pro.)

His mystique increased as fans saw him seated on Houston's bench during games, not taking off his warm-ups. The NCAA had ruled him ineligible to compete during that 1980–1981 season because he arrived mid-semester, although he had participated in a practice from the start. "Guys like Hakeem didn't just *show up*," says Fran Fraschilla, former Division I coach and longtime basketball TV analyst. "At that time, it was so unusual."

For a brief period, Olajuwon was an in-between student-athlete: he was living with Terry Kirkpatrick, a Houston assistant coach, and worked as a busboy in the cafeteria, but he wasn't immediately enrolled in classes. He was studying for his SAT. The whole thing seemed strange. "Lewis has sequestered Olajuwon in some secret dorm room," wrote the *Fort Worth Star-Telegram*.

Some players and coaches within the Southwest Conference (SWC), of which Houston was a member, wondered if his recruitment was legal. "There was always media speculation," says Tom Turbiville, who worked for the SWC as assistant information director from 1978 to 1984. "I was certainly not privy to anything illegal going on."

Many players who played for Houston at the time grew up nearby. "It was still really odd, I guess, to have a player emerge with that kind of talent who was not home-grown," says Michael Hurd, who covered SWC hoops for the *Austin American-Statesman*. "But to have a kid come over from Africa to play? It's like, 'Oh, what is this?' People had no idea what to make of him." Texas was also known as a football state at that time, so to have "a basketball player, and a basketball player not from *these here parts*, it was just this lack of understanding, and if I must say, tolerance, for somebody like that," Hurd adds.

Only two other African basketball players, cousins Dud Tongal and Ed Bona from Khartoum, Sudan, had previously starred at the Division I level. Tongal, who played for Fordham from 1978 to 1982, graduated as the school's all-time blocked-shots leader with 217 (he's currently third on the career list). He was relentless inside and had a pretty sky hook. Bona, about six feet eight, had a deadly jumper and was eventually inducted into Fordham's Hall of Fame in 2017.

Few in Houston had heard of Tongal and Bona, but people were nonetheless intrigued by Olajuwon. Reporters were clamoring to talk to him, but Lewis wouldn't allow it. He claimed that Olajuwon didn't speak English well enough. Of course, that was a lie. Olajuwon had spoken English since he was a child, given that English was the national language of Nigeria. Lewis, however unintentionally, fed into an exoticization of Olajuwon and ignorance about Africa as a whole.

As the *Philadelphia Inquirer* wrote, "Lewis had been coaching at Houston for 25 years. He had operated a regular foreign aid service, letting 200 or 300 gym rats from Tijuana to Tibet try out for his team. None had made it. . . . Neither would some Third World soccer goalie, especially one with a Nigerian mailing address."

El Paso Times: "Lagos . . . as in Nigeria. Nigeria? A basketball player?"

Fort Worth Star-Telegram: "The center is called 'Akeem the Dream,' mainly because it is too difficult to pronounce his real name."

Goldberg thinks that Lewis was trying to protect Olajuwon. He was seventeen, living in a new country, and didn't need any more attention or pressure. Besides, there were many upperclassmen, such as leading scorer Rob Williams, who were more deserving of press. However, the media shutout may have backfired. "The fascination [with Hakeem] grew because Guy didn't let him talk initially," says David Moore, who covered the SWC for the *Fort Worth Star-Telegram* at the time.

Back then, when reporters were allowed to watch practices, there was a coziness between Lewis and some reporters, Houston natives who were brazen homers. They agreed not to write about Olajuwon until Lewis gave them the green light. But the lone female sportswriter on the beat didn't play ball.

• • • •

TRACY DODDS WAS NEW TO THE *HOUSTON POST* WHEN SHE WAS assigned to cover the SWC. She was an experienced journalist, having previously covered the Milwaukee Bucks for the *Milwaukee*

Journal Sentinel. She had spotted Olajuwon at the end of the bench and wondered why he wasn't playing: "They weren't acknowledging that he existed."

She approached Olajuwon at practice when the coaches weren't looking. She asked him his name. How he came to Houston. If he was enrolled in school. What life was like in Nigeria. He answered her questions, then explained the stereotypes he faced in America: "He was explaining that people think of Africa as elephants and giraffes," Dodds says. Olajuwon told her he had grown up in a big city. She teased him that he had a bit of a southern drawl coming in, and he mentioned he had a British lilt because of the British influence on Nigeria's education system.

"Here," she said, handing him her spiral notebook, asking him to write his name and phone number. He wrote: "Hakeem Abdul Olajuwon." She didn't think twice about him writing "H" until a *Post* copy editor later informed her she had "misspelled" his name. "That's not how he spells it," Dodds told the editor. He didn't believe her. "Look, he wrote it!" she said. But she had bigger problems once she returned to the gym. "Guy Lewis—his head was exploding," Dodds says. Right before practice, he told her she couldn't write the piece on Olajuwon.

It was difficult enough being a female sportswriter in the early eighties, let alone in the Deep South. Her own editor chewed her out, too, saying she had tried to scoop her *Post* colleague, John Hollis, the Cougars beat writer. Her story never ran, but her exchange with Olajuwon offers a rare glimpse into the "H" versus "A" debacle. "Hakeem was so respectful, he never corrected anyone," says Eric Davis, the team captain. "It's because of who he is. And he doesn't want to embarrass anyone or make them feel bad."

Those characteristics only further endeared him to teammates, who embraced him. They came up with a new nickname for

Olajuwon: "Jelly," short for "Jellybean." Micheaux, the power forward, says: "Jellybean is a shake. It's a move, that you shake like jelly." Davis, on the other hand, says it came from the assistant coaches eating jelly beans at practice and giving some to Olajuwon. He loved them. There was also something effortlessly *cool* about Jelly, and Olajuwon took to the name. It stuck. So did other nicknames. Adams, the student manager, called him "Lagos." The papers started calling him "Akeem the Dream."

Olajuwon didn't remember how the name started but later recalled a moment during practice, that first season, when he dribbled from one end of the court to the other, dunking so easily that Lewis remarked that he made the play "look like a dream." It was perfect. It rhymed with "Akeem," and it captured his tantalizing potential, which appeared to be growing by the day.

· · · ·

OLAJUWON LONGED TO PLAY WITH HIS TEAMMATES THAT FIRST season. On game days, he'd cheer them on. "You got to win!" he'd tell them. According to the NCAA rules, he could be *at* practice with them, working out on the side, but was not allowed to play alongside his teammates. As a result, he kept himself in game shape by playing intramural pickup ball with students and even professors who walked into the gym. One day, he won thirty—yes, thirty—consecutive games.

He focused on getting bigger. He was only about 180 pounds, easily getting knocked around during intramurals. His coaches tried to fatten him up, giving him steak, potatoes, and Blue Bell vanilla ice cream. His favorite food was rice. Jollof rice from home. "If you would have let him," Davis says, "he would have only eaten rice." Sometimes, though, he'd show up with a bag of McDonald's burgers from the fast-food chain across the street. He quickly put on thirty-five pounds.

The coaches weren't sure if he had ever lifted weights before. His first day, he couldn't even bench-press a forty-five-pound bar with no additional weights. But he was diligent, never missing a workout. "He never once, ever once, complained about working," says Schverak, the assistant coach. "He wanted to get big. He didn't want to be pushed around."

Still, one day, Olajuwon walked into the coaches' office, frustrated. "I want to go home. They play too rough upstairs," Olajuwon said, according to Schverak, referring to the intramural pickup games.

"Akeem," Schverak said. "Whenever anybody gets near you, you slap that ball back the other way. And when you get the ball, turn and dunk on them."

Schverak remembers Olajuwon saying, "I can do that?" His response revealed how surprisingly deferential he was early on. Schverak nodded. "That's when he started getting a little bit tough."

• • • •

SOME REPORTERS ASSUMED THAT OLAJUWON EXPERIENCED CULture shock in Texas, but he really didn't. He was accustomed to living in a cosmopolitan city. Houston presented some unexpected differences, though. For example, Olajuwon didn't remember many people in Lagos having a car until age twenty-seven or so, and if they did, it was usually a small European car. In Houston he saw twenty-year-olds driving eighteen-foot-long Oldsmobiles and Pontiacs. And when they'd drive to fast-food places, ordering from the car window, Olajuwon was surprised to see that one talked to a machine and then the food was ready at the next window.

He didn't understand the slang his teammates used at first. "You'd say, 'What's happenin'?' and he'd have no idea what you were talking about," recalled forward Benny Anders, his roommate. But Olajuwon soon adopted their basketball phrases. When Olajuwon heard someone say "rock your world," meaning dominate a defender, he repeated the phrase over and over during one practice, cracking up his teammates with his all-too-proper delivery: "Now I am going to rock your world!"

He was fully immersed in the South. When he'd get treatment at the university's training room, Ernie Garza, a student athletic trainer, would play country music, often Larry Gatlin, a Houston alum. "I remember [Olajuwon] telling me that he liked it," Garza says, especially the 1979 hit "I've Done Enough Dyin' Today." Once, on a road trip to Lubbock, the team arrived at night. It was pitch black, and tumbleweeds rolled across the road. "What is *that*?" Olajuwon said. Jim Duffer, a team manager, started laughing and told him: "We are definitely in the country now."

But it was clear that Olajuwon had had experiences that his Texan classmates hadn't. When Olajuwon went to the training room, Garza would treat his knees, noticing a smoothness that he'd later learn came from helping in his parents' cement business. "If you've ever seen anyone who does concrete work, that handles concrete, or in his case, kneels on concrete, it files your skin away," Garza says. "His skin was smooth from that." Olajuwon told him about their business and what it meant to him. "He had more life experiences than Americans his age," Garza says.

Sometimes he felt homesick, often calling his parents, usually at midnight (7 a.m. the next morning in Lagos). He'd try to comfort himself by making *fufu* with Bisquick. Teammates made sure to check on him. "Everybody just wrapped their arms around him. I know he missed his family, but he was much loved," says Michael Young, the forward. "I've seen some nights he would cry because he missed his family."

Olajuwon became close to other teammates, too, including Drexler. The two would eventually become lifelong friends. Drexler was

talented, smart, kind, and all-out competitive. The two understood each other immediately, never giving up on possessions. They
became close off the floor, too, as Olajuwon began to open up about
his home life. Another teammate, cocaptain Lynden Rose, had family of Bahamian descent who made Olajuwon feel like he was one
of their own. The two would hang out off campus and talk about
politics and racism in the South.

Olajuwon had similar conversations with Davis, the team captain. Davis had been thinking a lot about what it meant to him to
be African American, and about the meaning of "home." Since the
day Olajuwon arrived on campus in his white dashiki—which Davis
thought was *beautiful*—he became more introspective about his
own identity: "That was at a point in America where we were debat-
ing, 'Are we Africans? . . . Are we African American?' For me just to
see him, it was kind of like, 'Wow. Wow! From Africa.'"

He was struck by Olajuwon's pride in Nigeria. "You have to see it.
You will not believe it," he'd tell Davis. Davis says he didn't know
much about Africa before their conversations. "Just to spend time
talking to him about Africa, it was like going to class every day,"
Davis says, adding later: "It instilled a different pride in me."

Olajuwon eventually stopped wearing the dashiki because too
many of his teammates had made fun of him for the rhinestone
decoration. "Akeem tried to tell us they were diamonds," Drexler
later said. (Olajuwon insisted they were real.) "We embarrassed him
into ditching it." Davis says they were trying to help him fit in. "We
should have all ran out and got dashikis," Davis says. "We were popular enough that, you know what? They would have set a trend."

Davis shared with Olajuwon what it was like growing up Black
in Chicago, and the two bonded over adjusting to southern life.
"There were some things that were still very strange to me in the
Deep South, and we would talk a little bit about the history of why

those things happened," Davis says. They discussed history, dating back to slavery.

Olajuwon told him that many Houston students held inaccurate views about Africa, with some asking him if he lived in "the jungle or a hut." "He was very shocked about the ignorance that many people in America had," Davis says.

Their conversations often turned to religion. Olajuwon explained to him the tenets of Islam (Davis was raised Baptist). "He spoke about everyone being brothers and sisters, and treating everyone fairly," Davis says. These conversations resonated with Davis so deeply that he eventually converted to Islam. "I still am grateful that he showed me a direction," Davis says. "I really am. And now, to have grandkids and children who are faithful, who are connected to, in my opinion, the most beautiful religion in the world."

Ironically, though, as Olajuwon was getting settled in Houston during his college years, he stopped practicing Islam. He still prayed by himself, but he wasn't nearly as observant as he had been back home. He didn't know where the mosques were. He "didn't understand [his] obligations as a Muslim," he'd later say. He partied, as college students do. In one of the rare instances Olajuwon mentioned religion to the press, he acknowledged in 1983 that he was indeed Muslim but claimed, "I'm not really religious."

He left his faith behind for the next decade, later recalling that he was occupied more with fitting in with those around him. It would take him many years to realize what he had lost.

CHAPTER 6

MOSES

NEARLY EVERY DAY IN THE SUMMER OF 1981, AFTER HIS FIRST PAR-
tial year at Houston, Olajuwon played at Fonde Recreation Center,
the spot to play if you were a talented ballplayer in Houston. There
were two no-frills courts separated by a blue plastic screen. There
was often no air-conditioning. Players frequently played shirts versus
skins. Everyone was out for blood. "If you wanted to find out what
game you had, you'd come to Fonde," says James Robinson, Fonde's
current recreation assistant. "If you ain't got it, you gotta get out.
Don't come back."

For months, Olajuwon had heard stories of the legendary court
and the pros who graced its hardwood, including Rockets players
Moses Malone, Robert Reid, Major Jones, John Lucas, Allen Leavell,
Caldwell Jones, Joe "Jellybean" Bryant (Kobe Bryant's father), and
Bill Willoughby. The Rockets players, who had made it all the way
to the NBA Finals in 1981 before falling to the Celtics, knew that
many of the kids who showed up at Fonde couldn't afford to attend
Rockets games, so they'd bring autographed shoes and gear for
them. "We welcomed them," said Reid, who gave an interview for
this book before he died in February 2024 at age sixty-eight. "They
saw good, hardcore, *where's your mama 'cause I'm gonna put this in
your face* basketball."

The first time Olajuwon walked into the gym, he knew he'd have to bring his best: he and his Cougars teammates were trying to prove they were on the Rockets' level. Olajuwon's teammates had battled the Rockets players many times before and knew the challenge that lay ahead. "Oh, they actually thought they could beat us," Leavell says.

Everyone seemed to have the same mindset, regardless of age: *You push me; I'll push you. We'll both get better.* The Rockets players were, in some ways, big brothers to the Cougars players. Fonde was more competitive than Rowe Park in Lagos, Olajuwon quickly realized, but it had the same kind of prestige. If you proved yourself there, you could walk around with a certain amount of respect. Puff your chest out a little farther.

Then he spotted Malone, the center everyone had been telling him about. Big Mo. The NBA's fiercest rebounder. The one his friend Yommy Sangodeyi had looked up to. Malone was the first player to play professionally directly after high school. He had been the number-one recruit in the country, and hundreds of college scouts hounded him. He was relentless on the glass, scoring at will. He was six feet ten but slender, with incredible quickness for a man of his size. He had unusually small hands, but every rebound was *his*. He once grabbed thirty-seven boards in a game. But what separated him, Olajuwon soon learned, was his intellect. And his timing. He didn't wait to box out until the ball was halfway to the basket like most players. He fought for position earlier, as soon as he sensed a teammate was *about* to shoot. And even more impressive? "He would study the rims," says Del Harris, Malone's former Rockets coach, now eighty-seven. "Some rims were real tight. Back then, early on, they didn't go around and check the rim tension." Malone knew every detail about every rim and studied every detail about every opponent.

Malone was everything that Olajuwon aspired to be: dominant, hard-nosed, skilled. He had an unshakable confidence, a swagger, that Olajuwon needed, too. Cedric Maxwell, former Celtics star and now a broadcaster for the team, remembers a game in which Celtics big man Rick Robey was guarding Malone. Malone took it almost as an insult. "You guys have Rick *Robey* on me?" Malone said to Maxwell. "I'm gonna get a hunnit rebounds!"

"A hunnit?" Maxwell said. "You gonna get a *hunnit?*"

"Yeah. You keep him on me. A hunnit rebounds."

Olajuwon didn't yet have that kind of swagger. He looked uncertain, often hesitating on offense. "He was scared of the contact. He didn't know what to do," Malone later said. "I worked with him, told him not to be afraid."

· · · ·

OLAJUWON INTRIGUED MALONE AND THE ROCKETS PLAYERS, although he was very much still learning. "He didn't have any clue what he was doing," says former Rockets guard Allen Leavell, "but his athleticism was off the charts. We knew he could be a great player if he learned the game." Everyone respected how hard he competed. "He was just this young sponge that had so much courage, and so much desire," says James Bailey, Rockets forward from 1982 to 1984.

Malone began to mentor Olajuwon, teaching him the intricacies of the post: how to set up, how to get the ball, how to be aggressive. Rather than verbally give lessons, Malone taught him by *showing* him: guarding him daily, embodying the hunger he hoped his protégé would adopt. Malone simply overpowered him. When Olajuwon caught the ball? *Smack!* Tried to seal him? *Smack!* Took it strong to the cup? *Smack!* "[Olajuwon] was struggling," Reid said. "Big Mo was *hitting* on him." But Malone saw potential in Olajuwon. "When [Mo] saw something that could be great," Reid said, "he pushed it." And Olajuwon loved the challenge. "Dream never backed down," Reid said.

In quiet moments between games, Malone would pull Olajuwon aside, offering morsels of wisdom. He took Olajuwon around in his Maserati, and the two would hang out at Frenchy's Chicken in South Houston. Malone was generous with his protégé as well. He bought Olajuwon stylish clothes and gave him his mint-condition hand-me-downs, including a striking cream-colored sports jacket.

"The thing that the young people forget about today—and I know Moses was taught this, I was taught this, and I'd say 95 percent of athletes that came up in the '60s, '70s, and '80s [were taught this]—is you give back to the game," says Michael Cooper, former Lakers guard and close friend of Malone. Malone died in 2015. "Whether it's materialistic, whether it's spiritual, whether it's emotional, you always give back. For him to help Hakeem along the way, a young man that I'm pretty sure Moses saw in [him] what we couldn't see: how great of a player he was going to be."

. . . .

NOW THAT HE WAS FINALLY ELIGIBLE TO PLAY, HYPE SWIRLED around Olajuwon as the 1981–1982 college season began. Much of it was over the top for the newly minted member of the active roster who had yet to play a single minute in a game. "An awesome, sweeping sky hook is implied by his middle name [Abdul] . . . ," one reporter wrote, referring to Kareem Abdul-Jabbar. "Akeem Abdul Olajuwon has to live with those expectations."

A *sky hook*? Olajuwon had yet to develop a consistent jump shot. Conference coaches were stoking the fire, too. One coach was ready to give his two cents, even if he didn't know Olajuwon's actual name: "If Abdul is what they say he is," Texas coach Abe Lemons said, "it's over for the rest of us." Lewis still wouldn't let Olajuwon speak to the press, so he tried to quiet the chatter himself. "I know damn well the alumni expect too much out of him," Lewis said. "They're playing him up like a savior. . . . Akeem hasn't even done anything yet." Lewis wasn't even sure Olajuwon would play. He was brutally honest with Olajuwon, too, telling him privately that he didn't know if he would ever score a point.

There was also a more pressing concern: Olajuwon was suffering from back spasms, unable to run without grimacing in pain. Sometimes he couldn't even bend over to pick something up off the ground. His coaches wondered if he was experiencing growth spurts. Maybe he wasn't used to weight training? Maybe his dorm bed wasn't big enough and his feet dangled off the end?

Each day before practice, Olajuwon hooked himself onto a machine called the "Rack" that flipped his near-seven-feet frame upside down for ten minutes to stretch his back. He watched as his teammates took the floor, laughing and smiling, and there he was, upside down, looking silly, feeling uncertain of his future. "I had heard rumors that he was never going to play again," says Ernie Garza, the student athletic trainer. Garza remembers Terry Kirkpatrick, an assistant coach to whom Olajuwon had grown close, telling him that Olajuwon was thinking about returning to Lagos. Garza wasn't sure if the rumor was true, but he remembered Olajuwon's pain. "It was debilitating," Garza says.

The coaches tried to find him the right treatment. They also helped him find a local acupuncturist. Mercifully, after just one session, along with all the stretching and treatment he had been doing at the university, he began to feel relief. The spasms eventually stopped, but Olajuwon had a lot of catching up to do as nonconference play began. He struggled against Seton Hall, getting called for goaltending a couple of times. Otis Birdsong, former Cougars star and twelve-year NBA veteran, was in attendance, wondering how

Lewis gave him a scholarship. "Hakeem was terrible," Birdsong says, laughing. "He couldn't walk and chew bubble gum."

But every day, Olajuwon got a little better. His teammates gave him no choice, bumping him and bruising him to help him get stronger. His main foe was Larry Micheaux, nicknamed "Mr. Mean" ("Mean," for short). One did not want to piss off *Mean*. Olajuwon battled, but Mean often got the best of him. "Punishing him," says Michael Young, the forward. That was intentional. "I didn't want to be easy on Hakeem," Micheaux says. The two mutually benefited, though. "I had to figure out a way to stop him from blocking my shot," Micheaux says. Olajuwon caught on quickly, too, and was able to hold his own.

Practices were often more intense than games. Fights sometimes broke out. During one practice Olajuwon caught a fingernail above his right eye and had to get stitches. But he wasn't always on the receiving end of blows. Once, Micheaux remembers him trying to fight guard Reid Gettys. Micheaux had to tell Olajuwon to back down before he could land a punch. His teammates respected that he played hard and was a workhorse during drills. "Either you fit in, or you fit out," Micheaux says, "and definitely he fit in."

He also continued to stand out with his uncanny skills. In one instance, while on the road, coaches spotted Olajuwon kicking a soccer ball around with random students before shootaround. Olajuwon dribbled around imaginary defenders and then bounced the ball off his knees. Then his head. The students stopped, amazed someone so tall could be so agile.

Lewis was furious: "Go get Akeem!" he screamed to Barron Honea, a student assistant coach. Honea said a prayer. *Please, Lord, don't let Akeem sprain his ankle.* Fortunately, he didn't, but the kicking would continue. Another time, before practice, instead of shooting, he stepped on *top* of the basketball, balancing on one leg while sticking out his other leg. He looked ridiculous, teetering back and forth. One fall could have injured him or, worse, ended his career. He finally stepped off but kicked the ball up toward his shoulder in one motion. His teammates just stared. They had never seen anyone quite like him before.

• • • •

OLAJUWON PLAYED SPARINGLY OFF THE BENCH AS NONCONFERENCE play in the first half of the season continued but had a breakthrough at the December 1981 Sugar Bowl Classic in New Orleans. He was nervous, playing in front of 7,955 fans at the Superdome, but scored twenty points in the team's final game against LSU, including thirteen in the final seven minutes, along with eight rebounds and three blocks. With four seconds left, and Houston up by two, he swatted away an eight-foot jump shot by LSU's Howard Carter. Drexler scooped up the loose ball and hammered in a dunk as time expired to win the tournament.

Afterward, tournament officials handed out awards, including MVP. Houston players began forming a tunnel around Olajuwon, as one might do in starting lineups; they were sure he would be named MVP. Olajuwon bent low, low-fiving everyone, slowly making his way through when the announcer said: "And the MVP is Howard Carter from LSU!"

From the *runner-up*. A couple of teammates walked over to Olajuwon, who had already started to walk toward half-court. "It's OK," they said, putting their arms around his shoulders. "Come on back, man."

The hits kept coming. As the season wore on, Olajuwon's playing time became more sporadic, and when he did sub in, he struggled with fouls against the SWC's top centers, including Texas's LaSalle Thompson. Olajuwon frequently got called for goaltending.

However, Thompson was still impressed, watching Olajuwon get a rebound, then throw it to point guard Rob Williams, then sprint to the other end, ready to score under the basket. "I hadn't even crossed half-court," Thompson says. "I was like *shit*, this guy. I gotta start grabbing his jersey so he won't outrun me."

Still, Olajuwon expected more out of himself. Soon thereafter, he walked into Lewis's office, telling him that playing basketball in America was harder than he had anticipated. His coach reminded him to be patient; he had been playing the game for only about *three years*.

He was still seen as somewhat of a curiosity by the press, someone easy to talk to and described by one reporter as possessing a "precious innocence." "He was so charming," says George Vecsey, renowned former *New York Times* sports columnist. At first, Olajuwon seemed to enjoy the attention. When one reporter asked him why he liked basketball, he smiled and said, "The media." He sometimes asked reporters when the story would appear in print: "Can you send me a copy?"

But he soon grew tired of being asked the same ill-informed questions. Reporters often painted Africa as a monolith, blending 54 countries, more than 2,000 languages, and nearly 1.5 billion people into a single stereotype. One local paper ignored the fact that Olajuwon had grown up in a middle-class neighborhood, describing Lagos instead as "a backdrop of poverty, overpopulation, and widespread illiteracy."

As the Nigerian writer and editor Dipo Faloyin noted in his 2022 book, aptly titled *Africa Is Not a Country*,

> For too long, "Africa" has been treated as a buzzword for poverty, strife, corruption, civil wars, and large expanses of arid red soil where nothing but misery grows. Or it is presented as one big safari park, where lions and

tigers roam freely around our homes and Africans spend their days grouped in warrior tribes, barely clothed, spears palmed, hunting game, and jumping up and down with ritualistic rhythm to pass the time before another aid package gets delivered. Poverty or safari, with nothing in between. . . . In reality, Africa is a rich mosaic of experience, of diverse communities and histories. . . . We sound different, laugh differently . . . our moral compasses do not always point in the same direction.

OLAJUWON TRIED TO EXPLAIN AS MUCH TO REPORTERS. However, one of them called him a "Watusi," a term he had never heard. *Sports Illustrated* also thought it would be clever to play on that term, calling Olajuwon a "Swatusi." ("Watusi" is an earlier name for the Tutsi people of Africa, an ethnic group historically from Rwanda and Burundi and stereotypically known for their height.) In another instance, after Olajuwon played well against Baylor, the *Fort Worth Star-Telegram* ran a short article titled "Baskeetbowl Been Bera, Bera Good to Me." In it, Olajuwon was described as "He may not look like Chico Esquela, but Olajuwon certainly sounded like the *Saturday Night Live* character." He was quoted as saying: "It was a very, very nice game. Very close, a very good crowd."

Some espoused lazy, racist tropes, and others questioned Olajuwon's mastery of English.

"[Olajuwon is] a 7–0 modern-day Goliath who swats basketballs away like he would flies in his native Lagos, Nigeria."

"Olajuwon arrived . . . with only rudimentary knowledge of the English language."

"He puzzles over some words, but he knows 'slam dunk' and 'bucket' and 'boards.'"

"[He] speaks in halting English but fluent Dunkese."

"The Dream speaks in broken English and deals in broken hearts."

One article even falsely claimed he was struggling to pass an English-language class and that he had turned in a five-page essay containing only three sentences.

Other articles highlighted the "Americanization of Akeem," as they often put it, tending to overemphasize Olajuwon's affinity for ice cream, assuming that he'd never had it before. (He had.) The bit spread, as *Newsday* titled one article: "The Story of Olajuwon: It's Hoops and Scoops." *Sports Illustrated* claimed he had downed thirteen scoops in one sitting. "Folks thought they knew him," says Eric Davis, the Cougars captain, "and I would laugh and say, 'You have no clue who this kid is.'"

To be clear, these articles didn't represent the viewpoint of all reporters. Many not only admired Olajuwon but also treated him with decency and respect, asking questions to genuinely learn more about his upbringing. But for some fans, it was another matter. During a road game at SMU in the early eighties, one opposing fan held up a sign aimed at Houston's predominantly Black team: "Cage the CouGros."

• • • •

YEARS LATER, AS HIS NBA CAREER PROGRESSED, OLAJUWON SEEMED to speak less candidly to the press, revealing little about his personal life. One can't help but wonder if these early college experiences had something to do with that. He was, in some ways, perpetually treated as an outsider, examined as if he were an exhibit rather than a human being. "I know some people think that when I was living in Lagos I was naked in the jungle and swinging in the trees. And I do not like it," Olajuwon said while in college. "I do not like it when TV only shows the bad things and then says, 'This is Lagos.' There are bad things, sure, but in Lagos we have designer clothes, big buildings, videos, and many other things that people enjoy in

America. TV doesn't show that, and I get tired of trying to explain it."

"Lagos is a big, vibrant city," he said in another instance. "We have a Copperfield store just like in Houston. We have videos in Nigeria. We have Pat Benatar." And another: "People didn't believe that I was an educated person."

One rumor repeated in papers throughout his college career held that Yemi, his older brother, was seven feet five. (Yemi was five feet ten.) It upset Olajuwon because he had never said this. The mix-up occurred when reporters had asked him if he "came from the Watusi tribe." When he didn't know what that meant, they informed him that Watusis were at least seven feet tall. Then, when they asked him if he was the shortest one in his family, he said "yes," and the next thing he knew, Yemi was seven feet five. That was Hakeem's intro-duction to American media.

Later, during his sophomore and junior seasons, he began toying with reporters, pretending to stumble for the right word, perhaps to point out the absurdity in questioning his mastery of English. He and Goldberg would laugh about it afterward. "He knew what he was doing," Goldberg says.

Olajuwon later publicly admitted it. During his junior season, journalist David Moore, now with the *Dallas Morning News*, asked him how he dealt with attention. Olajuwon said he pretended he didn't know English. "He always had that little mischievous glint in his eye," Moore says. "He was saying, like, 'It works. If these guys come at me and they don't know I speak English, why am I going to give them my time? They know so little about me.'"

Some did, however, including Ralph Cooper, a pioneering Black sports journalist of over fifty years in Houston who had inter-viewed everyone from Jesse Owens and Muhammad Ali to Mar-vin Gaye and Sammy Davis Jr. Cooper understood Olajuwon in a way others didn't, for he had been in Africa—Kinshasa, Zaire (now the Democratic Republic of the Congo)—for nine weeks for the famous 1974 Muhammad Ali and George Foreman fight. "Although he was dealing with some people who had no desire to know where he was from and what it was like," Cooper says, "he appreciated the fact that maybe some of us respected where he had come from." Cooper continues: "Before I went to Africa, I was not an African American. I was a Black American. When I came back as an African American, I could understand, appreciate more so what *he* did." Although some reporters tended to infantilize Olajuwon, portraying him as an innocent, happy-go-lucky, ice-cream-loving "manchild," as one newspaper called him, Cooper instead saw Olajuwon as self-assured and ambitious: "He gave off the persona that he was going to be somebody great."

Cooper grew up in Houston. He remembered when the university didn't admit Black students or athletes (Houston began admitting Black students in 1962 but didn't allow Black athletes until the next year). He says it's important to note that Olajuwon's college experience was near the Third Ward, a historically Black neighborhood that has served as a vibrant cultural hub for decades. Olajuwon learned not just about the legacy of the neighborhood but also of the history of the integration of the Cougar program itself, the first Texas university to do so.

· · · ·

DURING THE 1930S, AT THE HEIGHT OF JIM CROW SEGREGATION, the Third Ward became the city's most diverse neighborhood, a booming center for Black businesses. It featured Emancipation Park, a ten-acre site purchased by former enslaved people in 1872 to serve as a place to annually celebrate the end of slavery in Texas. The neighborhood was home to many Black newspapers, including the *Defender*, the *Informer*, and the *Forward Times*, that covered every aspect of Black life, including sports—something uncommon in mainstream papers. (One white man at the *Houston Post* in the 1950s, a copy editor, resigned because he didn't want to edit articles that mentioned Black athletes.)

By the sixties, the Third Ward had become the epicenter of the city's civil rights movement, but Houston quietly persisted in remaining one of the largest segregated cities in America. Nearby, Texas Southern University students staged the first Houston sit-in demonstration at the lunch counter of Weingarten's grocery store in the Third Ward on March 4, 1960.

Around that time, Guy Lewis had been trying to recruit local Black athletes to the university, including McCoy McLemore and David Lattin, but university policy prohibited it. Lattin went on to help Texas Western win the national championship in 1966 with the NCAA's first all-Black starting lineup. McLemore, who played for Drake University, then helped the Milwaukee Bucks win an NBA championship in 1971.

Lewis's progressive thinking had been influenced by his days on the basketball court at the local Jewish Community Center. The JCC was the precursor to Fonde, and it was one of the few places that allowed Black and white players to play together. "If there was a good basketball player in the Houston area, they were at the Jewish Community Center," says Ronnie Arrow, former coach at San Jacinto College in Houston and most recently at the University of South Alabama, who had spent many summers at the JCC.

Lewis became friends with Marvin Blumenthal, who ran the JCC and integrated the facility in 1958. Blumenthal may have influenced Lewis's efforts to integrate Houston's program. To be sure, Lewis, and many SWC coaches who would follow his lead, weren't determined to recruit Black players for purely moral reasons. "Those coaches needed Black players to win. That's the bottom line," says Frank A. Guridy, historian of sport and society and professor at Columbia University. His *The Sports Revolution: How Texas Changed the Culture of American Athletics* details the racial politics of sports integration throughout the state. For decades, SWC conference coaches refused to recruit Black players.

Houston football coach Bill Yeoman, who arrived in 1962, ended up signing star running back Warren McVea, the first Black football player at the university. Lewis had already begun integrating the basketball team by signing Don Chaney and Elvin Hayes. In 1964 Houston became the first major college in the South to integrate its athletic program with the recruitment of all three athletes. "[Yeoman] always said that Guy Lewis followed suit with him," says Robert D. Jacobus, a history professor at Stephen F. Austin State University who has published several books on the integration of Houston's sports teams. "But I'm not so sure of that. I think it was kind of a mutual thing, a simultaneous kind of thing."

Chaney and Hayes, both of whom eventually starred in the NBA, were trailblazers. Chaney recalls facing racism and discrimination, mostly on road trips throughout the state, especially when restaurants refused to serve Black players. "I was used to it, coming from Baton Rouge," Chaney says. "I was used to racism. I was used to walking in the street in Baton Rouge at night and people throwing cans and bottles at me and yelling obscenities." Many schools that desegregated their student bodies in the late 1950s and early 1960s still sought to shut out or limit the presence of Black male athletes on their football teams until the late sixties and early seventies.

Basketball fared similarly. Some fans threw cups filled with drinks and ice at players. Once, at a restaurant, the owner came over and told Cougar players: "There's a table over there that's going to leave if we serve you. You can go ahead and leave." A few times, Black teammates stayed on the bus, and their white counterparts brought out sandwiches to them. While traveling to an away game in San Jacinto, former Cougars cocaptain and later graduate assistant coach Jim Perry remembers seeing people burning crosses.

Houston continued to recruit Black players throughout the seventies and in some seasons boasted a predominantly Black team. "That wasn't well liked," says Otis Birdsong, who played for Houston from 1973 through 1977. He is African American and remembers fans shouting racist insults at him during some games. "What was tough for me was to try and deal and understand as a young kid in college the hatred and the racism when we're just trying to play sports. We're just trying to have fun."

By 1980, when Olajuwon joined the team, Houston was not so far removed from that era. And it needs to be stressed that Houston had a predominantly Black team. "And then you have a guy who comes all the way from *Nigeria* to be part of the team?" Cooper says. "You had some people who didn't want to see him there."

• • • •

OLAJUWON TRIED TO SHUT OUT THE NOISE AND FOCUS ON GETTING stronger. He blocked eight shots—a conference record—against TCU in February 1982, a good way through his first full season. "He was like a pogo stick," says Kevin Sherrington, former Cougars beat writer for the *Houston Post*. Olajuwon averaged a modest line of eight points and six rebounds off the bench. But Lewis noted his progress: "In this country, if a young man did not play basketball until he was 16, you'd say he'd be in trouble. But Akeem is working hard. He's going to get better." He liked that Olajuwon wasn't spoiled. "He's the nicest kid I've ever met," Lewis said. "He hasn't been told all the things that good young American athletes have been told."

Houston, posting an 18–6 regular-season record, peaking at number ten in the Associated Press poll on January 11, was unranked during the conference tournament. Refreshingly, Olajuwon was excited as the conference tournament began, so excited that he stood outside the arena talking to strangers walking by and selling the tickets his coaches had given him for friends and family. Because his parents were still in Lagos, he figured he'd sell the tickets and make a small profit. But someone alerted Turbiville, the SWC officer, who rushed outside and told Olajuwon he couldn't sell the tickets. "He had no idea this was against the rules," Turbiville says.

Houston eventually lost, 84–69, to fourteenth-ranked Arkansas in the championship game, which meant it lost the automatic bid to the NCAA Tournament. After the game, Jim Nantz, who had graduated from Houston in 1981 and was working as a public-address announcer for the Cougars, spotted Olajuwon in the locker room: "I see [Olajuwon] over in the corner, and he's almost inconsolable. He thinks the season is over. He doesn't realize we're going to get an at-large bid."

Nantz, now a Hall of Fame CBS Sports broadcaster, remembers nudging Eric Dickens, a backup guard, to tell Olajuwon the good news. "Hey, Akeem! We're still playing!" Dickens said. "We're going to be in the NCAA Tournament! We'll get an at-large bid!"

Olajuwon looked up, breaking into a big smile, thankful he had another chance to compete.

• • • •

AFTER HOUSTON, THE NUMBER-SIX SEED IN THE MIDWEST REGION, easily handled Alcorn State in the opening round of the 1982 NCAA Tournament and beat Tulsa in the second round, it faced a much steeper challenge in the semifinals against Missouri, number five in the Associated Press poll.

Malone dropped by Houston's practice leading up to the game. Olajuwon would be facing Steve Stipanovich, a surefire NBA first-round draft pick. Malone told reporters not to count Olajuwon out. "He is young," Malone told reporters. "A lot of people don't think he is strong, but I've played against this guy, and he is real strong and can jump real well. He's a good intimidator. He is aggressive. Give him another year of getting back to the summer and working on his game."

Olajuwon proved him right, dominating Stipanovich. Terry Kirkpatrick, the assistant coach, ran up to Olajuwon after the win over Missouri, beaming: "Son, tonight, you became a man."

Yet Olajuwon was still learning on the fly. After the Missouri win, he looked a bit green against Boston College in the regional finals, stepping in the lane too soon on a free throw. His coaches had to call a time-out and explain the violation to him.

Houston managed to break through to the Final Four in New Orleans, the first time since 1968. Before the game, Olajuwon looked around at the empty arena, more seats than he had ever seen before. *This must be big*, he thought.

Houston faced number-one North Carolina in the national semifinals. UNC was loaded with talent in James Worthy, Sam Perkins, and a freshman guard named Michael Jordan. The Tar Heels beat the Cougars 68–63, with Olajuwon playing only twenty minutes. He managed to grab six rebounds in an otherwise forgettable performance. UNC famously went on to beat Georgetown in the title game with Jordan hitting the championship-winning jumper.

Heading back to the locker room after the loss in the Final Four, Olajuwon looked upset. He wanted to become a bigger contributor. He knew he needed to improve his game. So, that summer, he went back to the basics. Back to Fonde. Back to Malone.

CHAPTER 7

SLAMA

OLAJUWON BATTLED MOSES MALONE FOR POSITION, POSTING HIM up, during one Fonde battle in the summer of 1982. Olajuwon was more aggressive than he had been, calling for the ball, sealing Malone with authority. Olajuwon's teammate, Clyde Drexler, pulled up for a jump shot near the free-throw line that clanked out. Olajuwon grabbed the offensive rebound and, instead of looking to pass back out, bounced the ball hard, then rose up . . . and up . . . and up . . . , shoving Malone out of the way before slamming it in.

Slamming *Big Mo* down.

A hush came over Fonde. And then everyone started jumping around and screaming: "Akeem!!! Akeem!!! Akeem!!!" Some players ran out of the gym and into their cars to go home; nothing could top what had just transpired.

Malone, who had stumbled to the floor, dusted off his shirt and looked Olajuwon in the eye: "About time!" Malone could have been resentful, or upset, but instead he was proud. His protégé had finally learned to push back, hardly resembling the player he had been a year ago. He no longer seemed fearful or hesitant. *He* became the aggressor. On one play he blocked Malone three times on a single possession. Malone called a foul on Olajuwon, who wasn't having it. "Mo!" he screamed. "Be a man!"

• • • •

Now a sophomore, Olajuwon had moved into the starting lineup for the 1982–1983 season. His teammates marveled at how much he had improved, but he still lacked a true jump shot. Sometimes his teammates wouldn't even throw him the ball. His sole purpose was to block shots, play defense, and rebound. Fearing that Olajuwon would commit a traveling violation, Lewis told the team: "Throw him alley-oops and that's it. Throw him anything else and I will take you out of the game."

His defense, though, was stellar. He regularly posted double-digit blocks and was terrifying in the paint, even if he didn't block the shot. "Shots Akeem Altered" could have been its own statistical category. "You decided not to go in the middle of the floor because he was there," says Chuck Anderson, a former SMU forward. "You were just scared to go in there." Michael Young, a Houston forward, would sometimes even *let* the opponent glide by him, knowing Olajuwon had his back. "I would spread out on the wing to start the fast break because I knew it was a block," Young says.

During his team's practice, SMU coach Dave Bliss hoisted a broom into the air, directly under the hoop, trying to prepare his players for Olajuwon's outstretched arms. "We're shooting over *this*," he would say, instructing players to shoot floaters over the broom.

Olajuwon had an uncanny ability to jump and recover, to be completely flat-footed and spring up again and again, almost like a volleyball player. So much of his handball and football background was evident in his coordination and timing. He slapped away passes that entered the lane. He'd cheat over earlier than most big men when he sensed someone was about to drive the baseline. "I got to teach him a whole bunch of things," says Donnie Schverak, the former Houston assistant coach, "but it was instinctive. . . . He was a once-in-a-lifetime athlete."

Olajuwon wanted to be *everywhere*. Float among positions 1 through 5. After he had a triple-double against Texas, with seventeen points, thirteen rebounds, and ten blocks in just twenty-five minutes, the *Houston Post* remarked that he was "basketball's first 7-foot point guard." But Olajuwon wasn't satisfied. When he found out he was fifth in the nation in rebounding, he felt even more motivated. "I can go for more," he said.

Cougars backup big man Gary Orsak experienced this situation every day of practice. He was Olajuwon's punching bag, constantly getting dunked on. He took pride in his job: make Olajuwon better, prepare him for the physicality of the postseason. "I had to do everything I could. Legal, illegal, it didn't matter, to slow him down," Orsak says. "I got in fights with Hakeem multiple times. I think my nose got broken six times." He might be exaggerating, but his nose still bears a scar from one of the fractures.

But during one scrimmage, Orsak did the unthinkable. When a seam opened, he drove through the middle and dunked on Olajuwon. Everyone was stunned. Lewis, who was already upset with the team's effort level that day, grabbed a ball and kicked it into the stands. "God dang it!" Orsak remembers him saying. "If Orsak can dunk on you, you're not working hard enough! Everybody get out of my gym!"

Players filed out, looking dejected. It was one of the best days of Orsak's life.

• • • •

BY NOW, OLAJUWON WAS FAR LESS SHY THAN HE HAD BEEN WHEN he first arrived in Houston. He usually had everyone laughing, befriending everyone. The team often ate at Capt'n Benny's Half Shell Oyster Bar. Once, while at a different restaurant, Olajuwon asked the waiter: "How big is the biggest steak you've got?" The waiter made a small circle with his hands. Olajuwon seemed disappointed. "Is that all? Well, then bring me two cheeseburgers." Everyone started cracking up.

Olajuwon just seemed more comfortable in his own skin. On the court, he sometimes belted out, "Get that out of here!" when he blocked a shot. Off the court, he looked sophisticated, stylish. His teammates soon found out about his love for fashion. When the team went to New York for a road trip, Micheaux realized that "Hakeem liked to shop."

He walked around campus with his portable cassette player, listening to reggae. He drove a red Buick. He loved Houston. The warm weather reminded him of Lagos. He was having a blast.

"He went from not wanting to dance, shy to dance with a girl," Young says, "and before it was all said and done, the guy's a great dancer."

Olajuwon would have to become even more extroverted because Houston was about to become college basketball's most famous high-flying team: *Phi Slama Jama*.

• • • •

THE NICKNAME EMERGED ON A SUNDAY AFTERNOON. THE COUGARS were dominating the University of the Pacific, dunking all over the place. The game looked like warm-ups, with players taking turns throwing down tomahawks with ease.

Thomas Bonk, a columnist at the *Houston Post*, watched in awe. "They did stuff I had never seen a college team do," he says. Brainstorming his column, he wondered: *What can you say about a blowout? Well, universities are a fraternity, so what do you call a dunking fraternity? You have to start with Phi. Hmmm. Slama sounds like Gama. Slam . . . as in dunk . . . Phi Slama Jama!*

So began his story on January 3, 1983: "As members of the exclusive college roundball fraternity *Phi Slama Jama*, the Houston chapter has learned proper parliamentary procedure. . . . If you're a *Phi Slama Jama*, you see how many balls you can stuff into a basket. . . . Whirling dunks, backwards dunks, rebound dunks, and one-on-one dunks. Stylin' and profilin', runnin' and gunnin', slammin' and jammin', mercy, what a life."

Houston was flooded with calls about the nickname. As Athletic Department marketing manager Perk Weisenburger remembers telling colleague Steve Holton, the athletic marketing coordinator, "We gotta use this." They called Bonk to ask for permission to use *Phi Slama Jama* on promotional material and gear. "Go right ahead," Bonk told them. "It was a throwaway line. You're free to use it."

The throwaway line sparked a national phenomenon. "I went nuts. I had T-shirts made," says Frank Schultz, who worked in the Houston Athletic Department. The university made jackets that said "Texas' Tallest Fraternity" on the back, with a Cougar dunking the ball. Each player had his name on the front. Even Bonk had one that said "Author." Players received flashy new uniforms made of red satin with white stars. When forward Larry Micheaux saw them, he said, "Wow. Is this a circus?"

Even in the pre-internet, pre–social-media era, the name went "viral." "It just kind of grew a life of its own," Bonk says. *Sports Illustrated* called Phi Slama Jama the "fastest, quickest, runningest, dunkingest, most creatively athletic college basketball team in years." By the end of the season, the Cougars would become the number-one-ranked team in the country. "It was wild," Weisenburger says. "It was so fun to watch."

Lewis came up to Bonk: "You realize you've created a monster." Bonk never received a dime from it. Like everyone else, he just enjoyed the greatness he was witnessing. Lewis encouraged an innovative, high-flying style that was fast and fun and creative. Drexler would make the unimaginable look routine, once dunking completely over the body of Memphis State's Andre Turner.

"You didn't want to get dunked on," says Jon Koncak, former SMU center. "Once they got that part going, when you were missing shots, and they were running back in transition and throwing the ball and alley-oops and all of that, that's when the game got out of hand really quickly."

Houston was now playing with a palpable passion. Joy. "As young adults, you don't really think about it until it's over," Young says, "but it was like being at Disneyland or somewhere. It was like, 'Is this really real?' I mean, a lot of fun. . . . Who would have ever thought, the way that team came about with a bunch of local guys and then Hakeem showed up." The team was so deep that anyone could get hot. It wasn't just on offense. "A lot of people don't think of [Houston] as great on defense, but we were really, really great on defense," says Rickie Winslow, a forward who joined the team in 1983. "The amazing open court in transition with the dunks was *because* we went against each other [in practice]."

National reporters started to attend Houston practices. Benny Anders, Olajuwon's roommate, explained to *Sports Illustrated* why he and Olajuwon worked so well together: "I drop a dime on the big Swahili, he got to put it in the hole."

Houston was no longer purely a football city anymore; basketball could no longer be referred to as "Thump Thump," either. "Phi Slama Jama changed the narrative," says Jay Goldberg. "It revealed Houston as a hotbed for basketball talent." Lewis wouldn't let his players get full of themselves, though—especially Olajuwon. One game, Ralph Adams, the student manager, remembered Lewis lighting into Olajuwon: "Akeem the *Dream*?! Well, that's bullshit! You're an effin' nightmare today!" Houston responded with a dominating win and continued to roll to a 24–2 record and the number-one spot in the Associated Press poll as postseason play began.

But before the regular season concluded, Houston faced Arkansas, arguably its biggest foe, on the road. Barnhill Arena was rowdy. Fans threw pennies, soda cups, ice, cigarette lighters, and even small cans of snuff at players on the court. Olajuwon hadn't seen anything like it, but Micheaux tried to calm him down: "Keep your head."

Although the crowd had grown so wild that Arkansas coach Eddie Sutton had to grab the microphone and tell fans they could be loud but to stop throwing things onto the court, it fell silent when the Cougars eventually won the tense matchup, Lewis's first-ever victory at Barnhill. The win clinched Houston's SWC title. But when cutting down the nets, they passed a middle-aged Arkansas fan who, according to a local paper, "mumbled something about a lynch mob." Those whispers were never too far behind.

• • • •

As the NCAA Tournament began, Houston was a fan favorite. The Cougars were the epitome of *cool*, with their dunks and flashy red uniforms. "It was a cultural moment," says Ben Osborne, former *SLAM* and *Bleacher Report* editor in chief. "It was just *fun*. I just hadn't really seen anything like it."

That was especially true for Houston natives like journalist Joel D. Anderson, host of the award-winning Slate podcast *Slow Burn*. "They were the first team that I loved," Anderson says. "I still have a Phi Slama Jama wall pennant." He adds that the team meant something to the downtrodden sports city in which the Oilers, Astros, and Rockets struggled. "In my experience as a sports fan, as a person from Houston, is you're always trying to remind people that you exist. And that, hey, we're doing things down here. You're always just kind of hoping somebody is going to validate your fandom. So, when Phi Slama Jama legitimately was great, and legitimately burst out, of course you're going to glom onto that."

Players couldn't walk anywhere without getting asked for autographs. "They owned the town," says Dale Robertson, a *Houston Chronicle* columnist for nearly fifty years. The Houston faithful hoped this was their year to win it all on the national stage. "They became more popular than the Rockets," says Barry Warner, former Rockets color commentator and play-by-play man. "They became Houston's franchise."

After defeating Maryland and Memphis to begin its 1983 NCAA Tournament run, top-seeded Houston would face a deep Villanova team in the Midwest Regional Finals. Olajuwon would battle star big man John Pinone, thought to have the upper hand in the matchup. But Olajuwon defended Pinone so hard the big man could hardly get a shot off. And when he did, Olajuwon blocked it. "He was so quick," Pinone says. "You could get him off his feet, and he'd get back on the ground, off his feet again, as quick as you were getting ready to shoot the ball."

Mitch Buonaguro, Villanova's assistant coach, turned to Head Coach Rollie Massimino and said, "Rollie, sit back and enjoy this game." Buonaguro caught himself becoming a fan of Olajuwon: "Pinone was an iconic player at Villanova, and he looked like a grammar school player in that game compared to the talent level of Olajuwon."

Olajuwon finished with twenty points, thirteen rebounds, and eight blocks in the Cougars' win. "Only eight? I thought it was like eighty," says Ed Pinckney, former Villanova forward who'd later face Olajuwon in the NBA. "We were saying, '*Man*, this dude,' I mean he is unbelievable. The ability to move that fast. . . . We just hadn't seen anyone like him."

Afterward, Olajuwon looked almost uncomfortable in the post-game press conference as reporters called him a star. "A star?" Olajuwon said, letting out a laugh. "I play. I just play. I do not think I am a star."

• • • •

HOUSTON MADE IT TO THE FINAL FOUR IN ALBUQUERQUE, NEW Mexico, and was set to play Louisville in the semifinals, another high-flying team. The Cardinals were nicknamed "The Doctors of Dunk." The game, which Houston eventually won, displayed so many dunks from both teams that Dick Weiss, renowned college hoops journalist and columnist, remembers forgetting the adage "No cheering in the press box": "The media lost it. I mean, we wanted to be part of the celebration. I remember screaming, 'Welcome to the twenty-first century!'" Weiss has covered college basketball for five decades. "To this day," he says, "I've never seen a stretch like that in the Final Four."

Louisville coach Denny Crum remembered not having a solution for Olajuwon. "It didn't matter what we did," Crum said. "He just did whatever he wanted to do."

Advancing to the national title game against NC State, Phi Slama Jama became more popular than ever. Once, after a media session and heading to the team bus, Drexler and Young called out to Goldberg: "Jay! Help!" Goldberg helped: "I had to literally fight them a path to the bus to get them on."

Fans were able to attend practice, watching Houston's customary two-on-one drill. Guard Dave Rose, who is only six feet four, dunked on Olajuwon. The gym went wild. "He took a lot of heat from the fellas," Rose says. Olajuwon burst into a smile. "David Rose," he said, walking toward him. "You're the luckiest man in the world."

The hype around Olajuwon seemed to grow even more now that he was playing on the biggest stage in basketball. One paper, referring to Patrick Ewing, wrote: "What's the name of that guy up at Georgetown?" Such a statement would have seemed ludicrous a year ago when Olajuwon could barely bench a forty-five-pound bar. Another wrote: "We could very well be watching the second coming of Wilt [Chamberlain]."

The media seemed smitten with him. He was friendly, funny. He joked to reporters that if he were any taller, he'd have trouble finding a wife in Nigeria. He was also the pride of his home country: Nigerian newspapers called him "King Akeem," opting for the same spelling as American papers. Ahead of the national title game, US reporters formed a semicircle around him at press conferences, peppering him with questions:

"Will anybody in Nigeria know about what you did today?"

"It will take time," Olajuwon said. "There are no Nigerian reporters here. Basketball is not very important there. Not like here."

"Well, what do your parents think?"

"They want me to graduate, get my degree, and come home."

"So, they don't know about the NBA? About you being a millionaire someday?"

"No."

"Have you thought about all this? I mean, have you thought about the fact that you'll be doing TV commercials someday? Do you know, really, what's going on?"

"It has been like a dream," he said. "A couple of years ago a coach pulls up in front of my house. Now I'm in school, playing basketball. It is like magic to me."

On the other hand, one reporter wrote that "he's living something that seems as if it came out of 'Babar Visits Paris.'" (Babar the elephant is a character in a French children's book series that has more recently drawn criticism for its racist depictions of Africans.) Another wrote: "Akeem Abdul Olajuwon's story is right out of Arabian nights, missing only the genie and the lamp." One Division I coach, incorrectly stating Olajuwon's home country, went so far as to say "Guys like that one from Algeria are hard to find. I guess you could go to Africa . . . and you never know what you might find. There might be one out there playing soccer, or maybe naked and just running around."

Few seemed to grasp what it must have been like to be in Olajuwon's shoes, to be asked dehumanizing questions about his culture, his country, again and again.

• • • •

HOUSTON WAS HEAVILY FAVORED TO WIN THE TITLE OVER NC State, the number-six seed in the West and unranked by the Associated Press poll heading into the tournament. The Wolfpack was a talented team, however, with senior guards Dereck Whittenburg and Sidney Lowe, as well as a tough front line in Lorenzo Charles, Cozell McQueen, and Thurl Bailey. "It was sort of like a David and Goliath," says Alvin Battle, a forward on NC State's team. But NC State believed it could pull off the upset. "We knew in our hearts that we were going to win that championship," Battle says.

Coach Jim Valvano's game plan was to try to slow Houston down, contain its quick guards, and, of course, keep Olajuwon off the boards. But Olajuwon was effective on the offensive end despite pressure from McQueen. "I pushed him further out from the block. I considered the shot that he was taking was almost like a guard," McQueen says. "After the third one, I said, 'Man! This guy can *play*.

This guy can play! Now, his confidence level is up. Now *I'm* trying to hold on for dear life.'"

It was a physical, back-and-forth game, one in which many players on both sides struggled to breathe because of Albuquerque's elevation. The game came down to the final play after Houston had lost a six-point lead in the final three minutes and nineteen seconds.

NC State had possession with forty-four seconds remaining in a game tied at 52–52. Without a shot clock, the Wolfpack swung the ball around and around against Houston's trapping zone, failing to get the ball inside the three-point line. With five seconds left, Benny Anders poked the ball away from Whittenburg, but the NC State guard recovered possession. With the Cougars scrambling and slightly out of position, Whittenburg heaved up a thirty-five-foot prayer from the top of the key. Olajuwon had ventured closer to the free-throw line than the basket, leaving the middle wide open. So when Whittenburg's shot fell short and to the right, Charles was in position to catch it and dunk it in one motion. NC State won by two, 54–52, as Valvano ran around the court, searching for someone to hug.

The Cougars were devastated. Olajuwon lay crumpled on the floor, covering his eyes, crying. He pounded his fist on the floor. Goldberg pulled him up, steering him to the locker room.

Reporters blasted Lewis and his game plan, but in the end, many players simply ran out of gas. "You could say we got lucky at the end," says Tom Abatemarco, former NC State assistant coach. "Well, we didn't get lucky. Why didn't Hakeem get that rebound?"

Reporters asked Olajuwon that same question. Olajuwon explained that he was conscious of referees calling goaltending and believed that he was too far out to make it—about six feet out by some reporters' estimates—so he boxed out the middle. He thought that somebody else should have boxed out Charles. Olajuwon has never publicly addressed responsibility for that final play, but he was distraught nonetheless. He was named Most Outstanding Player, the first player chosen from a losing team in seventeen years, but it wasn't much consolation. All he cared about was winning. And his teammates. With still-watery eyes, buttoning his red satin warm-up jacket, he declined to answer questions. "I don't want to talk," he said. "I want to go to the bus."

David Moore, the journalist, was able to chat with Olajuwon right before he hopped on. "What are you going to do now? Are you going back to Fonde this summer?" Moore asked him.

"Yeah, yeah," Olajuwon said, a tiny smile surfacing. "Stay cool. See you next year."

But would he?

. . . .

REPORTERS HAD WONDERED ALL SEASON WHETHER OLAJUWON would leave school early for the NBA or return to Houston for his junior season. Olajuwon maintained he wanted to get his degree before turning pro. Education had always been the primary goal for him and his family. He was a business technology major, and whenever he'd call his parents, they'd discuss academics, not basketball. "I want to play pro ball," Olajuwon said at the time. "But my parents, they don't like to hear that." They expected him to return to Lagos after graduation and join the family cement business. They didn't realize that pro basketball was not only a viable living but also a lucrative one. He told reporters that if he told his father how much he could be paid, his dad wouldn't believe him: "People ask me if I'm ready for the NBA now. I don't know. But I like school. I don't like it when people think all I do is play basketball for UH. They think I'm dumb. I'm going to get my degree."

It was exhausting, being in the public eye while contemplating such a big decision. He hadn't been home in three years, and he missed it. Some of his best memories came from his college years, but it wasn't always easy handling the pressure and attention. In a rare glimpse of vulnerability, and perhaps in an attempt to finally tell his own story, Olajuwon wrote a firsthand account of the difficulties he faced for the student newspaper, the *Daily Cougar*:

When I didn't play that first year, the press still wanted to know how well I could do this and how well I could do that. That is what I sometimes don't understand about the press. Maybe it's because when they come to you, treat you like you are friends and ask nice questions, you become trusting. And there have been times that I have read their articles afterward, and said, "Wait a minute. I didn't say that." And the next time you see them, and tell them, they just say, "Well, I'm sorry. I didn't really mean for it to sound that way." But there is nothing I can do about that. . . .

If they could take the time to get to know me, then it would be different, but instead they will get just a few quotes and then write a long story. Unfortunately, half of the things they put down aren't how it is, and this is where I have no control.

For a long time people thought that I was just in school to learn how to read and to play basketball. They didn't think that we studied in Nigeria, they didn't know that I knew how to play basketball, they didn't even know that I could speak. And a lot of the stories would make it look that way also. But later on, when some of them started talking to me, they could see the way that I talked, and it changed their minds.

Now, every day, it seems that there is somebody that wants to talk to me. Some people come from places that you have never even heard of, and often I wonder why they want to write about someone who is far away.

Although I enjoy the attention and the publicity, sometimes you feel like you are forced to be nice. Like anybody, there are times when you just want to be left alone. . . .

Sometimes I get a little scared when I think about leaving Houston, because someday I know that I will have to go. I want to play pro basketball, but I have to be sure when the time is right. . . .

When the time comes, it will be my own decision. That's the way that I really feel, because my parents aren't here. They don't know what I'm going through.

CHAPTER 8

NEXT

THE PUBLICITY OLAJUWON WAS RECEIVING ONLY INCREASED AS IT became clear he had been the missing piece Houston needed to compete at the top level. He was no longer learning the game; he was, especially on the defensive end, dominating it. Houston was now considered a powerhouse, and many US college coaches began to take notice. The best teams were no longer limited to the Big East Conference; there was talent everywhere. And, as Olajuwon forced many to consider for the first time, there was enormous potential abroad.

Some college coaches began contemplating a strategy: how can *we* find the next Olajuwon? His success at the Final Four motivated some to start thinking about recruiting abroad. "We're all copycats," says Jim Larrañaga, coach of the University of Miami, who has been coaching at the collegiate level for more than fifty years. "When Houston was getting to the Final Four . . . and Hakeem is just getting better and better, everybody's saying, 'Hey, I'd like to have a guy like that.'"

There are no hard data to turn to (the NCAA started keeping track of international players as a separate demographic category only in 2012), but many longtime coaches and experts felt as Larrañaga did: change was on the horizon, and Olajuwon may have contributed to the increase in international players on US rosters. "I don't think there's any doubt that he did," says Richard Lapchick, renowned human-rights activist and scholar who led the South African sports boycott during apartheid. He had first traveled to Africa in 1967 and has seen the growth up close.

Longtime NBA executive R. C. Buford had a similar feeling in 1983, when he was a graduate assistant coach at Kansas. Facing Olajuwon and the Cougars in a nonconference game, the first play of the game remained etched in his mind: Olajuwon blocking Greg Dreiling's hook shot with his underarm. That night, Buford was certain that basketball was headed for global expansion and that a new pipeline would emerge between the United States and Africa, allowing players like Olajuwon to dominate.

He was correct, but a "pipeline" wouldn't form for some time. "There was this Olajuwon phenomenon that had people's hopes and expectations probably out of whack," Buford said. Change *was* happening, though, beginning within the Southwest Conference. And Houston's rivals had to find a way to catch up.

Bill Brown, then an assistant coach at Arkansas, happened to hear about a talented player in Lagos who was reportedly six feet eleven. Brown quickly boarded a plane for Nigeria. "It was a chance of possibly securing another young man like Olajuwon," says Brown, who gave an interview for this book before his death in 2023 at age seventy-one. "We were going to do everything we could to see if we could get that done."

Brown, a Black man who had been born in Toledo, Ohio, was excited to travel to Africa. But he landed amid widespread political instability. That night, he slept in the airport on top of his luggage. The next day, he met the player, who turned out to be far shorter than promised. "It would have been nice if I would have found a player," Brown said, "but at the same time, I felt connected, a little closer to Hakeem."

Around the same time, Rob Evans, a Texas Tech assistant coach, traveled to Mozambique to scout a six-foot-ten player that Chris Pond, the Central African Republic coach who helped get Olajuwon to the States, recommended. But Evans found the player to be too old for NCAA restrictions. "He was a very good player," Evans says. "I remember the last thing he told me was, he really wanted to come."

Evans and Brown were among an increasing number of assistant coaches making trips to Africa, enough of a trend that the *New York Times* headlined a 1985 article with "Basketball Recruiters Now Journey to the Bush." Indeed, not everyone embraced the demographic changes emerging within the sport. "Now hold on just a minute" began a 1982 *Boston Globe* story. "Ever since 1891 when Dr. James Naismith hoisted an old peach basket atop a pole for his students at a Christian training school in Springfield, the game of basketball has belonged to Americans . . . Akeem who? . . . How can the son of a West African cement dealer be an All-America candidate?"

That attitude seemed to reflect the growing sentiment toward international athletes in general. The same article asked the reader to "say Goran Skoko 10 times fast," referring to a Fordham player from Yugoslavia, before mentioning an Indiana University player from Germany: "Would you ever call your future Celtic offspring Uwe Blab?" Another article mentioned that Olajuwon's "a Nigerian. A foreigner. There's suddenly talk that intruders such as Akeem have absolutely no business competing in this country's own national championships, such as the NCAA basketball tournament."

The late Billy Packer, college basketball commentator and voice of the NCAA Tournament for more than thirty years, espoused similar sentiments. He said on a broadcast during halftime of a 1984 Houston-Virginia game that if a coach could win an NCAA title by recruiting "foreigners," as he called them, he wouldn't bother to develop American athletes. Packer later said that international players were "taking away the scholarships from your kids and mine." He added, incorrectly, that some soccer teams representing colleges didn't have an American citizen on their roster. "Are these our national championships or not?" Packer said.

Of course, not everyone shared that opinion. "It's a great game, why not share the game?" said Digger Phelps, former Notre Dame coach and analyst. "It can be the least complicated road to peace." Many other college coaches felt that way as well, excited about expanding their recruiting pool. LSU's Hall of Fame coach Dale Brown told one of his assistants at the time, "Get me a big man, even if you have to go to the planet Uranus." But Bill Brown, who had a Yugoslavian player and a Dominican player on his roster in 1984–1985, suggested that the rise of international players was a fad "like the hula hoop."

Lou Carnesecca, the former St. John's coach, had been ahead of the curve, already traveling abroad to coach clinics for about a decade. In June 1982, before Olajuwon's sophomore year, Carnesecca led a team of Big East college players to Angola. "It was being called 'dunk diplomacy' because we had no diplomatic relationships with Angola," says Lapchick, who went on the trip. The hope was to improve US relations with Angola in the same way "Ping Pong diplomacy" did with China in the 1970s.

When asked about his motivation for the trip, Carnesecca also mentioned recruiting: "Well, I can't say it's all altruistic. Especially if I see someone like that," he said, pointing to Dud Tongal, the seven-foot star for Fordham.

In many ways, Tongal's story has been lost over time. Although Olajuwon is recognized as the first true international basketball superstar, Tongal and his cousin, Edward Bona, who both grew up in Khartoum, Sudan, were two African players who came to America about a year or so before Olajuwon.

Tongal was relentless inside and had a pretty sky hook. Bona was a lethal shooter. Drafted by the Suns, Bona ended up playing professionally in England for eight years. Tongal died at age fifty-four in 2010 while working in Qatar following his professional basketball career there. "We were trailblazers," Bona says. "Dud had a chance. He should have played in the NBA for a while." That was Tongal's dream. Like Olajuwon, both Tongal and Bona helped pave the way for other African players who came after them. All their stories are connected, interwoven threads in a shifting American hoops landscape.

One afternoon in 1978, Columbia coach Tom Penders spotted what appeared to be a seven-foot-tall man behind his team's bench, whom he'd later discover was Tongal. Columbia was facing City College of New York (CCNY), and Tongal was visiting his relatives in New York, one of whom was a diplomat working with the United Nations. That cousin came to know Floyd Layne, CCNY's coach, and told him about Tongal. Layne helped him obtain a visa to move to New York.

That summer, Tongal flourished in the famous NBA Pro-Am league held at CCNY. But after finding out that CCNY didn't offer scholarships, he looked elsewhere. Penders was soon hired at Fordham and offered Tongal a spot. Bona joined the year after. "It was like a dream come true," Bona says. They had long hoped to go abroad for their education because a civil war was raging in South Sudan. The pair eventually helped Fordham reach the NIT for three straight years, from 1981 to 1983. "I got a little bit of criticism from New York area coaches, saying we're depriving American kids of scholarships," says Penders, who later happened to coach the University of Houston from 2004 to 2010.

Tongal and Bona encountered some who doubted their abilities because of where they were from. "We played for the Sudanese national team, and they thought we didn't know how to play," Bona says. "They thought we were all projects—people that needed a lot of work to develop—which wasn't the case." Tongal and Bona also happened to be cousins of Manute Bol, also from South Sudan, who would later make his mark in the NBA. The cycle continued: Bol helped mentor South Sudanese star Luol Deng, who became a two-time NBA All-Star and who is also Bona's nephew.

All of them, Bona says, were inspired by Olajuwon. "Hakeem was a dreamer," says Gbemisola Abudu, NBA Africa's first vice president and country head of Nigeria. "He gave everybody permission to dream." That included another group of pioneering African players who arrived in the States shortly after Olajuwon. Akin Akin-Otiko, Olajuwon's former Lagos State teammate, went on to star at Oral Roberts from 1983 to 1987. Olajuwon's biggest foes from the Central African Republic, Anicet Lavodrama, Fred Goporo, and Bruno Kongawoin, starred for Houston Baptist in the early 1980s. Lavodrama was drafted in the third round of the 1985 NBA draft, eventually playing thirteen years at the highest professional level in Spain. Goporo and Kongawoin also played professionally. The trio represented the Central African Republic in the 1988 Summer Olympics.

Yommy Sangodeyi, Olajuwon's former teammate back in Lagos, moved to Texas in 1981 to play for Sam Houston State. Olajuwon had recommended him to the coach, Robert McPherson, remembering his friend. "We had never seen Yommy play. There wasn't film or anything," McPherson says. "But the description that we got, we felt like it'd be worth taking a chance on. And certainly he was." Sangodeyi thrived, leading the team in scoring during the 1983–1984 season.

He and Olajuwon stayed at each other's apartments, seeing each other most weekends. They cooked together. They frequented a reggae club in Houston, both being fans of Bob Marley. Sangodeyi, who eventually was drafted in the third round by the New Jersey Nets in 1984, ended up playing over a decade professionally in Italy, Sweden, Spain, Israel, Turkey, Argentina, and Brazil. He told the local papers in 1984 how far his protégé had come, from fumbling the steps for a layup to garnering comparisons to Chamberlain. "In Nigeria, he wasn't good," Sangodeyi said. "Now he's All-World. He's Mr. Universe. Sometimes, when I see him play, I can't believe it's him. If I hadn't seen him for a few years and someone told me, 'That's Akeem,' I [wouldn't] believe him. I'd say, 'No, no, no. He is not the same Akeem.'"

Sangodeyi remained friends with Olajuwon until his death in 2020. "He was extremely proud of Hakeem," his wife, Delphine, remembers. But Sangodeyi, an oft-forgotten pioneer himself, had laid the path for Olajuwon. Inspired him.

• • • •

Olajuwon's height, once a source of shame in his youth, was now admired. His talent and NBA potential made him famous in Lagos. "We haven't pressed for him to come home," his father, Salam, said at the time. "We don't want him to lose concentration, and he might if he came home a hero."

"At the airport, in the shops, anywhere I go [in Nigeria]," his mother, Abike, said, "once they realize I am Akeem's mother some stare at me as if I am from the land of spirits, others come to say hello to me, they are all very proud of him."

In 1983 *Sports Illustrated* even sent a reporter, Curry Kirkpatrick, to Lagos to conduct interviews for the first extensive national profile of Olajuwon. Olajuwon couldn't go—it was midseason—but gave

Kirkpatrick shoes and clothes to take to his brothers, and told him that he needed to visit Fela Anikulapo-Kuti, the musician and political activist, and spend time at his shrine. "[Olajuwon] told us: You've *gotta* go see him," Kirkpatrick says. He remembers Olajuwon handing him a gift to give to Fela. In a publisher's note that ran after the story, Kirkpatrick called Fela Olajuwon's "boyhood hero."

It's possible Olajuwon may have encountered Fela because they lived in the same neighborhood in Surulere. And for Olajuwon to instruct Kirkpatrick to see Fela to demonstrate the quintessential Lagos experience suggests an admiration for Fela and, perhaps, a window into Olajuwon's political leanings at the time, given Fela's antigovernment and anticorruption lyrics. Fela had been arrested, detained, framed, and imprisoned on numerous occasions, his music constantly suppressed, his residences frequently attacked and destroyed.

Arriving in Lagos, Kirkpatrick, as well as Bill Campbell, a *Time* magazine photographer, made an appointment to see Fela, suggesting some kind of connection with Olajuwon. "Everybody couldn't just get in and go to see him," Kirkpatrick says.

Kirkpatrick and Campbell eventually arrived at Fela's shrine at about one in the morning. Fela didn't perform until 3 a.m., the crowd aching for him and his band to begin. They eventually gave Fela Olajuwon's gift. "He was so happy to receive these gifts from Hakeem," Kirkpatrick says. "He knew all about Hakeem because everybody in Nigeria knew about Hakeem after that season, and the publicity he got from the Final Four."

· · · ·

As the 1983–1984 college season began, Olajuwon looked dominant, swatting anything that came into the lane. NBA executives and scouts viewed him as a top draft pick should he leave school early. Now in his junior year, Olajuwon said he would take his time with his decision, but scouts were convinced he was more than ready.

Jerry West, then the Lakers' general manager, remembered being floored by Olajuwon's unique combination of size, agility, and skill. "You saw this incredible player in college and said to yourself, 'Oh my gosh, I haven't seen someone play like him,'" West said. During one game that West attended, he was sitting in the VIP section with some trustees and other notable alums from the opposing school who didn't seem to know much about basketball. Josh Rosenfeld, the Lakers' director of public relations from 1982 to 1989, sitting with West, remembers one person saying that Olajuwon's "not that good; he's just bigger than everybody." West turned around and politely said, "Excuse me, but he's one of the five best players on the planet right now."

Olajuwon had a taste of the next level from many conversations with Clyde Drexler, who left for the NBA that year, as well as from continuing to play pickup games against Moses Malone. But a trip to Indiana in the summer of 1983, where he met Celtics star Larry Bird, further introduced him to the NBA. Cougar teammate Renaldo Thomas, who is from Gary, Indiana, was working a camp with Bird and asked Olajuwon to tag along. He sat in the bleachers next to about four hundred high school players and two hundred coaches, awaiting direction. "Akeem, get down here," Bird said. "I want to use you a little bit."

Bird challenged Olajuwon to a game of one-on-one. Olajuwon didn't have time to be starstruck, playing against the NBA's greatest shooter in the heartland of hoops. He defended Bird as hard as he could, and Bird uncharacteristically missed a half-dozen shots. Olajuwon won, 4–0. "I couldn't score on him today," Bird said. "But I guarantee you I'll score on him someday [in the NBA]."

Olajuwon was headed for stardom, but he was in many ways still a young man, who, along with Thomas, borrowed a limousine from the father of a friend, hitting all the McDonald's drive-thru windows in town. "My life is not real. It's like, what you say, a fantasy," Olajuwon said.

He'd see his name in the papers and wonder if it was really him that they were writing about. Later in the year, at a nonconference tournament, the Cougars attended a Four Tops concert. Drummer Melvin Franklin acknowledged the players from the stage, finishing with "Akeem, big guy, good luck to you."

Olajuwon paused. *How did he know who I was?*

· · · ·

AS THE SEASON CONTINUED, OLAJUWON BECAME MORE DEMONstrably competitive on the floor. He was fiery, even getting into a couple of fights. One game, at UC Santa Barbara, Olajuwon was ejected for punching UCSB forward Scott Fisher in the face. The game had come down to the wire, and Fisher had to intentionally foul him because he knew Olajuwon didn't shoot free throws well. "Fisher!" he remembers Olajuwon saying after Fisher had taken a hack. "You foul me again, and I'll box you!" The referee hadn't called the foul, so Fisher fouled him again. "Next thing I know I've been punched in the face," Fisher says.

Another time, against Virginia, Olajuwon and six-foot-eleven center Olden Polynice went at it all through the game. Olajuwon had had enough of Polynice pushing him, and he elbowed him in the neck. Olajuwon received a technical foul. Later on in the season, after Olajuwon had a superb game, Craig Roberts, a longtime Houston radio and TV host, complimented him in the locker room afterward: "Well, looks to me like your *game* did the talking today."

"[Olajuwon] just blew up," Roberts says, "ran across the locker room coming at me with fists clenched." Lewis stepped in, calming Olajuwon down, telling him that Roberts was complimenting him. Lewis often told Olajuwon: "Don't lose your temper. It's always the second guy that gets caught, not the instigator." Olajuwon was rarely the instigator of the fights. Players shoved him in the post because they couldn't stop him. This would be a tactic he'd see (and have to learn to deal with) in the pros as well.

Going into the Final Four, which Houston had reached for the third straight year, Olajuwon knew it would be just as physical. Houston would face Georgetown and Patrick Ewing in the title game, considered the premier matchup of centers, which would have been comical to say during Olajuwon's freshman year when his own teammates told him to watch a TV special on Ewing. "[We] want you to play like this guy," they said.

Olajuwon and Ewing had gotten to know each other through various NCAA programs, bonding over their love for reggae and Peter Tosh. And they respected each other on the court. "I'm like, 'Dear God! He's so quick, so agile,'" Ewing later said. "He's an amazing competitor."

Georgetown had Olajuwon's number, though, suffocating him every time he caught the ball. Olajuwon was uncharacteristically ineffective, playing with four fouls—three in the first half. He took only nine shots and finished with fifteen points. Houston lost 84–75, falling short of a national title for the third straight year.

It was a crushing defeat. Afterward, Olajuwon said Houston didn't play as a team, calling his teammates selfish. Phi Slama Jama—one of the best teams in the history of college hoops—would never win a championship. Olajuwon soon declared that he was leaving early for the pros.

It was a tough decision, one he constantly mulled, talking with his family, his coaches, and his friends, especially Drexler. The two leaned on each other. Drexler was a model for him, a guide whom Olajuwon cherished as he contemplated the move.

Olajuwon decided it was the best time for him to go to the NBA. There was a strong chance he would get to stay in his beloved Houston. The decision just felt *right*. And he finally felt ready to test his game against the world's best.

CHAPTER 9

TOWERS

SINCE 1966, THE NBA HAD USED A COIN TOSS BETWEEN THE LAST-place finishers in its two divisions to determine which team would secure the number-one pick, a system that would disappear in 1985 with the advent of the NBA lottery. In May 1984 the Houston Rockets and the Portland Trail Blazers were to flip a coin to determine which team would get the first pick and a chance at Olajuwon.

The Rockets had finished last in the Western Conference. The Trail Blazers had been the recipients of the last-place Indiana Pacers' first-round pick, which they'd acquired in June 1981's Tom Owens trade.

Although Michael Jordan had also entered the draft, at that point he was not yet anointed the future of modern hoops. If Houston lost the coin flip, though, it would likely take Jordan with the number-two overall pick.

Back then, teams believed they couldn't win without a dominant big man. The idea of taking a guard like Jordan was not just risky but also illogical. The NBA was vastly different from today's game, where three-point shots rule. Back then, everything flowed from the inside to the outside. "If you didn't have a good center," says former Lakers assistant coach and executive Bill Bertka, who coached some of the all-time-best big men in Wilt Chamberlain, Kareem

Abdul-Jabbar, and Shaquille O'Neal, "you weren't going to have a good team."

Mike Thibault caught a glimpse of Olajuwon long before anyone thought he was NBA material. Then a Bulls assistant coach and director of player personnel, scouting was one of his main duties. Thibault had attended one of Olajuwon's first college practices. "When he could barely play," Thibault says.

Thibault happened to come to Houston's practice to watch another Cougars player. But something about Olajuwon fascinated him. The kid played so *hard*. And as Olajuwon broke out during his next two seasons, Thibault kept coming back to Houston's gym. "It was just such a dramatic change from when he was young," says Thibault, now general manager of the WNBA's Washington Mystics.

Thibault was splitting his time between Houston and North Carolina, watching about ten of Olajuwon's practices and ten of Michael Jordan's because the Bulls were in the hunt for a top-five pick. Rod Thorn, then Bulls general manager, was also impressed by Olajuwon. "For a young guy, he just moved very, very smoothly," says Thorn, now eighty-three, "like most big guys can't do. . . . He would have been our number-one pick had we gotten it."

On the eve of the coin flip, Rockets staff went to Jimmy Weston's bar on Manhattan's East Side to discuss strategy over some Irish whiskey. Weston gave them a clock in the shape of Ireland, with twelve Irish coins in a circle to represent each hour, for luck. It was the same place the Rockets had convened for last season's momentous coin flip, when they won the right to draft Virginia's seven-foot-four Ralph Sampson, national Player of the Year, with the number-one pick. Sampson had been the most highly touted college player in the nation, his hype akin to LeBron James of the current era. If the Rockets drafted Olajuwon, they'd have not one but *two* seven(ish)-footers.

Olajuwon would again be listed on official pro rosters as seven feet tall, as he had been in college, despite standing somewhere between an inch and an inch and a half under that height. Jim Foley, then Rockets director of public relations before becoming the team's longtime radio broadcaster, ultimately went with seven feet, despite some in the media complaining that he wasn't *really* that tall.

"Look," Foley remembers telling them, "he's been seven feet tall for the last three years at the University of Houston, and we got an owner here who's going to pay him about a million bucks a year, so I'm not going to shrink him. So, he remains seven feet tall."

It added not just to Olajuwon's mystique but also to what Houston fans were beginning to call the "Twin Towers"—the tantalizing possibility of having Sampson and Olajuwon ruling the Rockets frontcourt for years to come. "They just felt that by calling [Olajuwon] a seven-footer, that would make him more, you know, bigger than life," says Bill Worrell, the Rockets TV play-by-play announcer for forty years.

When the Rockets won the coin flip, Foley tore off his jacket and shirt. "I had a T-shirt underneath that said 'AKEEM,'" Foley says. "We were all excited. Houston was going crazy about us getting the Twin Towers."

"There's no way you don't take Olajuwon," says Steve Patterson, who was working in the organization at the time and would eventually succeed his father, Ray Patterson, as Rockets general manager in 1989.

Olajuwon would get to stay in the only American city he had ever known, and the Rockets would have their best chance yet to rejoin the list of NBA title contenders for the first time in the post–Moses Malone era, which, to this point, had featured two straight seasons without a playoff berth. (Malone was traded to Philadelphia in September 1982.)

Portland, licking its wounds, turned its focus toward Sam Bowie, a talented center out of Kentucky who had once shown even more promise. Then he suffered a fractured tibia that was discovered after the 1980–1981 season, causing him to miss both of the next two seasons. He played all of 1983–1984, but his health was a major concern for teams heading into the draft. Still, Portland appeared willing to take the risk, for it already had guards in Clyde Drexler and Jim Paxson, and needed a center. The Trail Blazers didn't even see Jordan as a viable pick at number two, which has haunted the franchise ever since.

Thibault, on the other hand, wanted the Bulls to pick Jordan at number three, not because he was clairvoyant but because he thought Jordan possessed a competitiveness he had never seen before. And Thibault had coached Hall of Famers in his previous stint with the Lakers. "After being around Magic and Kareem before that," Thibault says, "I had a hard time thinking this, but I said, 'I might have found a guy who is more competitive than them.' Every drill he wanted to win."

"Everybody thinks what a great job we did in getting Jordan," Thibault says, "[but] if we would have had the first pick, we would have taken Hakeem." Thorn felt the same way. "To think that Jordan would become what Jordan became was a real reach," Thorn says. "I wish I were prescient enough to think that he was going to be as good as he turned out to be. My feeling was, he's gonna be really good, and hopefully he'll be an All-Star someday, and hopefully he'll make our team a lot better."

Thibault even remembers one Bulls front-office member saying to him, after drafting Jordan, "Is Jordan really as good as you say? He better be good." However, Jordan wasn't always a lock at number three. Many potential trades were offered to the Bulls in the weeks before and even on the very day of the draft, which was arguably the most consequential in NBA history.

. . . .

THE BULLS HAD TO BE PREPARED FOR PORTLAND TO PULL A SUR-prise and steal Jordan at number two. They needed a backup plan. "We weren't probably going to take Bowie," Thibault says. "We were scared off by all the medical stuff." Instead, the Bulls focused on Sam Perkins of UNC and Charles Barkley of Auburn. "In all candor, I would have taken Sam Perkins," Thorn says. Perkins was an all-around player who could pass and score. Thorn says he thought the six-foot-six Barkley was "too small" to be an effective rebounder in the NBA.

Rumors flew left and right, including one that claimed Portland was attempting to trade the number-two pick to Houston to get Sampson. The Lakers reportedly offered several players to the Rockets, potentially even star James Worthy; the Rockets were adamant that they were never contacted.

Another rumor had the *Rockets* trying to trade Sampson to the Bulls for the number-three pick, which might have given the Rockets Olajuwon *and* Jordan—a dynamic duo that would have undoubtedly altered history.

The Rockets did discuss the trade briefly, but nothing materialized. Meanwhile, the 76ers, picking at number five, were trying to send guard Andrew Toney and the number-five pick to the Bulls for the number-three pick, meaning that Jordan would have gone to the 76ers. Billy Cunningham, the 76ers coach, was a former UNC player and liked Jordan a lot. Thibault says some Bulls owners wanted to draft a center no matter what. "They would've been happy if we could have traded with Portland to get Bowie," Thibault says. "We absolutely did not want to do that. We wanted Michael."

About a week before the draft, Portland general manager Stu Inman privately told the Bulls' Thorn that he was going to select Bowie, meaning that Jordan would be available for the Bulls.

Nothing was guaranteed, though. "We kidded the night before about locking our owners in the room so that they couldn't change any picks on us," Thibault says. "But we basically prayed right up to the draft that we were going to get Michael."

Heading into the Felt Forum at Madison Square Garden on draft day, June 19, 1984, the Rockets were giddy with anticipation about drafting Olajuwon. The place wasn't very well lit or very well attended; the NBA wasn't the billion-dollar enterprise of today. The league held a predraft party at a small Italian restaurant nearby. Olajuwon was thrilled to be there, dapper in a black suit and white tuxedo shirt with a red bow tie. His parents had flown in from Nigeria, beaming at how far their son had come. It was the first time they had seen him in three years. It was an emotional night for them. His mother, Abike, was shocked at the number of cameras and reporters present.

Longtime Bucks broadcaster Eddie Doucette and St. John's coach Lou Carnesecca served as the draft broadcasters. When describing Olajuwon, Carnesecca said it was a good thing for opponents he had started playing only five years earlier. "Thank God," Carnesecca said. "He'd be unbelievable."

Now reflecting back on the draft, Doucette remembers Olajuwon's "immense, immense talent," he says, but also his humility, awaiting his fate that night: "He was grounded." As planned, the Rockets selected Olajuwon number one. He became the first African player to ever be the first pick. He flashed a bright smile, holding up his new Rockets jersey as cameras flashed back at him. He shook Commissioner David Stern's hand. It was official. He was now an NBA player.

"This is the best thing that ever happened to me," he told Doucette that night, beaming. "I'm just very lucky to stay in Houston." However, potential deals behind the scenes were cropping up left and right among other teams. Thibault remembers one with the Jazz that would have sent John Stockton, who'd eventually fall to number sixteen, to the Bulls, to be a tandem with Jordan. Thorn remembers Dallas being interested in trading up for the number-three pick to get Jordan. However, none of that mattered once Portland picked Bowie at number two, allowing Jordan to go to Chicago as the third pick. It remains one of the all-time missed opportunities in the NBA.

Even after all Jordan has accomplished, though, it's a testament to Olajuwon's legacy that to this day you never hear people say *Houston should have drafted Jordan.* Olajuwon was just that transcendent. But even *he* wasn't sure of his true potential at the time. "It's a completely different league," he said ahead of his rookie season in 1984–1985. "I know that I have to prove myself. I hope the coaches and my team aren't disappointed in me."

* * * *

OLAJUWON NOTICED HOW PEOPLE LOOKED AT HIM DIFFERENTLY, treated him differently, now that he was in the NBA. He had more money than ever before, buying a custom-made blue Mercedes mini-limousine *and* a Porsche 944. He had a giant home, sophisticated and lavishly decorated. He even had his own signature sneakers, signing a deal with Etonic to produce shoes named "Akeem the Dream."

"I'm still the same person. I just have to be myself," he said in 1984, before returning to Lagos for the first time that summer. He spent several weeks there. It was a meaningful trip, one that reminded him of how far he had come—and how much things had changed. How much *he* had changed. Now that he was famous, he sensed that some friends were afraid to approach him. He also felt like he couldn't relate to some of them anymore, either. His family, on the other hand, embraced him. He finally had his parents' blessing to pursue professional basketball. They had been skeptical, but when Yemi, his older brother, visited Hakeem the previous summer in Houston and reported back that Hakeem had his head and heart in the right place and that his decision to turn pro wasn't irresponsible, they relented. Salam and Abike told Hakeem they would pray for him.

Beginning when he was drafted and continuing through the first few years of his NBA career, Nigerian newspapers boasted about both his achievements and his demeanor. Adekunle Olonoh, of *Punch*, wrote: "He is quick-footed; he is a good scorer and the best shot blocker. Simply put, he is AWESOME." Banji Ola, also a journalist for *Punch*, noted that Olajuwon was "a good ambassador of Nigeria and Africa . . . [he is] humble and cool headed." Phil Osagie, a journalist for *Quality*, wrote that "he has made Nigeria more popular in the U.S. than a dozen ambassadors put together. . . . Another Hakeem would be hard to find. His determination [domination] of a game which Americans gave to the world and a game that is best played by Americans is remarkable." Another edition of *Quality* declared that "the house he lives in looks like something out of a megabucks Hollywood movie. . . . Akeem is indeed the miracle man of basketball."

While on his trip back to Lagos, Olajuwon visited his old stomping ground, Rowe Park. His former teammates were proud of him, including Tari O. Preh, the veteran who'd trained with him. "We thank God," Preh says, "that when he went, he was able to excel." Many of Olajuwon's old teammates and coaches were pleased to see that he hadn't changed much in terms of his humility, his spirit. His witty sense of humor. Fame didn't seem to shake his core. He seemed happy to just be *home*.

But even he, too, could see how many more Nigerian kids were playing hoops. His success had motivated many to take up the sport. "Every young ball player now wants to play basketball," says Ganiyu

Otenigbade, his former Lagos State and Muslim Teachers College coach. Agboola Pinheiro, who coached him on the Buffaloes, the Nigerian team, echoes the sentiment: "Hakeem was the eye-opener. Because of Hakeem, we had more people come into basketball. More families allowing their children to play and leaving football for basketball, leaving tennis for basketball."

Otenigbade eventually visited Olajuwon in America, as did Coach OBJ, who coached Olajuwon in the 1980 tournament in Morocco. Coach OBJ brought a group of Nigerian players who he had been training to New York when the Rockets played the Knicks at Madison Square Garden. Later that night, Olajuwon invited the team to his hotel. Coach OBJ marveled at how much Olajuwon had grown. "He just wished everybody well on the tour," Coach OBJ says, "because he knows what he went through when he first came to America. . . . He was just excited for us."

Other former teammates, still in Lagos, such as Gbade Olatona, read articles about Olajuwon with pride. People would ask Olatona and other teammates, "How come you guys are not in the US? Why are you not playing in the NBA? Why don't you want to travel?"

"I laugh," Olatona says. He'd simply respond with "America had gotten their dream."

• • • •

THE HYPE SURROUNDING HOUSTON'S TWIN TOWERS INCREASED AS training camp neared, as did the hope of building a dynasty that could compete with the Celtics and Lakers, as well as the 76ers.

Moses Malone immediately helped the 76ers not just make the NBA Finals for the second straight season but actually win in 1983 with a 4–0 sweep of the Lakers.

Ticket sales at the Summit, where the Rockets played, soared. A downtown Houston billboard said, "THE FUTURE IS NOW."

Referring to the Twin Towers, *Sports Illustrated* wrote about "the young millionaires who have greatly altered the Houston skyline— and may someday do the same to the NBA's." John Lucas, Rockets veteran point guard, told reporters that "I think there's going to be a commandment around the league. Thou shalt not come into the lane against this team."

Olajuwon and Sampson weren't the first pair of skyscrapers to team up. The Lakers had George Mikan and Vern Mikkelsen. The Knicks had Walt Bellamy and Willis Reed. The Warriors had Wilt Chamberlain and Nate Thurmond (later, when Chamberlain was traded, Thurmond paired up with Lucious Jackson).

But Olajuwon and Sampson weren't just tall; they were back-to-back number-one picks, players who seemed to be of a different mold than the traditional, bigger, less mobile center. "The uniqueness of it was that they were both really young. Sampson being in his second year, Olajuwon being a rookie, was definitely part of it," says Curtis M. Harris, a basketball historian. "It was great marketing, Olajuwon playing at University of Houston and Sampson being a huge college star himself. . . . And just how athletic they played, too. It made them more dynamic."

Even more so than Olajuwon, Sampson yearned to play guard, to push the ball up the court, dribble, and pull up for jumpers. But coaches would tell him to go back into the paint and stay in his lane. Olajuwon presented a thrilling opportunity for Sampson: he could play power forward and face the basket while Olajuwon could play center and fill the back-to-the-basket role. Reporters, though, wondered how the pair would work together. Some called it a "great experiment." Would there be enough room for them? Would they get in each other's way?

Sampson's path couldn't have been more different from Olajuwon's. Whereas Olajuwon came to hoops later in life, Sampson was praised practically as soon as he touched a ball as a child. He was nicknamed "Stick" for his skinny, lanky frame, and strangers had been gawking at him since he was a teenager. He was seen as an aberration; he couldn't get into cars without twisting himself into a pretzel.

Sampson once felt compelled to give a speech for a high school class assignment that began with "Yes, I am seven feet four." He went on to say: "I have two eyes, two ears, a nose, a mouth. Like everyone else, I have normal feelings. I get hurt inside, too." But he wasn't allowed to be sensitive; he was expected to dominate. Sampson was hailed as the next great center, a generational player who graced the cover of *Sports Illustrated* fresh out of high school.

So many college coaches called the family home that sometimes Sampson pulled the phone off the hook or pretended to not be at home. When he visited Virginia, he was given a helicopter ride over Charlottesville and shown the top of University Hall, where someone had painted the words "Ralph's House." The attention only heightened once he arrived at Virginia, setting the record books ablaze. He remains the Cavaliers' career leader in rebounds, field goals, and blocked shots. "He was so gifted, so phenomenal," says Bob Rathbun, Atlanta Hawks play-by-play broadcaster who formerly called UVA games for Jefferson-Pilot Sports.

Even pro teams were after him. Detroit and San Antonio reportedly prepared to offer him a million dollars while he was still in high school. Celtics coach Red Auerbach tried to recruit him, but Sampson wasn't interested. He wanted the true college experience. "Red was absolutely furious that this guy wouldn't come out after his freshman year," says Peter May, who covered the Celtics and the NBA for more than three decades for the *Hartford Courant*, the *Boston Globe*, ESPN, and the *New York Times*.

The attention was almost too much to bear. "There were times that he just had enough, he just had to get away, like really get away, disappear for a couple of days," says Lee Raker, Sampson's Virginia roommate and teammate. Sampson deflected whenever he could, asking reporters to interview his teammates instead. "[There] wasn't a selfish bone in his body," says Jim Larrañaga, the Miami coach who served as an assistant coach for Virginia at the time.

That's why Sampson wasn't threatened by Olajuwon's arrival. On the contrary, he was eager to share the spotlight, have a rest from its glare. "I admired his career," Sampson says, adding later: "I had welcomed the opportunity." And as the Rockets' training camp began, Sampson quickly saw why so many coveted the rookie. Olajuwon was a work in progress, but one thing would become abundantly clear to Sampson: "He gave everything he had every game."

· · · ·

OLAJUWON HAD NEVER RUN SO MUCH IN HIS LIFE. THE TWO-A-DAY practices were brutal. He still had much to learn. He had to pay close attention, memorizing eight plays on the first day alone. And when Rockets coach Bill Fitch told him to run a backdoor play, Olajuwon looked for the gym's *actual* back door.

He was determined to excel, but he hadn't lost the sense of wonder and excitement: basketball was still relatively new to him. "He was a wide-eyed phenomenal player that was just *happy*," says Kevin McKenna, briefly on the Rockets during that training camp. "He was very hardworking, very serious when it came time to play and everything, but he was just happy."

Fitch, who died in 2022, was a stickler for detail. He was extremely knowledgeable about the game. He was a former marine drill instructor, as his father had been before him, and preached discipline. "As tough and mean as you could be," says Carroll Dawson, a Rockets assistant coach at the time who'd eventually become the Houston general manager in 1996. He and Fitch remained friends up until Fitch's death. "He was cut out of the old cloth," says Dawson, now eighty-six.

Fitch was known as a builder; the Hall of Famer would take struggling teams and turn them into contenders, like the Cavaliers in the early 1970s and the Celtics in the late 1970s and early 1980s. He led Boston to the 1981 NBA Championship before moving on to the Rockets in 1983. Things had to be run a certain way. *Fitch's* way.

He had an unusual sense of humor. In Olajuwon's third season with the Rockets, he made a joke out of reporters saying he put certain players in a doghouse by bringing an *actual* miniature doghouse to the locker room with twelve cloth dolls bearing the number of each player. He had unique methods of recruiting, too. In 1962, while at North Dakota, he recruited a young Phil Jackson, who'd later coach the Bulls and Lakers dynasties. Despite facing a major blizzard with more than twenty inches of snow, Fitch drove to Jackson's high school sports banquet as a speaker. Then he called Jackson up to the podium and said, "I want you," as he locked a pair of handcuffs around Jackson's wrists. He was eccentric, to say the least.

Yet Fitch was a good match for Olajuwon because he was a teacher at heart, always prepared. He was ahead of his time in terms of studying film. His nickname was "Captain Video": he was one of the first NBA coaches to embrace video replay. When he was with the Celtics, he'd often carry two VHS recorders under his arms. Jeff Twiss, then Celtics director of public relations, remembers a day when Fitch ran out of his beloved VHS tapes. Twiss and other staffers had to scramble all around Boston to find more. "He went through so many tapes, and he saved a lot of them. No recycling," says Twiss, now Celtics vice president of media services and alumni relations.

Fitch challenged Olajuwon, saying he'd give him fifty dollars if he grabbed twenty or more rebounds in a single game. Once, as Olajuwon was preparing to shoot a free throw before practice, Fitch dropped a hundred-dollar bill next to his feet and said, "It's yours if you can make it." Olajuwon missed but started cracking up. "Dream liked it, because he wasn't getting a big contract yet," says Craig Ehlo, former Rockets guard. "It didn't last long because Dream's pride came out and said, 'I'm supposed to make free throws.'"

Olajuwon stayed late after practices, launching free throw after free throw. Carroll Dawson often worked out with him. Dawson was known by his peers as a basketball genius, a terrific big man's coach. He and Olajuwon worked together tirelessly that first season. The coach played a crucial role in shaping Olajuwon's offensive development when Olajuwon's repertoire was quite limited. "He was just a spring chicken in this game," Dawson says.

But Dawson remembers how quickly Olajuwon picked things up. He saw a tremendous amount of potential: "He was as athletic as anybody I've ever seen in my life. I get chills thinking about it now, and it's been a long time." Dawson would feed him in the post, and they'd labor on his jump hook, up-and-under, and baseline jumper—things he'd need to develop to become a more complete player, not just a defensive stalwart. "When you come back tomorrow," Dawson would say, "we'll do the very same thing." Some players might find the drills boring, but Olajuwon's competitive nature drove him to try to master the mundane.

Another renowned coach, Pete Newell, saw those same traits ahead of Olajuwon's rookie campaign. Olajuwon had attended Newell's famous Big Man's Camp that summer in 1984, which profoundly affected his still-developing offensive skill set. Newell, who had led the US team to gold at the 1960 Olympics, in addition to coaching at Cal and serving as general manager for the Lakers, built his reputation on developing the game's best centers. Both in dress and demeanor, he resembled more of an Ivy League professor than a basketball coach, appealing to players' intellects, explaining not only the *how* but the *why* behind a move.

His biggest lesson? "Footwork," Newell once said, "that's the whole thing." He taught that players were right-footed or left-footed, just like people are right-handed or left-handed. Most players, Newell thought, were underdeveloped in one foot, not as comfortable stepping, driving, or defending on that foot. Olajuwon was mesmerized. He started to learn how to apply the quick foot speed he already possessed. He was excited to attend camp each day, riding in a rental car with then Kansas City Kings forward Eddie Johnson, who'd later join him on the Rockets. "A lot of the things that he incorporated came from the teachings of Pete Newell," Johnson says. "It made him a dominant player."

It would take time, but Newell could see that Olajuwon had a high basketball IQ. He could read instantly what the defense was giving him. "Who taught you to move your feet like that?" Newell asked him.

"No one," Newell remembered Olajuwon saying. "I play soccer." That soon became evident to his Rockets teammates, too. Whenever he stood on the sideline, he'd kick the ball with his feet or bounce it off his knee. Once, Olajuwon was telling McKenna and Ehlo about his football exploits as a kid. "I can kick a basketball over my head and kick it off the backboard," Olajuwon said.

"No way," McKenna said. "You can't do that." Olajuwon smiled. He pointed to the other end of the court before pulling off the circus trick. They were stunned: a six-foot-ten, 255-pound center just did a bicycle kick, launching the ball some 75 feet. "It was crazy," McKenna says.

Dawson and Rudy Tomjanovich, then a scout and assistant coach with the Rockets, were not as thrilled. They came over and scolded

Olajuwon. "Don't you ever do that again!" they said. The future of the franchise couldn't injure himself playing *soccer*.

. . . .

A COUPLE OF HOURS BEFORE THE ROCKETS' FIRST GAME OF THE season, Olajuwon called Fitch. "Coach, can you tell me how . . . how we go . . . to the game?" Fitch laughed, telling him that players and coaches would meet in the lobby and then take a bus to the arena. Olajuwon paused. Fitch then realized that Olajuwon, who cared about how he presented himself both in terms of dress and demeanor, wanted to know what attire was appropriate to wear to the arena. He didn't carry himself as if he was entitled, and he didn't want to make a mistake.

He was perhaps a little *too* eager in his debut. The first few minutes of the opener against the Mavericks were forgettable. Olajuwon, who was in the starting lineup, clanked his first dunk off the front rim. He kept fouling, getting beat on defense. Fitch benched him for the rest of the first half. He wanted to teach the rookie, who had collected a whopping thirty-five fouls in the previous seven exhibition games, that he had to defend smarter.

Sampson comforted Olajuwon at halftime, telling him to breathe. "The ball is coming to you, so go ahead and do your thing," Sampson said. "I'll be on the other side [of the basket] if you miss, so don't worry about it." Olajuwon came out of the locker room and began to resemble the number-one overall pick that he was, hitting a shot sixteen seconds in. He scored the team's first nine points as if suddenly realizing basketball is basketball, no matter if at Rowe Park or an NBA arena.

On one play, Olajuwon leaped up to block center Kurt Nimphius, causing him to dish to Brad Davis. Davis thought he had a clear shot at the rim until Sampson came charging toward him, swatting the ball back to midcourt. Olajuwon and Sampson smiled at each other, and Houston escaped with a win. They were just starting to learn each other's habits.

It took a little time for the Twin Towers to adjust to each other. "A lot of growing pains," says Bill Baptist, a Houston-based photographer who worked with the Rockets for more than thirty years. Olajuwon was learning to play as a true center, figuring out when to flash to the ball, when to screen away. The two big men sometimes accidentally posted up on the same side, but eventually, after about a month or so, they found their groove: Olajuwon in the low post, Sampson up high. "We were double trouble," Sampson says. "If I couldn't get it, he would get it. If he couldn't get it, I would get it."

Even if neither blocked the shot, they intimidated guards from even challenging them at all. "Teams had nightmares trying to come to the basket," says Allen Leavell, former Rockets guard. "You might get by the guards, and you might miss Dream, then Ralph was waiting. It was tough for players to score inside."

During one game Rockets guard Robert Reid was defending Celtics floor general Dennis Johnson when Reid dropped back, giving Johnson plenty of space. "A whole freeway lane open," Reid recalled.

"Reid," Johnson said, "what are you doing?" Reid turned his head back to Sampson and Olajuwon, their arms raised tall as tree trunks, and said, "You feel lucky?"

"Man, y'all wrong! Y'all *wrong!*"

CHAPTER 10

DIFFERENT

OLAJUWON WASN'T AFRAID TO BATTLE THE NBA'S PREMIER BIG men, including the Celtics' Robert Parish. Olajuwon reminded himself how, early in college, some said he'd have trouble cracking the lineup because he hadn't grown up playing hoops. Being a late bloomer didn't stop him then, he reasoned, so why would it now?

His Rockets coaches marveled at how talented he was for someone still so new to the game and its history. When Fitch asked him to help Celtics coach Red Auerbach tape a segment for his show, *Red on Roundball*, Olajuwon didn't know who Auerbach was. He didn't know Celtics lore, either, as Fitch tried to explain that some thought there were ghosts at the famed Boston Garden.

John Lucas, the Rockets guard, gave him a tour when the Rockets were in town to play the Celtics, showing him the creaky, dead spots on the parquet court, as well as the retired jerseys and championship banners on the rafters above.

"Well," Lucas said, "what do you think?"

"This place is a dump," Olajuwon said.

To Olajuwon, a basketball court was just a basketball court. And he wasn't very impressed with this one, no matter its history. He was more focused on the game, and, as it commenced, he soon realized he had his work cut out for him. Parish quickly slipped in front of him, beating him for an offensive rebound and put-back. But Olajuwon also showed Parish he wasn't going to back down. "Hakeem was, excuse my language, alllll up in yo' *shit*," Parish says. "He was all up in it! He had this uncanny knack of just coming out of nowhere."

"You know I don't say this about many players, but during Hakeem's premium years, I would have bought a ticket to watch him play. . . . That's how much respect I have for his game," Parish says. "He brought it every dang night, and I respect that, because that's how Larry [Bird], Kevin [McHale], and myself approached every game. Hakeem had the attitude that we had. We didn't come to your town and your arena to play a game. We came, excuse my language, we came to take the fuck over. And that's the attitude Hakeem had." That attitude, Parish says, led Olajuwon to believe "he's the baddest MF in the building, and that's why he was not afraid of us. Because he felt like he belonged on the floor with us, and he played that way, too. He played with tremendous confidence and arrogance. And that chip on his shoulder."

However, the Rockets' veterans had to temper Olajuwon's confidence just a little. He was a man of few words but often said, "Give me the ball, man!" even if he faced a double-team. It wasn't because he was selfish but because he was so skilled, and so mobile; he knew he could score no matter how many defenders were thrown at him.

Once, as Olajuwon shot over two defenders, Rockets guard Allen Leavell said, "Dream! If you come back out with the ball, you can reset it. You don't need to take that shot!"

"Allen!" Leavell remembers Olajuwon saying. "They pay me to take that shot!"

Another time, Leavell looked for Olajuwon, but he wasn't open. So Leavell faked to him and took the layup himself. He missed.

"Allen! Why didn't you pass me the ball?!"

"Dream, I had a layup!"

"But you *missed* it! I could have had a dunk!"

"Well, have you ever missed any dunks?" Olajuwon just looked at him blankly.

Another game, Olajuwon fought for position, posting up. Reid drove to his side, but Olajuwon was getting clobbered inside. "Bob-bee! Bob-bee! Give me the ball, man," Olajuwon said.

"Dream, you got three guys on you!"

"That's OK. I dunk on everybody."

He had a point. The bigs couldn't match his catlike quickness. "Olajuwon was just something *different*," says Jack McCallum, a renowned *Sports Illustrated* journalist and author who covered that era of hoops. "You tend to say he changed that position."

He'd outrun the guards in sprints during practices. In games he'd often rack up more steals than the guards, too. Sometimes he'd be the farthest defender from the offensive player racing the other way in transition but would somehow beat everyone else down the court for the chase-down block. He played with a certain pride, an unquantifiable competitiveness. "Hakeem is the type, he ain't gonna let you beat him," says Robert Barr, former Rockets strength coach who eventually served as vice president of basketball affairs.

That he was becoming such an offensive threat surprised his coaches more than anything else. "We were so happy that he was turning out the way that he was turning out because we sort of felt we were going to have just a defensive presence and didn't realize all these wonderful things that he developed, too," Tomjanovich says. "He was learning the NBA game, but he continued to awe us, and then do it again. It was just, 'My God, he can do that, *too*?'" A little baseline jumper there, a little shimmy to the center there. He had soft hands, hands that just found a way to the ball. "It was pretty amazing to watch that for a guy who got into the sport late in life. That's very rare to see that kind of a touch."

Olajuwon challenged himself to add more moves to his offensive arsenal, practicing them against teammate and friend Jim Petersen. "I was his sparring partner," Petersen says. "You know, Muhammad Ali needed someone to spar against." Petersen, now the television analyst for the Minnesota Timberwolves, felt that Olajuwon was almost more ruthless in practice than in the games. And he was much stronger than defenders realized, with his broad base and solid core that made him practically immovable off the block. Then he'd shoot a fadeaway, light as a feather. "Dream could do things that no normal person could do," Petersen says.

Olajuwon kept getting better and better, dropping forty-two against the Warriors in December 1984. It was only his twentieth NBA game. "I remember him coming into the league like a freight train, man," says former Hawks Hall of Famer Dominique Wilkins, now Atlanta's vice president of basketball operations. "He was just awesome. I don't care what era you're in, because what he did and how he did it, and the type of player he was, was undeniable." Remembering his first time guarding Olajuwon, Wilkins says, "He was a *phenomenon*. The best all-around center I've ever seen. I was holding on for dear life. He just ran me over."

• • • •

OLAJUWON, AVERAGING 20.7 POINTS, 11.8 REBOUNDS, AND 2.3 blocks per game, was voted a reserve for his first All-Star Game, joining Jordan as one of two rookies to earn the honor. "It really doesn't seem real to me. This is all a little surprising," he said at the time. "If anyone had told me I'd be in the All-Star Game my rookie year, I would have doubted them very, very much. . . . Sometimes, I really don't believe it myself."

The All-Star Game, though, was a bit of a letdown for Olajuwon. He didn't play much. "Big fella," Sampson said to Olajuwon, "in an All-Star game, you gotta sprinkle minutes." Olajuwon shrugged. Sampson, who had started the game, put his arm around him. "It'll come."

Sampson looked after Olajuwon, as did many Rockets players who saw him as a younger brother. They'd remind him to bring his coat on East Coast trips. They enjoyed his playful personality. He cracked everyone up while shooting a commercial for McDonald's. During each 60-second take, he had to eat a Chicken McNugget. It took him more than 100 takes, so he indeed ate *100* Chicken McNuggets in one sitting.

He wasn't afraid to laugh at himself. "He never came off as being better than anyone," says Hank McDowell, former Rockets forward. "He was a superstar from the get-go, but he never really seemed like a superstar." They respected his kindness, the way he always said "thank you" to bellmen who offered to take his bags. He'd refer to Jim Foley, then the Rockets public relations director, as "Mr. Foley": "To this day, he still calls me Mr. Foley. I gave up trying to get him to call me Jim."

Olajuwon relished his time with teammates and coaches off the court as well. He and Barr frequented IHOP for pancakes and eggs. Olajuwon then began inviting Barr to his home, where he'd cook Nigerian food for him. "I could not believe it," Barr says. "We had fish, rice, vegetables. I'm like *holy crap*. Dream could actually cook! It was amazing."

Carroll Dawson remembers one road trip where he and Olajuwon stopped to get coffee. "Let me have two donuts and a coffee to boogie," Dawson told the barista. Olajuwon couldn't stop laughing at the strange-sounding request. To this day, whenever he sees Dawson, he belts out: "Coffee to boogie!"

His teammates and coaches appreciated his sense of style, too. Olajuwon knew from a young age that his outfits would affect how people perceived him. He wore bright-colored fabrics and was partial to cashmere and linen. He'd wear skinny ties with bright colors and bold patterns. He rarely shined his shoes; he'd just buy another brand-new pair. He'd tell Cedric Maxwell, who'd eventually join the Rockets, that his passion for fashion came from Lagos. "Maxey," he'd say, "you gotta go to Lagos. Lagos makes New York look like a tiny town. You can do anything in Lagos."

Olajuwon also relished elegant suits, at one point having forty-five tailor-made suits from shops in London, Paris, and Milan. He even designed his own clothes, enjoying visiting fabric stores and envisioning an outfit, then creating something that seemed both regal *and* modest. Unique. "I don't like to wear things that everyone else wears," he once said. "I've always wanted to be different."

That creativity, which would later land him a fashion spread in *GQ* wearing a custom-made wool suit along with a multicolored Hermes silk tie, was only just beginning to reveal itself on the basketball court.

• • • •

As much as he was enjoying his time with his teammates and coaches, and breaking out as one of the league's best young players, he still experienced some of the same stereotyping he had in college. The *Atlanta Journal-Constitution* once wrote that Olajuwon was "a new American hero whose very success is predicated on his own innocence. He does not know enough about our part of the world to have been corrupted by it." *ABC News* ran a Sunday segment in 1984 in which broadcaster Dick Schaap said, "Once a soccer player, Olajuwon is still learning the subtleties of basketball and English, and while he occasionally stumbles on both, his progress is impressive."

Scholar Munene Franjo Mwaniki, author of *The Black Migrant Athlete*, contextualizes these depictions of Olajuwon within the broader history of American exceptionalism and racism in that they position Olajuwon as a "charming media novelty, as outside and above the 'normal' corrupting influences of even his home country and city." Olajuwon is described as "a model minority against either the backdrop of Africa(ns) or African Americans," Mwaniki writes. "In each instance Olajuwon 'benefits' but blackness as a whole is restigmatized."

. . . .

THE ROCKETS, WHO WENT FROM 29–53 IN THEIR LAST PRE-Olajuwon season to 48–34 in his rookie year, faced the Jazz in the first round of the 1984–1985 playoffs. But the hard-fought series is remembered not just for the 3–2 Utah victory but for one defining play: "The Punch." Billy Paultz, former Jazz center, nicknamed the "Whopper," remembers it well. The fifteen-year veteran and three-time ABA All-Star can't escape it. He's often asked about "The Punch" at his job at a car dealership. "Hey, check this clip out," customers say to him, showing him the moment on YouTube. "Forty years later," Paultz says.

He had one task during the fifth and final playoff game: shut down Olajuwon. Because that wasn't entirely possible, he did the next best thing: pester Olajuwon. "You couldn't stop his quickness. It was just tremendous. . . . Really unparalleled," Paultz says. Olajuwon had been schooling seven-foot-four Mark Eaton, who went down with a knee injury as the Jazz trailed by eight.

"Come on, get in," Frank Layden, the Jazz coach, said to Paultz. "I decided to start annoying Hakeem," Paultz continues. "I figured if I'd just start jabbing him in the ribs a little bit, just to catch him off his game a little bit. I was doing it where nobody could see it."

A little bit turned into a lot. Reid shouted from the bench: "Whopper's hanging on Dream!" The referees didn't flinch. Olajuwon kept scoring but grew more and more agitated.

"He finally broke," Paultz says. Olajuwon walked over to Paultz, coldcocking him in the face. "It was like, *dang, Dream*! But that was Hakeem," Reid said. He had been that way in college, too, most notably punching UCSB big man Scott Fisher. Olajuwon wouldn't back down.

Surprisingly, after punching Paultz, Olajuwon didn't get ejected. "That's the way it was back then," says Robert Falkoff, then the Rockets beat writer for the *Houston Post*. "It fired the Jazz up so much."

Paultz remembers the referee telling him "I'm not trading Olajuwon for Paultz," which he took to mean "I'm not ejecting a star like Olajuwon in the last game of the series." Olajuwon was eventually fined $1,500. He fumed afterward. Craig Ehlo, the Rockets guard, remembers him upset not so much at Whopper but saying, "That motherfucking Mark Eaton's never going to win another game against me!"

A few weeks later, when Michael Jordan was named the 1984–1985 Rookie of the Year, Fran Blinebury, the Rockets beat writer for the *Houston Chronicle*, called Olajuwon for comment. Olajuwon, who was the runner-up, expressed elation for Jordan, saying he had more than earned the award. Blinebury then obliquely alluded to The Punch. "If you had to do it all over again," Blinebury said, "would you change anything?"

"Yes, I would probably punch that old man," Blinebury remembers Olajuwon saying, referring to the referee. "And if I keep reading what you are writing, I will punch you out, too."

Blinebury laughs at the memory because the two became close as the years wore on, but *this* version of Olajuwon was not yet as mature as he'd eventually become. He had a short fuse then, smoldering, often on the verge of outright combustion. He felt that players were trying to disrespect him, punk him, and he wasn't going to allow that to happen.

Referees, meanwhile, weren't quite sure how to handle Olajuwon, not only his demeanor but his footwork as well. It was so quick, almost as if he were dancing, that they weren't sure at first if he was committing a travel violation. What's more, opponents had to find a way to somehow adjust to Olajuwon: adjust to something they had never seen before.

CHAPTER 11

SHAKE

RICK MAHORN, PISTONS POWER FORWARD AND CENTER, HAD OLAjuwon right where he wanted him. He dipped his shoulder into the Rockets' big man, backing him down before gently pulling away for the shot. Olajuwon lost his balance and fell to the ground but quickly popped up. "You won't get me with that move again," Olajuwon said as the two ran down court, according to Mahorn.

Now Olajuwon was on offense, pushing Mahorn back, faking one way, spinning the other way, then swishing a buttery fadeaway jumper. Now *Mahorn* was on the ground. "Sorry," Olajuwon called out to him. "Did I . . . *shake* you?"

Olajuwon started laughing. Mahorn, one of the original Detroit "Bad Boy" Pistons, scowled: "The hell outta here with that bullshit!" Only now, more than three decades later, can Mahorn admit that Olajuwon had gotten him good. "In my mind, you know back then, I was a Bad Boy, I'm like, 'Mothafucka?! You ain't shake *me*! You just made a shot.'" But deep down, he knew it wasn't any old shot. "It was something new. It wasn't Abdul-Jabbar's sky hook. It wasn't Bob Lanier's [left-handed hook] shot," Mahorn says, adding later: "He *perfected* moves. We call it stealing, but he ain't steal anybody's moves."

Olajuwon was in his second NBA season, and his offensive repertoire wasn't just coming along—it was developing its own manual.

He moved like a guard, shaking left, shaking right, pirouetting this way, that way, falling away for a silky jumper. It was a thing of beauty, the way he made off-balance shots look like layups. If he was fading, especially toward the baseline, the defender knew he was cooked. Olajuwon had such a high arc that he once called the technique "putting [the ball] to the moon." "I never saw a shot like he had from that angle," says Jack McCallum. "I mean it looked like he was going to hit the edge of the backboard. The only person I've ever seen do that is Larry Bird, and that was in fool-around shooting games. It's an incredible shot."

Olajuwon didn't just move; he *flowed*. "If he ever got you in what we called the popcorn machine," says Ralph Sampson, the former Rockets center, "once you jump up in the air, and you make that move, he knew it, and then he could counter that move into something else. He was deadly with that Dream Shake." And then after embarrassing someone, he'd start giggling, like a teenager. He played with sheer joy, which came not from racking up video-game statistics but from losing his man completely. Sometimes he'd even miss the shot because he himself was so distracted by the thought that two people could start in the same spot and, in a blink, he could make his defender believe he was going one way, then change directions on a dime to go the other way while his defender lay helpless. "That is art," he would later say. "It is art to keep someone frozen like that until you are gone."

Olajuwon turned the court into his own canvas. He was bright red in a black-and-white era. "I am not an artist who paints or draws," Olajuwon continued. "I look at basketball like an artist looks at painting. When you look at basketball as an artist, you get so much joy from the fakes and the creativity. That is the part that is so much fun."

• • • •

"Shake" seemed the only way to describe such a quick move, according to Bill Worrell, the longtime voice of the Rockets, who coined the name "Dream Shake." He initially called the move on live broadcasts the "shake and bake" or even casually in conversations as doing the "dipsy do." "I just needed to come up with something that was as regal as he was, that kind of fit his style," Worrell says. "It's just that he was such a blur. I always thought of making a milkshake. Just putting stuff in a blender and shaking it up."

Stuff. That would be the arms and legs and hearts of some of the most elite centers in NBA history, men much bigger and taller than Olajuwon. Kareem Abdul-Jabbar, Patrick Ewing, and, later, David Robinson and Shaquille O'Neal—Olajuwon shook them *all.* He had to use his quickness and creativity out of necessity because as strong as he was, he wasn't going to outmuscle those players. He wore them out by constantly moving. "He was probably one of the first really versatile big men," O'Neal says. "One of the first big guys to be able to step out."

And he had this unflappable confidence about him. "Just give me the ball, man!" he'd tell his teammates. "Talk to me, man!" When Dream was hot, Dream was *hot.* Worrell knew he needed a name for the move that matched that kind of pizzazz and felt he had to run the name by Olajuwon before using it. The two were sitting at a Cleveland airport on a road trip when he asked Olajuwon's opinion. "That is good," he remembers Olajuwon saying. "I like that."

The Dream Shake kept evolving. Take away the middle? He'd spin baseline. Take away the baseline? He'd spin middle, fake once, twice, maybe even a third time, then score. He had a counter for every counter. "You could see the look of desperation on the defender's face," Tomjanovich says. "That little distance there, eight to ten to twelve feet, is, I think, one of the harder shots in basketball, and to do it with big people pushing on you? . . . It was pretty amazing that he could just keep that soft touch with all that physical play inside."

Olajuwon approached basketball with the same creativity he did with fashion. Having just one move, in his eyes, was like having one outfit; one wouldn't wear the same outfit to the party as one would to the gym. He needed to have multiple moves—multiple outfits—revealing his wardrobe slowly while continually adding new pieces.

Players had no choice but to respect him:

Michael Cooper, former Lakers guard: "You got kind of mesmerized in watching him."

Bill Walton, Hall of Fame center: "His footwork is an extension of his character, his mind, his spirit, his soul, his vision. . . . He was quick as could be, and quickness is not a physical skill. Quickness is a mental skill. His mind just goes so fast." Walton gave an interview for this book before passing away in May 2024 at seventy-one.

Vlade Divac, former Lakers center: "If you're not ready, he'll kill you."

Gary Payton, former Sonics guard: "He always tricked you. . . . He used to give you fits because he was so light on his feet."

Robert Reid, former Rockets teammate: "It was just like the *Swan Lake* ballerina."

Kenny Smith, former Rockets teammate: "He's one of the few players that was indefensible. Because the shots you were basically saying, 'Hey, we want to force you to make, take,' those are actually the shots he was *looking* for. He was like, 'Oh, you want me to spin baseline, fake towards the rim, and fade away and shoot? That's the shot I want to take.'"

Mychal Thompson, former Lakers center and now serving as the team's radio analyst: "He was a combination of LeBron, Jordan, and Kobe in a center's body. . . . He's gotta change his nickname. He's no dream. He was a *nightmare*. . . . It was exhausting and demoralizing trying to guard him. . . . I had to really practice—like an opera singer. I had to warm up before the game and start learning how to say, 'Help!' in a really loud voice."

Cedric Maxwell, former Celtics center and current Boston broadcaster: "He was unreal. . . . Hakeem was doing the Eurostep before the Eurostep was invented. The spin move on the post was like putting your clothes in a dryer. That spin move, it was like you can't even watch it, it was so fast."

That's because Olajuwon studied guards, ever since that day in Lagos when he saw a teammate dribbling between his legs without looking. That was challenging, and that thrilled him; he didn't want *easy*. He felt the traditional back-to-the-basket big-man game was . . . boring. "I never really liked being a center," Olajuwon later said. It was far more fun, he realized, grabbing the rebound, dribbling all the way down the court, and *creating*. Stop and pop. Dunk. Even he never knew what was next.

That thrilled fans—but gave some referees pause.

• • • •

ED T. RUSH, FORMER LONGTIME NBA VETERAN REFEREE, REMEMBERS studying Olajuwon's film more closely than he did the film of other players. "The study of his footwork was like none other. I mean, we had not seen a big man put himself in that kind of position on the court and do those kinds of things," Rush says. "Initially, I think when he first came in the league, we got some of those plays wrong, because it just looked like, 'Wait a minute. That can't possibly be legal.'"

Many weren't sure if Olajuwon was traveling. "If a player is doing something that nobody else can guard," says Don Vaden, another former veteran NBA referee, "you think, 'OK, well, he's got to be doing something illegal.' . . . He was just a magician with the ball." Still, it was challenging to determine with the naked eye which foot was Olajuwon's pivot foot. "It's like boom, boom, boom, and he's gone," Rush says.

Olajuwon forced referees to prepare a little harder for Rockets games. They'd often watch a series of his moves in their pregame meeting. "We would look just to make sure," Rush says. "It was pretty amazing." And, most importantly, "It was not illegal," says Bob Delaney, another former veteran NBA referee. Referees also realized that they, too, could get caught reveling in his moves. "I do remember a couple times just thinking to myself, 'I don't care who it is, there's no guarding this guy. He's unguardable,'" says Bill Spooner, another former veteran NBA referee.

Even more impressive, Olajuwon was only twenty-three, a second-year pro only just beginning to realize his powers. "He knew he was unstoppable," Ralph Sampson says.

His former teammates and coaches in Lagos weren't surprised. They had seen traces of the shake and of his quickness, his agility, his fakes, while he played football. When he was running to the ball in football and his defender would chase him from behind, he'd have to shake in one direction in order to evade him, confuse him, and ultimately control the ball and sprint in the other direction. He was not as helpless on the basketball court early on as some portrayed him to be. "He was not the overnight American wonder phenomenon that they want to make the world believe," says Oritsejolomi J. Isebor, his former Leventis Buffaloes teammate.

Beginning hoops at a later age actually worked in Olajuwon's favor, allowing other muscle groups to develop first. He was more of an athlete first, basketball player second, which is why Anthony Falsone, former Rockets head strength and conditioning coach and Olajuwon's personal fitness trainer, called him "Athlete."

Whereas many have acknowledged how *football* helped foster Olajuwon's hand-eye coordination, speed, and change of direction, *handball*'s influence has been underestimated. Handball is all about mobility, pivoting, faking a defender one way, then shooting over him the other way. Olajuwon constantly reverse pivoted, possessing the spatial awareness and lateral foot speed to know where he and his defender were—and would be—at all times. That ultimately helped him pull off his signature Dream Shake on the basketball court, feeling where his defender was, intuiting which way to spin.

But many didn't realize that the *shake* was influenced by something else. Or, more accurately, *someone* else: Yommy Sangodeyi, his boyhood hero and friend. "Yommy taught him the greatest move Hakeem used in playing in the NBA," says Agboola Pinheiro, who coached him on the Buffaloes. "I wanted [Hakeem] to be an identical player [to] Sangodeyi, and that was his greatest move in the NBA. That's the Dream Shake."

Sangodeyi wouldn't just shake people; he would rarely miss the shot that followed. Gbade Olatona, Olajuwon's former Lagos State teammate, says, "Yommy had this clinical touch, wrist touch, after he does the shake, and then faces his opponent. . . . He has a way of finishing it, you see his wrist dangling like, 'Heeeeeeey,' already calling it." Sangodeyi worked on the shake religiously. "It was almost scientific," says Delphine Sangodeyi, his wife.

Delphine cautions against giving her late husband full credit for the move. "I think it was not [Yommy] that created it alone. . . . Yes, it was Yommy, but it was also Hakeem," she says. "It doesn't just belong to somebody." Rather, the move was a blend: "I think the Dream Shake was really the fruit of their friendship," Delphine says, "and the respect for each other and closeness that they have."

Like music. One artist shares a song with another; then the listener adds his or her own flavor to it. There were bits of Sangodeyi, and bits of coaches Carroll Dawson and Pete Newell. Bits of football, bits of handball. Inspiration rarely flows back to a single beat.

• • • •

AFTER DEFEATING THE SACRAMENTO KINGS AND DENVER NUG-gets early in the 1986 playoffs, the Rockets made it to the Western Conference Finals against the defending champion Lakers. It was a surreal experience for Olajuwon, taking the court against Magic Johnson and Kareem Abdul-Jabbar, the two players he saw grace *Ebony* back in Lagos. The Showtime Lakers, coached by Pat Riley, were the overwhelming favorites. "It was a challenge to [Olajuwon]," says former strength coach Robert Barr. "He said, 'To be the best, he's gotta beat the best.'"

Abdul-Jabbar had known of Olajuwon's prowess much earlier, after he had asked Lynden Rose, Olajuwon's former college team-mate who had been drafted by the Lakers in the sixth round in 1982, whether the "big African kid" was legit. "Oh, he'll be your heir apparent," Rose said. "He's that good."

That much was clear by the end of the series, although one wouldn't have known it from the Rockets' 119–107 Game 1 loss. At one point, the crowd of 17,505 rose for a two-minute standing ova-tion after Johnson dropped a no-look bullet pass to a slashing James Worthy. Riley was so confident he gave his players a day off: "Go to the beach."

But that confidence, that hubris, backfired as the young and hun-gry Rockets stole the next three games to take a 3–1 series lead. It was Olajuwon's coming-out party. He was no longer just one of the Twin Towers but a gloriously talented player in his own right, exploding for forty points in Game 3 and thirty-five in Game 4. To watch twenty-three-year-old Olajuwon against thirty-nine-year-old Abdul-Jabbar was to say to yourself *Here is the future.* West, then

Lakers general manager, thought, "This guy is going to get better every year."

Abdul-Jabbar still took it to Olajuwon, dropping thirty-one points in Game 1 and thirty-three in Game 3, but other times, he looked helpless. *Sports Illustrated* quipped that the Lakers might have had better luck if they had "tried to tie [Olajuwon's] shoelaces together." When Abdul-Jabbar showed up to Lakers practice with his team down 3–1, he seemed . . . vulnerable. "I remember at practice, Pat Riley [turned] to Kareem and said, 'How can we help you?'" says Josh Rosenfeld, the Lakers' director of public relations from 1982 to 1989. "I think it was one of the few times in his career that Kareem didn't have an answer for someone. It was one of the very few times in his career that somebody was better than him. I think he realized that, and it had to be hard."

Olajuwon had thirty points in Game 5, spinning and scoring at will. The Lakers, knowing Olajuwon had a quick temper, substituted nearly every big man on him to ruffle his feathers, including Mitch Kupchak. In the third quarter, Kupchak kept elbowing and shoving Olajuwon, who finally snapped and punched Kupchak. The two tussled as referee Jess Kersey desperately tried to get between them, finally grabbing Olajuwon by the waist as the big man continued to swing at Kupchak. Olajuwon and Kersey fell to the floor. In the ensuing chaos, someone punched Kersey in the head. "I don't know which one of you just punched me in the head," Kersey said, "but if I find out, you're going to be ejected."

"Jess," Bill Fitch, the Rockets coach, said to him, "I know who punched you."

"Who was it?"

"It was Kareem and Magic."

Olajuwon and Kupchak were both ejected. "[Olajuwon] was very, very upset that he did that," says Craig Ehlo, former Rockets guard, "but it also showed that there was a lot of fight in that dog. He didn't want to go down."

"He lost his cool," Ehlo says, "but you could tell, it kind of sparked us." The game came down to the last minute. With the score knotted and just over a second left, Sampson, about twelve feet from the basket with his back to both defender Abdul-Jabbar and the rim, nailed an off-balance prayer of a shot, one that bounced on the front rim, then on the back rim before falling through the net as the buzzer sounded. The Rockets won, 114–112, advancing to the NBA Finals.

"I hate talking about it because we were supposed to kick their ass that game," says Cooper, the Lakers guard. Sampson was the hero, but Olajuwon had been lethal. It didn't matter who the Lakers assigned to him; he had his way with them all. "Hakeem was on a mission," Cooper says. "He literally put that team on his shoulders." Cooper laughs because now, all these years later, the two are friends. But then? "Enemy for sure."

"He is truly that wolf in sheep's clothing," Cooper says. "Hakeem comes off as nonthreatening, but, shit, *I'm going to kick your ass and I'm going to do everything I gotta do.*" Off the court, Cooper says Olajuwon is different. "You think somebody that big and intimidating would have a fierceness about them, but he is so timid and so likable and so courteous. It was a pleasure playing against him. I hated him. But I also had to love him."

. . . .

THE ROCKETS FACED THE CELTICS IN THE FINALS. THEY BELIEVED they were on the verge of shocking the world. "We felt we could do it," Sampson says. The Celtics were loaded with Larry Bird, Danny Ainge, Dennis Johnson, Robert Parish, Kevin McHale, and Bill Walton. "It was the deepest, richest, greatest frontcourt of all time," says Bob Ryan, the Hall of Fame journalist who covered the team for the *Boston Globe*. Many consider the 1986 Celtics the NBA's all-time greatest team. They went 40–1 at home that year. "We were playing so well," says Ainge, who is now the CEO of the Utah Jazz, "we felt like we were going to beat anybody. But I think we definitely had respect for the Rockets and what they did to the Lakers."

The Celtics weren't just confident—they were, in some ways, superstitious. When the Celtics played an early-season game in Indianapolis, Bird and Walton went back to Bird's childhood home. Walton scooped dirt from where Bird first began playing as a young boy, packing it into a mason jar. He kept that jar in his bag throughout the season, occasionally sprinkling bits of it for inspiration. It was *Bird's* team, but no one acted as if he were better than the other. Dan Shaughnessy, longtime sports columnist for the *Globe*, remembers "how secure they were in their own greatness. There was not a lot of ego."

Approaching tip-off for Game 1, Olajuwon walked up to Parish and said: "What's up, big Chief?" That was Parish's nickname, but it also showed Olajuwon wasn't intimidated. That was clear as play began, with Olajuwon Dream Shaking Parish early. "Great move, big fella," Parish remembers saying to him as the two ran down the court.

"He had me *allll* the way turned around," Parish recalls.

Parish then remembers catching the ball in the post and outmuscling Olajuwon before softly laying the ball in. "Way to go, Chief," Olajuwon said. "I guess that's a little payback, right?"

"Yessir! That's *payback!*"

The Celtics, though, were too deep and too poised, winning the first two games. Olajuwon had thirty-three points and twelve rebounds in Game 1 but struggled to find his rhythm in Game 2. He told reporters afterward that he was "ashamed" of himself. He was refreshingly honest. He tended to be hard on himself, hanging onto mistakes.

Olajuwon came back with a vengeance to help the Rockets win Game 3, but the Celtics stole Game 4 in Houston to hold a commanding 3–1 series lead. Olajuwon wasn't going to give up. "The tougher the game got," Ainge says, "the tougher he was. And I always respected that about him."

The Celtics' front line felt it. "Just the hardest elbow I ever received," Walton said. "He was a rock. My whole body just went numb." But what stood out about Olajuwon more than anything was his mentality. "He was the only person on the Rockets not scared shitless," says Jack McCallum.

Olajuwon led the Rockets to a 111–96 Game 5 victory, tying a then-Finals record with eight blocks, but the game ended in a brawl as Sampson and Jerry Sichting got into a fight. Celtics players were *pissed*. Up 3–2, the Celtics headed back to Boston and were ready to end the series. "I've never seen a team more focused in my life than when we lost that game," Ainge says. "As we sat and listened to the celebration in Houston, there was a lot of frustration and anger in our locker room." Nobody said a word on the plane ride home. Practice the next day was so intense that Celtics coach K. C. Jones ended the session early. He didn't want anyone to get hurt, and he knew the team was ready. "There was no way we were losing Game 6," Ainge says.

Tensions were high at the Garden. Bird was so fired up he could feel his heart pounding through his chest, a feeling that lasted until the final buzzer when he thought he might have a heart attack.

Rockets players just tried to focus on their play. But Boston was so in sync that, at halftime, Bird changed his uniform, something he never did; he felt so confident of victory that he wanted to have two championship uniforms. Indeed, the Celtics ended up winning the title with a 114–97 rout.

As disappointing as the loss was, Rockets players were filled with hope. They felt as if they were merely scratching the surface of a bright future in which they'd compete for many championships. But that isn't how history played out. It would be a painful road ahead, one that Houston couldn't quite figure out how to overcome.

CHAPTER 12

PRIDE

SONICS CENTER MICHAEL CAGE KNEW THERE WAS ONLY ONE WAY to stop Olajuwon: foul the crap out of him. "I got in fights with him—on purpose," Cage says. "And he took swings at me when I kept pushing him. But I'd have to damn near get thrown out of the game just to get under his skin."

"You can't let Olajuwon be Olajuwon," says Cage, now a broadcast analyst for the Oklahoma City Thunder. "He'll score forty on you. Maybe even fifty."

During one game, on March 3, 1989, Cage and Olajuwon battled underneath the basket in the first half. Olajuwon grabbed the offensive rebound after an Otis Thorpe miss and tried to go up strong, but Cage clobbered him and nearly threw him to the ground. "I was hitting him," Cage says, "kept hitting him."

Olajuwon had had enough. He finally took the bait. *Got him,* Cage said to himself, grinning. *Finally. I got him.* "He just turned around and took a swing on me," Cage says. A quick left-handed jab to the mouth. Cage needed four stitches. Olajuwon was fined $5,000. Cage and the Sonics were thrilled, winning 118–108. "I got a lot of fines, and I got a lot of fouls against Olajuwon," Cage says. "I said, 'Hey, a thousand dollars? OK. I'm making a million. I'm good if we can win the game.'"

The Sonics' strategy was a common one at the time, as effective as the one described in *The Jordan Rules*, in which opponents resorted to similar tactics because they couldn't stop Michael Jordan. "Everybody knew Dream had a quick temper," said Robert Reid, the Rockets guard. "I mean he was hell."

Even Olajuwon himself admitted so. "I have a quick temper," he said in 1988. He wasn't typically the instigator of fights; he just couldn't help but react. Opponents elbowed him and punched him in blind spots on the floor the referees couldn't see, given that there were only two of them. "A lot of shenanigans that weren't caught," says Jeff Twiss, the Celtics vice president of media services.

Olajuwon had to defend himself and would rack up countless technical fouls and ejections during his early years in the NBA, even leading the league in technical fouls during his second season. In addition to the Billy Paultz and Mitch Kupchak fights, there was also a fight with Kurt Nimphius. Once, after scuffling with Danny Schayes, Olajuwon grabbed referee Jack Madden by the elbow and was ejected. Later, against the Sonics, Olajuwon and Clemon Johnson exchanged punches. Then there was John Shasky. Greg Kite. J. R. Reid. "When you got him mad, he'd let you know about it," says Mychal Thompson, former Lakers center. "He was no pushover. No punk."

Olajuwon was no more aggressive or physical than any other player; it was just a brutally physical era of basketball. This was the era of the infamous "Bad Boy" Pistons, where Rick Mahorn once described elbowing Mark Price of the Cavaliers, leading to a concussion, as a "love tap." In 1989 the *New York Times* reported that there were nineteen violence-related incidents involving thirty players on sixteen teams. Players played through injury. There was no load management as there is today.

"We beat the crap out of each other," Cage says. "If you didn't get ejected, you had no respect from us." Seattle was another very physical team, and probably Houston's toughest foe, especially in the playoffs. Defense was the Sonics' identity. "We wanted to turn you over. We wanted to frustrate you into making mistakes," says George Karl, former Sonics coach.

But Olajuwon still found ways to put up astronomical numbers, even with the obligatory double- and triple-teams swarming him. They'd send two or three people at him before he had time to think. "[Seattle center] Maurice Lucas was one of the best enforcers in league history," says Nate McMillan, former Sonics guard and long-time NBA coach. "The only way Maurice could, or thought he had a chance of guarding Olajuwon, was to be dirty, be physical, foul him hard."

The elbowing, the pushing, was, in retrospect, the ultimate compliment. Olajuwon was too intelligent and too savvy to be stopped any other way. "We had so much respect for him . . . ," Cage says. "We were amazed that we couldn't get him to play the dirty game we played." He would see Olajuwon score through the most brutal of fouls and think to himself: *Somebody needs to check that guy's heart because he's not human.* "He kicked our ass, man," Cage says. "There's very few players in my fifteen seasons that I ever had that kind of anxiety, if you will, like how do you stop him?"

Gary Payton, the Sonics' floor general, remembers how much effort he and his teammates expended in trying to get Olajuwon "out of his comfort zone," Payton says. "He got mad really fast. What we were trying to do is really, really agitate him. And what I did to agitate him is I would go on him fast and hit his arms and his wrists, and they weren't calling calls like that. . . . He would always get frustrated and complain and then that would get him out of his game. . . . It started working to our advantage."

Olajuwon's ejections hurt the Rockets. He couldn't stay on the floor, and the losses mounted. Rudy Tomjanovich, then a Rockets coach, would often walk him back to the locker room after ejections. "We'd watch the game from the locker room," Tomjanovich says, "and he'd be sorry that it happened and that his emotions got away from him."

. . . .

Assistant Coach Carroll Dawson tried to reason with Olajuwon, explaining how much his teammates needed him to stay on the floor. "That didn't work. We tried everything," Dawson says. "His temper was just, he didn't really control it that much. It was kind of an explosion."

Referees often bore the brunt of it. "He was hotheaded," says Fran Blinebury, former Rockets beat writer for the *Chronicle*. "He called them the nastiest things you've ever heard," Blinebury says, adding later: "I talked to many referees through the years. They just despised refereeing his games because he was out of control."

Once, Don Vaden, former veteran NBA referee, called a foul on Olajuwon and remembers him saying, "God will judge you in the end!"

"Yeah," Vaden said to Olajuwon, "He probably will. But he's not going to be able to help me right now."

Bob Delaney, another former NBA referee, remembers a similar instance in which Olajuwon said to him, "God will punish you for this call." Delaney laughs: "I remember just thinking to myself, 'I think that God has more important things to do than worry about these calls.'"

During another game, referee Bill Spooner didn't call a foul that Olajuwon thought he should have. Olajuwon had tumbled to the floor. Spooner remembers Olajuwon gathering himself and, while running back on defense, clocking him in the stomach. "It was one of those where you know when you get hit in the stomach and you're not expecting it and it just kind of like, takes your wind away? And he just kind of popped me, and took my wind away," Spooner says. "And I stopped, and I ejected him."

The next time the two saw each other, Olajuwon apologized. "I am so sorry," Spooner remembers him saying. "I just meant to talk to you. I didn't mean to hit you."

"I know," Spooner said. "I didn't expect you to do that. And you caught me just right."

"Well, you kicked me out," Olajuwon said, "so I guess I deserved it."

"*Guess* you deserved it?! You hit me in the stomach, knucklehead. Next time you want to talk, just tap me on the shoulder and we'll talk all you want."

Jack McCallum, the former *Sports Illustrated* journalist, wrote a story about the Rockets' disarray. After the story ran, Olajuwon ran into McCallum, holding up a page of the story ripped from the magazine. "I talked to you for a long time. You don't even write anything about me!" McCallum remembers Olajuwon saying. McCallum tried to explain that the story was much longer than that page and only complimentary toward Olajuwon, but Olajuwon couldn't be dissuaded.

On and off the court, Olajuwon was a competitive person. For him, basketball was about pride. About honor. Practices were like real games to him. At some point, he'd challenge nearly every person on the team to one-on-one, not leaving the gym until he won. "He didn't just want to beat you," says former strength coach Barr. "He wanted to beat the crap out of you." He cared deeply for the game, and he expected those around him to as well.

Olajuwon didn't mind physical play, but this felt different. Players were trying to test him. In Lagos he had learned to surmise from afar someone's intentions. He remembered seeing people in the middle of what appeared to be a calm argument suddenly knocked out cold on the street. He felt if NBA players wanted to say something to him, they could speak to him from a proper distance. He almost *had* to respond with force, he felt, because if they were coming too close to his personal space, they were instigating a confrontation, intending to fight.

One reporter wrote that Olajuwon had a "reckless, undisciplined style," describing his actions as intrinsic traits rather than a justified response, possessing a "temper that has raged out of control." Olajuwon's image as a whole was not especially tarnished: he was widely known for being a magnificent, passionate, burgeoning talent. But articles written at the time also often emphasized his ejections.

One has to consider the context in which Olajuwon's actions—and other Black players' actions—were scrutinized. This was the era of the "War on Drugs," in which Black men—and athletes—were often criminalized. The majority-Black NBA was perceived by the white establishment and white fan base as "being violent, criminal, and out of control," wrote scholar Theresa Runstedtler in her 2023 book *Black Ball*. She continued: "They were labeled as ungrateful, undisciplined, and even immoral. The idea of the 'troublesome' Black basketball player came to define the decade."

• • • •

MEANWHILE, THE ROCKETS, ONCE A YOUNG, SCRAPPY TEAM ON THE rise, struggled to close out games.

Sampson, in the middle of his fourth and final All-Star season, slipped against the Nuggets on February 4, 1987, and suffered a major cartilage tear in his left knee. He had knee surgery and missed the next twenty-seven games of the 1986–1987 season. When he was playing, though, Fitch often called him out for being too soft, for not wanting to be a true center. Sometimes Sampson was even booed by Rockets fans.

The Rockets continued to unravel as several players were suspended for drug use, including John Lucas in 1986. Mitchell Wiggins and Lewis Lloyd were both banned from the NBA for cocaine use in 1987, although they were permitted to apply for reinstatement after two years. Olajuwon no longer had a reliable point guard.

The 1986–1987 season ended in disappointing fashion with a double-overtime playoff loss to the Sonics in Game 6 of the Western Conference semifinals. Although the effort was wasted, Olajuwon put on an incredible show, dropping forty-nine points, twenty-five rebounds, and six blocks while being triple-teamed in fifty-three minutes of play. Nobody could guard him. "He was hot as a firecracker," McMillan says. At that point, Sonics coach George Karl realized there wasn't much his players could do to stop Olajuwon: "It was magical. I admired him kicking my ass, I guess, is the best way to say it."

But Houston's hopes of a dynasty were quickly dissipating. The following season, in December 1987, Sampson was, to the surprise of many, traded to Golden State. The Twin Towers era was over. But to this day, Sampson isn't bitter, despite the way everything turned out. He loved playing with Olajuwon and fondly remembers the team's 1986 Finals run. "It was one of those most magical rides that we all respected and loved," Sampson says. "I think most of us wished we would have stayed together for another couple of years, but that didn't happen."

Olajuwon became the undisputed leader of a team fundamentally different from the one that had drafted him. He had to figure out how to get the most out of *this* team, and that was frustrating for him. After a tough loss to the Lakers, he was brutally honest with the press: "Everybody is just out there playing, but we don't play together."

Later that season the Rockets lost, 3–1, to the Mavericks in the first round of the 1988 playoffs. Olajuwon further isolated himself, criticizing the playmaking abilities of point guard Eric "Sleepy" Floyd as well as the effort level of center Joe Barry Carroll. Olajuwon maintained he wasn't trying to bad-mouth his teammates. He wanted to instill a sense of urgency within the group, but his relationships with teammates continued to sour.

Meanwhile, off the court, he had allegedly assaulted a clerk at a convenience store near his home in May 1986. Accompanied by Lita Spencer, his girlfriend at the time, he denied that he hit the clerk but said he was "verbally abused and cursed by the cashier." Olajuwon was ordered to pay $150 after pleading no contest to an assault by contact. Later, he allegedly assaulted a TV cameraman and photographer who came to his house, seeking comment for a story in 1988. The photographer claimed to have received several stitches afterward. But no legal charges were ever made public.

Coach Fitch was fired later that June with three years remaining on his contract. Don Chaney, the former Cougars star, took his place. He was looking forward to coaching Olajuwon, a player he felt was "special." He had known about him for quite a while, considering they were both Houston alums and had both been coached by Guy V. Lewis. "I was so in awe of him and his ability," Chaney says. But Chaney had to find a way to help Olajuwon become a better leader. Olajuwon was learning a fundamental truth the hard way: one man can't win a ring.

CHAPTER 13

DARKNESS

WHEN OLAJUWON FELT A TEAMMATE WASN'T GIVING FULL EFFORT in practice, he'd pull him aside and say, "You do not love the game." Those six words could cut *deeply*. "It was serious. Like, 'Oh shit.' It wasn't like a teammate telling you that. It's like a principal telling you that," says Matt Bullard, former Rockets forward.

You do not love the game was old school, an insult that attacked not talent but heart. Bullard, who played alongside Olajuwon for nine years and considers him a friend to this day, says the phrase came from a good place, of wanting to inspire, to instill the passion he possessed. Olajuwon couldn't shut off that part of himself, and his competitiveness was arguably his best trait as a basketball player. But at this point in his career, during the late 1980s and early 1990s, "he just didn't know how to embody that as a leader," Bullard says.

"Hakeem was not very patient back then," Bullard says. Still, Bullard and many teammates knew deep down he was right. "If I screwed up, and he was angry at me and yelled at me, it was like, 'Yeah. You're right. I fucked up. I'm going to try to be better,'" Bullard says.

Olajuwon wasn't urging his teammates to do something he wasn't willing to do. He gave full effort on both ends of the floor, becoming the first—and only—NBA player to record more than two hundred blocks and two hundred steals in a season in 1988–1989. That was desire. Effort.

Love.

But the distance between Olajuwon and his own teammates continued to widen. Robert Falkoff, the *Houston Post*'s Rockets beat writer, remembers sitting with Tom Nissalke, former Rockets broadcaster, at an airport. Back then, teams flew coach. The two spotted Olajuwon. "There goes Bruce Springsteen," Falkoff recalls Nissalke saying. "And the rest of us are merely roadies."

· · · ·

CHANEY'S FIRST ORDER OF BUSINESS WAS WORKING WITH OLAJUwon to pass out of the double-team. "That was probably one of my obstacles with him," Chaney says. "I remember him saying, 'Well, I can score on two guys. I can make the basket. I'm going to throw the ball to an open guy, and he misses the shot?!'" Chaney laughs. "He had a point there."

To his credit, Olajuwon usually *did* make those shots. And it wasn't as if he was a selfish passer; he was just so dominant that many times it didn't make sense to give up the ball. He had also more than earned the right to call for it. He was already one of the best centers—best *players*—in the league. "There was nothing he couldn't do," says Tim McCormick, former Rockets center, now TV analyst for the Pistons. "Any perceived weaknesses were just based on the fact that he didn't have a childhood of playing basketball."

But he didn't have enough support. Rockets management had brought in many players in the late 1980s who were either inexperienced or past their prime. "They weren't quite ready," says Bill Worrell, the longtime Rockets broadcaster. "Hakeem had to take on more of the load."

To put it more bluntly: "He needed some better teammates," Bullard says. "He couldn't do it all himself. He was *trying* to do it all himself."

Olajuwon and Chaney would talk about leadership and how to lead vocally and not just by example. "I think it took him a while to understand that there's a way to approach things and speak to his teammates," Chaney says. He tried to explain to Olajuwon that a leader has to be firm and direct, yet supportive, making sure that teammates know that the leader is in their corner. "That's a hard thing to do," Chaney says, "especially when you're not used to being a leader."

Chaney explained to Olajuwon that both he and his teammates had to trust one another. He had to pass it out to his teammates to instill confidence and trust in them, and they had to make the shot to validate his confidence and trust in *them*. Trust took time. Olajuwon would later insist that it was not a matter of trust, but he was clearly still learning how to navigate a team without Sampson. "It was a process," says Purvis Short, former Rockets forward. "He became the true focal point, the true leader of the Rockets, and really established himself. I think all great players go through that 'process' if you will. You saw it with Jordan. With LeBron. From a talent standpoint, there's no question of how talented they are. On any given night they can give you thirty. . . . But true greatness arrives when you can kind of harness all of that talent to the benefit of your team."

Sometimes teammates missed shots, and Olajuwon wouldn't kick the ball back out. "It was tough because we were all searching around and trying to figure out how we could help him, and how he could help us," says Mike Woodson, former Rockets guard and current head coach at Indiana University. "And that took some time." Olajuwon would also let his teammates *know* he wasn't pleased if they didn't feed him the ball. Jim Petersen, the former Rockets forward, remembered an instance when guard Allen Leavell missed several consecutive shots. "Dream was getting angrier and angrier every time Allen didn't throw him the ball, because Dream could pretty much score at will," Petersen says.

Houston called a time-out. "Hey, motherfucker, throw me the ball!" Petersen remembers Olajuwon saying to Leavell.

"Hey, fuck that, Dream," Leavell said. "I had an open shot."

"You fucking throw me the ball! You wanna fight me?"

"Not really."

Olajuwon was developing a reputation for being difficult to play with. He didn't like to be told "no." Some teammates were upset that Olajuwon publicly criticized them in the press. When Kenny Smith, former Rockets teammate and close friend, joined the team in 1990, he remembered hearing stories about Olajuwon screaming at point guards during games and telling the coaches to take them out on the spot.

Olajuwon even got physical with some of his teammates, including Vernon Maxwell. "He's gone after a couple people before," says Robert Barr. "Because he took that stuff serious. He didn't wanna just be out there, you know, bullshitting around." But to be clear: "Nothing to hurt somebody. He had a couple of incidents, but that was just him. I didn't mind that at all. If someone wasn't doing his job, he's gonna get on you."

Smith felt there was also a lack of communication between Olajuwon and his teammates, and he surmised that Olajuwon may have felt misunderstood. On one occasion, during an informal shootaround before practice, rookie Dave Jamerson didn't pass Olajuwon the ball back after he had made a shot. *Shoot until you miss* was the customary rule, and Olajuwon kept making his shots. Jamerson refused to pass him the ball even after Olajuwon called for it multiple times. Smith, who was present, remembers Olajuwon slapping Jamerson and saying: "Do not disrespect me. Give me my chance when I make my shot!" Jamerson was just goofing around, but Olajuwon perceived Jamerson's behavior differently, unable to respond in a more measured way.

A bit later in Olajuwon's career, the Rockets were getting beat in Seattle, and Maxwell's own temper was about to explode. He was cussing referees out; his nickname was "Mad Max" for a reason. Then Maxwell spat on the floor. Olajuwon was aghast. "Would you stop being so disrespectful?" Olajuwon said, according to Smith. "Just get in the locker room. Stop spitting!"

Maxwell then spat on the *locker-room* floor. Olajuwon stood up and grabbed Maxwell, and the two started fighting. Maxwell later claimed that he threw a chair at Olajuwon, breaking glass that splintered across the room. He allegedly picked up a piece of glass and said that he intended to "stab" Olajuwon.

Bullard remembers Assistant Coach Larry Smith and forward Otis Thorpe breaking the two apart. "It was really and truly a knockdown, drag out fight between those two. And if we didn't have Otis Thorpe or Larry Smith on our team," Bullard says, "they might still be fighting right now."

· · · ·

MEANWHILE, RUMORS SPREAD ABOUT OLAJUWON'S LIFESTYLE outside of basketball. His partying. "Living the NBA life," as some former teammates described it.

"He wasn't doing nothing crazy," Barr says. But like many NBA players of that era, one in which the league provided beer in the locker room after games, he enjoyed the nightlife. Leonard Armato, Olajuwon's former agent, recalled a trip he took with Olajuwon to Munich, Germany. Armato also said that Olajuwon didn't do anything "crazy." "By other athletes' standards," Armato says, "it was probably timid and mild." But he acknowledged that "it wasn't something anybody who was a devout Muslim would ever do."

Shortly before the start of the 1988–1989 season, Lita Spencer, his former girlfriend, sued him for breach of contract, alleging he promised to marry her if she proved she could bear children, forcing her to bear a child out of wedlock. The two had a baby girl, Abisola, in July 1988. Spencer claimed Olajuwon caused her to suffer "extreme mental anguish, humiliation, and disgrace."

Although she eventually dropped the lawsuit, there seemed to be more headlines about Olajuwon's off-court conduct than his on-court performance. In addition to allegedly assaulting the TV cameraman, the convenience-store incident, and a host of on-court fights, there were also rumors of drug use, which Olajuwon flatly denied. He told reporters at the time he was willing to pay a thousand dollars to take a test and clear his name. But the press questioned his moral compass, depicting him as immature, selfish, and egotistical, having strayed far from the charming "kid" they had admired just a few years before.

"Dr. Jekyll and Mr. Olajuwon," wrote the *Houston Chronicle*. "For as long as we've known him Akeem has been a Dream. But lately he's beginning to look like Freddy Krueger. It's a real *Nightmare on Elm Street*. . . . The former innocent from abroad . . . threatening to bring the entire Rockets franchise crashing down in ruins. For as Akeem goes, so go the Rockets."

"Akeem Wearing Out His Welcome," wrote the *Houston Post*, calling him "a self-centered center, a problem that won't correct itself on the court overnight . . . [who has had] an embarrassing litany of foulups."

Olajuwon would later reflect back on this time period, calling it his "dark years." But his troubles began even earlier, when he first came to the United States. Being a member of such a famous team, Phi Slama Jama, Olajuwon found himself exposed to the crowds in nightclubs, at parties. "I think that he saw the lifestyle when he came to the US, and it was different," says Ibrahim Arch, his close friend and former vice president of Olajuwon's off-court venture, DR34M. "And then you see the lifestyle of the NBA players . . . you see all of that. And I don't think that's the lifestyle that he saw for himself."

He was trying to find himself, and he couldn't escape an uncomfortable feeling that tugged at him when he was alone, away from the lights. Away from basketball. He was making millions of dollars but still felt spiritually empty. "Now you're an NBA player, you have a big contract. Materially, you're successful," he later said, "but you're not fulfilled, because you know the most important part of your life is . . . missing."

Olajuwon, number 7, had a breakout performance at the 1980 AfroBasket, dominating on both ends of the floor.
Credit: Silva Canembo

Angola's minister of education, Ambrósio Lukoki, hands
seventeen-year-old Olajuwon the MVP award at the 1980
AfroBasket after the teenager led Nigeria to a bronze medal.
Credit: Silva Candembo

Olajuwon poses with a fan after losing
the 1982–1983 national title game to NC
State.
Credit: UH Libraries, Special Collections

During college, Olajuwon was known for his defense but began showing glimmers of offensive potential.
Credit: Bettmann

Life began to change fast as Olajuwon was drafted in 1984. He had more money than ever before, and he took pride in his car purchases.
Credit: Bettmann

Getting drafted to the Rockets as the number-one overall pick in 1984 was one of the happiest days of Olajuwon's life.
Credit: Bettmann

The Twin Towers, Olajuwon and Ralph Sampson, were poised to become a powerhouse in the late 1980s.
Credit: Bettmann

Michael Jordan edged out Olajuwon for Rookie of the Year in 1985, but the two are forever linked. Olajuwon was famously selected before Jordan as the number-one pick in 1984.
Credit: Bettmann

In the late 1980s, Olajuwon emerged as one of the top young players in the league.
Credit: Focus on Sport/Getty Images

New York Knicks star Patrick Ewing and Olajuwon battle during a fierce 1994 championship series.
Credit: Bob Strong/AFP via Getty Images

Olajuwon teamed up with former college teammate and close friend Clyde Drexler to win a title in 1995.
Credit: Smiley N. Pool/Houston Chronicle/Hearst Newspapers via Getty Images

Olajuwon torched David Robinson in the 1995
Western Conference Finals.
Credit: Jeff Haynes/AFP via Getty Images

Shaquille O'Neal has long maintained that Olajuwon was his toughest competition. The two battled
in the 1995 NBA Finals as the Rockets won their second straight championship, sweeping Orlando,
4–0. Olajuwon was Finals MVP.
Credit: Allsport/Getty Images

Olajuwon, left, and his teammates celebrate winning the 1995 NBA Championship.
Credit: Robert Sullivan/AFP via Getty Images

Olajuwon spent his final NBA season as a member of the Toronto Raptors.
Credit: James Nielsen/AFP via Getty Images

Representing the US Olympic basketball team at the 1996 Olympics in Atlanta was a moment of great pride for Olajuwon, who had become a US citizen a few years before.
Credit: Smiley N. Pool/Houston Chronicle via Getty Images

Islam is not just a religion to Olajuwon. It guides every aspect of his life and his relationships, and he remains deeply devoted to the faith.
Credit: Jerry Holt/Star Tribune via Getty Images

These days, Olajuwon still attends many University of Houston and Houston Rockets games.
Credit: Bob Levey/Getty Images

CHAPTER 14

FOUND

HENRI DE YBARRONDO, A HOUSTON LAWYER, HAD SEEN OLAJU-won from time to time at a distance. He had been part of an ownership group with the Rockets, and the two were often in the same spaces. Ybarrondo, twenty-eight years his senior, saw someone in need of help, a young person surrounded by what Ybarrondo called "wolves," with many people wanting things from him. Ybarrondo felt for Olajuwon, who seemed lost and lonely. He thought the superstar needed someone both to listen to him and to hold him accountable.

The two had initially met years before through Lita Spencer. But when Spencer filed the lawsuit against Olajuwon, he and Ybarrondo reconnected in 1988 when Ybarrondo represented him. What was initially a business relationship, which included representing Olajuwon behind the scenes both as a lawyer and financial adviser, became more of a friendship, a family dynamic. Their relationship became, in Ybarrondo's words, "all-encompassing."

Over the years, Ybarrondo didn't want to share his role in Olajuwon's life because he didn't want attention or credit for helping Olajuwon through some of his darkest days. He was comfortable with sharing this part of the story for this book because, he said, it was an important part of Olajuwon's transformative journey.

He recalled asking Olajuwon about his values in life, the kind of person he wanted to be. Olajuwon was willing to be introspective and vulnerable. "He listened," Ybarrondo said. Olajuwon admired and respected Ybarrondo as the two became closer. They bonded over their shared love for art, design, and style. Ybarrondo was devoted to his Catholic faith and seemed morally grounded. He was equally nurturing and stern. "Henri [was] a very, very, very kind guy," says Ibrahim Arch. "He was one of the people that I think was influential in Brother Hakeem's life."

Olajuwon began coming over to Ybarrondo's home on holidays. Ybarrondo counseled him that he needed to become more patient; the older man saw how quick-tempered he was on the court. "We needed to change his whole view of life," Ybarrondo said. That began with reevaluating what money meant to him. "The first thing I told him to do was change his lifestyle." Although he had a beautiful home, a contemporary, Moroccan-style house with an extensive collection of abstract paintings and custom-designed décor, "He didn't need a beautiful house," Ybarrondo said. He believed that Olajuwon needed to become more frugal and recommended he sell his home. According to Ybarrondo, Olajuwon then moved into a one-bedroom place for a brief period of time. "That dramatically changed him."

Ybarrondo was trying to teach him that material things wouldn't truly fulfill him. As part of their dialogue, they read the book *Happiness Is an Inside Job* by John Powell. The 1989 book's essential premise is that one should not seek happiness from external things or people. They dissected each chapter as if it were a university class. "A classroom of one," says Ybarrondo's son, Henri Jr.

Ybarrondo thought Olajuwon needed to detach from material wealth. He had a black Mercedes-Benz. He collected expensive, limited-edition handcrafted timepieces and watches, and he had a large collection of designer clothes.

But what did it mean to truly be *happy*, not just wealthy? Powell's book spurred the two to ask deeper questions about happiness. Would he finally access true joy once he had a certain amount of money in his accounts? When he had won a championship? When he had won a certain number of MVP awards? Ybarrondo knew that none of those things would *truly* fulfill him. "The book was the perfect vehicle," Ybarrondo said. "He realized that buying things don't make you happy."

Olajuwon and Ybarrondo often discussed the "trap" of comparison. They discussed the book chapter by chapter, and they found other homespun lessons in it as well, such as "pride listens for applause, sniffs for incense. Pride is lonely without recognition and reward. Humility quietly knows that 'I have nothing which I was not given.' Humility is grateful, not grasping."

The book, along with his conversations with Ybarrondo, had a profound effect on Olajuwon and the spiritual transformation on which he was about to embark. "Henri became a mentor to him," says Fran Blinebury, the former Rockets beat writer for the *Chronicle*. "Henri I think deserves a lot of the credit for helping get Hakeem to . . . get a handle on [his] emotions. . . . Henri . . . got a hold of him and deserves a lot of the credit for helping Hakeem grow into the adult who got back to his Muslim roots."

Olajuwon, who would give copies of *Happiness Is an Inside Job* to many of his closest friends in the coming years, influenced Ybarrondo, too. Ybarrondo cherished their friendship and took pride in watching Olajuwon grow spiritually. In an interview for this book, after nearly an hour of reflection on this time period, at times struggling to speak, Ybarrondo uttered the most clear-throated sentence of the interview: "It was like raising a child." After a beat, he tried to pinpoint what he felt was missing for Olajuwon.

"Family," he said. "Nigeria."

. . . .

ONE AFTERNOON, AFTER A PRACTICE EARLY IN THE 1988–1989 SEA-
son, Olajuwon found himself alone on the court in Houston. As
he later recalled, he spotted someone cleaning the court who seem-
ingly appeared out of nowhere. He had never noticed him before.
He studied the man's face, his features. Then the man, as if pulled
by some force, walked up to Olajuwon, respectfully greeting him.
"Mr. Olajuwon," the man said, "are you Muslim?"

Olajuwon was taken aback, processing the question. He wasn't
observant and hadn't been for nearly a decade. Of course, he was
raised Muslim, but it had been many moons since he had attended a
service at a mosque. When he arrived in the United States in 1980,
he lost that foundation, in part because he didn't hear the Call to
Prayer. He didn't know where to find a mosque and sometimes even
attended church with friends. But with this stranger, this man cleaning the hardwood, awaiting his answer, Olajuwon felt . . . something. "Yeah," he finally said. "I'm Muslim."

The man asked him why he hadn't seen him at the mosque.
"There's a mosque close by. Would you like to go to *Jumu'ah*?" the
man said, referring to Friday prayer. Olajuwon was surprised. He
hadn't known there was a nearby mosque. It was about five minutes
away. He agreed to go. Excitement washed over him as he approached
the building that Friday. He opened the door, and all eyes turned to
him. *Is that . . . Akeem Olajuwon?* People were shocked to see him.

Olajuwon scanned the room. He saw people of many different
nationalities and felt a warmth inside. It was one of the happiest days
of his life. And then he heard people responding to the Call, about
three hundred men reciting in unison. Goose bumps traveled along
his body. Ordinarily three to four minutes long, the Call seemed
endless to him in that moment. He lost himself in the beauty of the
melody. He was in Houston, but he was also in Lagos, a young boy

walking to school with the rhythm of the Call echoing through the city.

He felt it all coming back to him: the feeling of his knees on the floor, the sound of the prayers. The feeling of belonging. His parents. His mother up before the sun offering gratitude to Allah. All this time, he had been intently searching for something and didn't even realize that what was missing had been there all along: His foundation. His faith.

He began to cry.

* * * *

OVER THE NEXT FEW WEEKS, HE BEGAN "SOUL SEARCHING," SAYS Ameer Abuhalimeh, the director of Olajuwon's Islamic Da'wah Center. He met Olajuwon a little later, around 1997 or 1998, he recalls, but had many conversations with Olajuwon over the years about this introspective period in Olajuwon's life and how Olajuwon rediscovered his faith. During this time, Olajuwon began to see that some of the people he associated with didn't have direction in their lives and that they were more concerned with acquiring material things than gaining spiritual knowledge, as he had been.

By this point, Olajuwon had been in the United States for nearly ten years, and he now began reflecting on how fast his life had changed. Phi Slama Jama was fun and exciting and incredible; he didn't have many worries but had to adjust to so many things at once, from basketball to school to a social life. At times, that was overwhelming. He realized he had been living as he wanted to but not in accordance with the tenets of Islam. "When you move to a new country, it's like, 'OK, people are doing it this way. I'm doing it this way.' And you try to kind of reconcile," Abuhalimeh says. "And sometimes through that reconciliation, we fall into a kind of confusion and an anxiety, you know? . . . Hakeem realized: He's living in different cultures. He's exposed to different norms and traditions, and he's playing this game, but there are certain things that he's missing. . . . And that's when I think he suddenly stopped and found himself. . . . [He] realized, 'I am a Muslim. I need to live it to the fullest.'"

As Olajuwon racked up ejections, alienated teammates, and faced legal issues off the floor, he realized that he lacked patience. Maturity. If he wanted to become a better person and, by extension, a better athlete, he felt he needed to return to his foundation. He never "discovered" Islam as some erroneously claimed at the time. He *returned* to Islam. And in his return, his reclamation of his heritage, he considered that he hadn't been as grateful to God as he should have been for the success that he had so quickly attained and the gifts bestowed upon him.

The teachings and values of Islam that he had been raised with remained within him. But now he needed to put them into practice, from patience to peace to compassion to mercy to selflessness. Faith gave him a framework for how to act toward others. Islam's emphasis on social justice, its commitment to community and helping others less fortunate through *zakat*, or charity, resonated with him as well. Wealth was seen as a sign of Allah's blessing and, of course, one's hard work, but Allah's law limited its pursuit and accumulation.

The reward, Olajuwon was learning, was giving to others. He became more motivated to do good deeds for the benefit of others rather than for himself. He had to let go of some ego, he now understood. That isn't easy for anyone, let alone a world-class athlete in the hypermasculine world of the NBA. But ego wasn't the same thing as confidence. He now concluded that confidence— genuine self-assuredness—came not from individual willpower but from a higher being.

It comforted him, too, knowing a community of people was willing to help him for no other reason than the kindness in their hearts. That first day he came to the mosque, many embraced him, coming up to him and saying, "We didn't know you were a Muslim." The imam gave him his number and a handful of Islamic books to study. Hasan Tulbah, who was praying there that day, had also approached him, and the two eventually became good friends, with Tulbah serving as a kind of mentor. Olajuwon would call him, asking how to handle different situations, such as navigating prayer during a hectic travel schedule or how to face the Kaaba in Mecca from a hotel room. Tulbah recalled a humble person, eager for knowledge, and felt compelled to nourish that desire.

Olajuwon also became close with a spiritual leader named Sheikh Mohammed Rashad Khalil, a relationship that lasted for decades until Khalil's death at age seventy-eight in 2006. Sheik Rashad, as Olajuwon called him, was from Egypt and was one of Houston's most respected Muslim spiritual leaders and Islamic scholars. His impact was worldwide: he was often asked to speak at Islamic scholarly events around the globe. He had a profound effect on Olajuwon, always encouraging him to "be true to Allah," Olajuwon later recalled.

Ybarrondo and Olajuwon also grew closer. Ybarrondo began to share some parts of his Catholic faith with Olajuwon while Olajuwon did the same with Islam. They noted commonalities between their faiths but would also discuss the differences. Sometimes those conversations, as Henri Jr. recalls, became spirited: "Neither giving an inch but always respectful. Always very thoughtful about it. It was a nice exchange of ideas."

Otis Birdsong, the former University of Houston and NBA star, stayed in contact with Olajuwon after initially seeing him play his first season of college ball. Birdsong had retired from the NBA in 1989 but still kept his eye on the league. Birdsong had become more devoted to his own Christian faith and had been attending a Bible course. Olajuwon, now exploring religion more pointedly, was curious and asked him about his beliefs. "He came to Bible class with me," Birdsong says. "To this day, he still asks me about it from time to time."

Olajuwon seemed rejuvenated, grounded in newfound purpose and support from his friends, his Muslim community. Although he had been raised Muslim in Nigeria, it was in the United States, through community members and books, where he grasped a more profound understanding of the faith than he ever had before.

Ybarrondo took pride in seeing Olajuwon's growth. "It gave me great joy," he said. "He [now] lives his life in an honorable way." Henri Jr. thinks that the friendship of Olajuwon and his father was not fate but "providence." He explains: "Providence is an exchange you have to respond to. It's effort, answering an invitation. It's not, 'Well, it's fate.' Fate takes agency away. My dad has to give a damn, he has to be able to listen, and vice versa."

Maybe something similar had happened to lead Olajuwon to the mosque that first day. When, years later, Olajuwon was telling his friend Ibrahim Arch about the man who was cleaning the floor, who had asked if he was Muslim, Olajuwon realized that he never saw that man ever again. He didn't remember what he looked like, either. He never got the man's name.

"Can you imagine the reward that person got?" Arch says. "Because what happens, we believe, is that when you do a deed like that, and you guide someone to goodness, everything they do thereafter, it's as if *you* did it. So, every charity Hakeem did, every prayer he made, *that* person benefits from it."

Arch himself is moved by retelling the story, as he gets emotional. "Who knows," he says, "maybe it was an angel in the form of a man. Who knows. But it's a beautiful thing."

• • • •

OLAJUWON SPENT THE NEXT FEW MONTHS PORING OVER THE Qur'an, getting his hands on every Islamic text he could find. "He refocused his attention to it," Abuhalimeh says, "and made the determination that he needs to learn it, and execute it, and practice it at the highest level." Islam requires that kind of discipline and work ethic, Abuhalimeh says. "He [Olajuwon] always tends to do so in every aspect of his life, to perfect everything that he touches, to perfect everything that he does," Abuhalimeh says, "and that's the approach that he's taken towards Islam."

Olajuwon focused on adhering to the five pillars of Islam, starting with performing *ṣalāt* (ritual prayer) five times a day, beginning at approximately one and a half hours before sunrise. He vowed to never let the sun catch him in bed. As with his mother, Abike, he felt it was the most beautiful time of day, even if waking up was difficult at first. Then his body adjusted; he began to beat his alarm clock. He'd pray, then read the Qur'an until the sun came up.

He followed the other pillars as well: *shahādah* (profession of faith), *zakāt* (charity), *sawm* (fasting during the month of Ramadan), and *hajj* (pilgrimage to Mecca).

Mornings at the mosque, he would work with someone who was teaching him *tajweed*, the rules of reading and recitation of the Qur'an, which is an art form in itself. He labored to memorize the verses and chapters in proper rhythmic cadence. He started to play a cassette in his car of readings from the Qur'an to further hone his recitation.

After Rockets practice, he'd return to the mosque and then visit the home of one of his Muslim friends, where he'd study more. Islam wasn't a hobby, a casual activity, or even merely a religion; it was now a way of life. And he knew there would be no separation between his work life and his personal life because they were guided by the same Islamic principles. "Basketball is not just a job now," Olajuwon said. "It's an obligation, an act of worship."

He asked Coach Chaney if practice could be scheduled around his prayer time, and Chaney obliged. They didn't talk much about religion, though; Olajuwon was just privately going about his business. "I'm Protestant," Chaney says. "I didn't have a problem with that at all. My brother had practiced Islam. I knew what he was going through at that time, so I knew a little bit about the religion itself."

Olajuwon read the Qur'an on the plane on team road trips. Every trip he challenged himself to learn different *ayat*, or verses, recording three or four and bringing them to practice. He felt calm, grounded, listening to and reciting the verses. "His whole perspective on things changed," says Robert Barr. "It made him a better person because he became more laid-back and more reserved. He just did his thing. Did his study and did his work, and that was it." He also seemed calmer on the court, more amiable with teammates.

The Rockets' struggles didn't dissipate during the 1988–1989 season, though, which ended with another playoff loss, this time to the Sonics in the first round. But as frustrating as things were, the newly grounded Olajuwon didn't lose hope.

• • • •

THE NEXT SEASON, 1989–1990, WAS ONE OF HIS BEST. ALTHOUGH HE was still learning how to lead his teammates, his own play flourished. During a breather in the middle of one game he was dominating,

Carroll Dawson, the assistant coach, said, "Dream, you might get a quadruple-double."

"What is that?" Olajuwon asked. Dawson was amazed that someone so dominant on the court didn't know; Olajuwon was *still* learning the game even with more than a decade of experience under his belt.

Kenny Smith once experienced a similar revelation, asking Olajuwon where he liked to receive the ball: "I think I can throw it to you at the elbow and you can use your ball-handling skills," Smith said.

"What is the elbow?" Olajuwon said. Smith had even more respect for the big man once he explained the elbow: Olajuwon had managed to morph into such a talent while still not knowing some of the most basic terms of the game.

Similarly, when Dawson explained the quadruple-double to Olajuwon that night on the bench, he was equally impressed. Dawson told Olajuwon it had been done only twice before. Ever. "Oh, OK," Olajuwon said, nonchalantly.

About a month later, he nearly pulled off the feat. On March 3, 1990, against Golden State, Olajuwon was *everywhere*. One had the sense that he wasn't merely playing the game; he was directing it from the rafters. "I saw him do some things I ain't seen since," Dawson says. The coach was sure Olajuwon had secured the quadruple-double. But when the buzzer sounded, Olajuwon was one assist shy: twenty-nine points, eighteen rebounds, eleven blocks, nine assists (and, for good measure, five steals).

Viewing the game film afterward, Rockets staff detected an uncredited assist. Or so they claimed. "After the game, they [Dawson and Rudy Tomjanovich] said, 'Oh, come on, we gotta get an assist for Hakeem. Let's look at the film,'" says former Rockets media relations director Jay Goldberg, who had reunited with Olajuwon after filling the same role at the University of Houston. They found a hockey assist: an outlet pass that Olajuwon had thrown to one player, who then passed to another player, who scored. "That's really not an assist," Goldberg said, but he went ahead and notified the league.

Dawson had Olajuwon sign the stat sheet, and he framed it for his office. Two days later, though, the Rockets received a call from the league saying one of his assists indeed didn't count. "I was furious," Dawson says. *How am I going to break it to Dream? He's going to be brokenhearted.*

But Olajuwon was chipper as ever. "That's OK, CD," Olajuwon said, referring to Dawson. "I'll get one next game." Dawson laughed. *Yeah, right.* As brilliant as Olajuwon was, even someone with the nickname *Dream* might not be able to pull off such a superhuman feat twice. But thirteen games later, against the Bucks on March 29, Olajuwon finally did it: eighteen points, sixteen rebounds, eleven blocks, and ten assists in a 120–94 win, joining Nate Thurmond and Alvin Robertson with the third quadruple-double in NBA history. "It was a phenomenal thing," Dawson remembers.

He continued his dominant play, posting a career-high fifty-two points and eighteen rebounds against Denver in April. But the Rockets lost the game, epitomizing the state of the team; it couldn't get over the hump, no matter how well Olajuwon played. After finishing 1989–1990 with a mediocre 41–41 record, the Rockets lost in the first round . . . *again.* The Lakers won the series, 3–1.

Olajuwon was still in his prime. His window to win a title wasn't exactly closing, but it wasn't looking promising, either. Something still wasn't working in Houston. "After this season, I have to concentrate on which direction I want to go. I love Houston. I'd like to play here. But the only way is to win," he said. "I'd rather have a championship-contending team than be an All-Star individual."

The only thing he seemed to be able to control was himself. His devotion to his faith.

• • • •

IN UNDERSTANDING HIS RESPONSIBILITIES AS A MUSLIM, HE NO longer drank alcohol. When Michael Hurd, the former *Austin American-Statesman* writer who had covered him in college, took him to lunch for an interview, he noticed how intently Olajuwon scanned the check afterward. Olajuwon wanted to pay, but Hurd had ordered a glass of wine. "I cannot pay for that," Olajuwon said.

"Why?"

"Because I'm Muslim. I cannot drink, and I cannot pay for alcohol."

He fasted during Ramadan. He no longer wore gold, getting rid of his gold bracelets and watches. He used to love buying silk scarves, Hermes or Chanel, and then creating designs and patterns for shirts to be made. The scarves were some of his favorites, but it was *haram*, or prohibited, for men to wear silk. As difficult as it was giving up those habits, he also realized just how attached he had become to material things. He could almost hear Ybarrondo's words, reminding him that happiness had to come from within.

Of course, he still loved architecture, and his most recent home was as elegant as ever, but it was white, understated. He loved the minimalistic styling of modern architects, such as Luis Barragan, the Mexican architect with his long, brightly painted walls, as well as the classic Palladian style and traditional Islamic architecture with its geometric styling. His home was inspired by the modern architect Philip Johnson, who even inscribed a copy of his book *The Glass House* to Olajuwon: "From the artist to an even greater artist."

Whenever Olajuwon traveled to other cities for games, he always noticed the city's architecture first. His home was, and still is, filled with architecture and design books. That passion extended to collecting prayer rugs of many hues—scarlet, lime green, pastel blue—all from various countries. He especially appreciated his 150-year-old rug from Turkey.

But he was no longer tied to any material object, any giant home, in the way that he had been before. "What he found in redefining, or revisiting, or in the soul-searching journey that he took of going back to his faith," Abuhalimeh says, "I think that gave him the most fulfillment of any other experience in his life."

* * * *

OLAJUWON WAS STILL NAVIGATING HOW TO BECOME THE LEADER his team needed. When Kenny Smith joined the team ahead of the 1990–1991 season, he felt he had to gain Olajuwon's respect early on. "Akeem, if you ever scream at me like you have to other point guards," Smith said, "I will never throw you the ball."

"Yes," Olajuwon said, "you will."

"No." Smith was adamant. But as the weeks wore on, he began to empathize with Olajuwon and try to get to know him better. One afternoon on a bus ride, Smith spotted an open seat next to Olajuwon; it was almost always open. Smith sat down and continued to do so for the next few weeks. One of those rides, he remembers Olajuwon saying: "Kenny, you know you're the first person that sits next to me and talks to me?"

"Really?"

"Everyone just assumes I want to be left alone and that I know everything." A beat passed. Something in Olajuwon loosened. "I appreciate it," he said. "Come to my house. Tomorrow," inviting Smith over for dinner. Smith said he wished he could, but his brother was in town. Olajuwon invited his brother as well, and he cooked fish for them.

Olajuwon began opening up to Smith, telling him that he was in the process of recommitting to Islam. He told Smith, before anyone else, that his name wasn't actually "Akeem." "It's *Ha*keem," he said. Publicly announcing the change was important to him, and he planned to do so soon. Smith appreciated Olajuwon opening up to him. He had allowed him into his home, and his heart, telling him something that nobody else knew. Maybe Olajuwon's hard shell was softening.

Soon thereafter, following a game against the 76ers in March 1991, a staffer came up to Goldberg: "Hey, Akeem is looking for you." Goldberg went to the weight room, knowing he might find Olajuwon there as he sometimes lifted after games. This time, though, Olajuwon was sitting on a bench in the weight room, hands clasped. "Jay," he said, "do you think it would be OK if I switched my name? Put an *H* in front of my name?"

He explained that he wanted to go back to the proper Arabic spelling of Hakeem, which means "a wise man" or "doctor" in Arabic. He didn't think the misspelling mattered much when he first came to America. It was easier to just go with "Akeem" because he thought that most Americans struggled to pronounce "Hakeem." And, as some of his former college teammates suggest, he didn't want to seem somehow disrespectful or ungrateful by correcting an elder.

When he'd call his mother over the years, she would ask why his name was spelled differently in America. Returning to his faith, in his eyes, meant also returning to the original spelling of his name. "But if you don't think it's OK . . . ," he said to Goldberg.

"Hakeem, it's your name," Goldberg said. "That's how you want it spelled, then that's how it's going to be."

"He knew the furor it would cause," Goldberg says. "And I'll tell you: I got it in the neck from the NCAA, the NBA. 'What are we going to do with the record books?"' Goldberg told them: "Look, deal with it. It's the man's name."

His coaches and teammates embraced the change. They welcomed other changes, too. Sometimes they'd be sitting on the bus, waiting for Olajuwon. The coaches would inform players that he was praying. "The entire bus would accept that," Bullard says, even sometimes waiting twenty or thirty minutes. "We respected him."

But Olajuwon wasn't much for publicly discussing the changes he was making; he was simply trying to live his life according to Islam's tenets. It wasn't for show. It certainly wasn't for media attention. He was just trying to become a better version of himself.

The changes happened imperceptibly; it wasn't as if he left one season with an incorrigible temper and came back the next the embodiment of peace. "It was gradual over time," Bullard says. "And I don't think any of us really were that aware of how profound the transformation was until we were able to look back on it a few years later."

• • • •

THINGS SEEMED TO BE TURNING AROUND AS HOUSTON FINISHED the 1990–1991 season with fifty-two wins. Chaney was named Coach of the Year. But for the fourth straight season, Houston lost in the first round, this time to the Lakers in a sweep. It was frustrating, falling short *again*. Craig Roberts, the longtime Houston radio and TV host, passed by Olajuwon. Unprompted, Olajuwon simply said to him: "Enjoy the journey." "I had no idea what he was talking about or that it had religious significance in his mind," Roberts says, but the words stuck with him.

Olajuwon was now *living* those words. His life was changing so profoundly outside of basketball that his perspective within the sport was shifting, too. He was still determined to win a championship, but he was also moving closer to a sense of peace about it. Winning was no longer his highest priority; pleasing God was. He often recited one of his favorite teachings—Surah 8, Verse 29: "Oh, you who believe, if you obey and fear Allah, he will grant you Furqan [criteria to judge between right and wrong] and will expiate for you your sins and forgive you and Allah is the Owner of a Great Bounty."

CHAPTER 15

PERSPECTIVE

LATER IN THE SUMMER OF 1991, THE TWENTY-EIGHT-YEAR-old traveled to Mecca to perform *hajj*, the annual pilgrimage. The *hajj* takes place each year between the eighth and the twelfth day of the twelfth month of the Islamic lunar calendar. Hasan Tulbah, Olajuwon's friend from the mosque, had been describing the magnificence of it to him. Tulbah was born in Mecca, and his family's home was five minutes from the Kaaba, the center of Mecca and the most sacred site in Islam, representing the metaphorical house of God.

Olajuwon was buoyed with a sense of excitement when he stepped onto the plane headed for Jeddah, Saudi Arabia. He heard many other pilgrims on the eighteen-hour flight reciting the Qur'an. They all had shed their everyday clothing in favor of sanctified garments—seamless white pieces of cloth for men, any plain garment for women—that signify *ihram*, a state of purity.

It moved him, seeing so many people of different backgrounds and nationalities fulfilling the same purpose. It didn't matter what one's class status or occupation was; everyone was equal before God. Here he wasn't *Hakeem the Dream*, NBA superstar. Only a handful of people recognized him. When they did, many were surprised; at this point, few knew that he practiced Islam.

He remembered when his parents had performed *hajj*. He knew how much it had elevated their level of faith. They weren't able to go until they were in their sixties; he was grateful to go at just twenty-eight. "I began truly to appreciate my life at that moment," he later recalled. "I looked at people who had saved money their entire lives just to afford to come here and saw how blessed I really was."

He heard the Call wherever he walked: "You could almost breathe it." He was amazed at the swell of worshippers walking counter-clockwise seven times around the Kaaba. He resolved to take his walk at a less busy time but was astounded to find that even going at 2:30 in the morning, there was still a large crowd. It was one of the most beautiful sights he had ever seen, watching everyone bow at once, resembling to him a giant wave.

Olajuwon found it profoundly moving to pray in the exact place that the Prophet Muhammad (PBUH) had. And it touched him, seeing so many focus on the core values of Islam, including kindness, humility, discipline, and compassion. He returned home with a deeper sense of what it meant to be Muslim and was determined to implement what he had learned into his everyday life. He felt a sense of inner peace and security.

"[Islam] I think just completed him," says Ibrahim Arch. "It completed his life. It's not so much that it changed him—I think that it was just a continuation of who he was already, but it just refined it."

• • • •

AS THE ROCKETS GEARED UP FOR THE 1991–1992 SEASON, team-mates, coaches, and friends noticed that Olajuwon appeared more mellow. "He became easier to coach. He started listening," Dawson says. "He was not a rebel anymore. He was a team player." He also carried himself with a confidence that couldn't be shaken. "It seemed like when he really turned to Islam that he calmed down quite a bit," says Jim Foley, the former Rockets broadcaster. Perhaps the late David Nordstrom, a former Rockets equipment manager, put it best before he died in 2001: "When he got into the pros, he was like a college kid. He got all this money, got rich, did all the crazy things. Then he grew up."

Olajuwon became even more disciplined. On road trips, he'd wake early to pray, so early that some of his teammates, upon finding out they were rooming with him, would request to change rooms.

Olajuwon's focus translated onto the court, where he now had far fewer outbursts and fights. Rudy Tomjanovich, a Rockets assistant coach at the time, noticed the calm conviction Olajuwon now had when speaking to teammates. "His spiritual journey, me seeing that happen to him, I went out and tried to develop a better spiritual life myself," Tomjanovich says. "Just trusting in God, doing the right things."

. . . .

OLAJUWON BEGAN COMMUNICATING BETTER WITH TEAMMATES. He and Vernon Maxwell, the fiery guard he had previously fought, reconciled. They sat on the team plane next to each other after one game, talking for hours. Afterward, Maxwell came up to Smith. "Kenny," he said, "I think I'm gonna become a Muslim."

Smith laughed: "He converted you on the flight?"

"No, no, no. He just told me that warriors like me need to be Muslims to redirect our energy."

It's unclear if Maxwell did look into Islam, but he and Olajuwon nonetheless came to an understanding of each other. The same thing happened with referees. Olajuwon no longer talked back to them or earned ejections. Ed T. Rush, the former NBA referee, certainly noticed. Every once in a while, during dead-ball situations such as free throws, the two would have brief conversations about religion. Rush is a devout Christian.

"Hey, Ed," Olajuwon said, "let's talk about it. Your God is a forgiving God?"

"Yeah," Rush said. "I know yours is too."

"You know, Ed, some of those calls, they're hard to forgive."

Rush laughed. "If I miss a call on you," he said, "can I ask you to forgive me? And then you can ask your God if he'll forgive me?"

"OK. But will *your* God forgive you?"

The two smiled. Such a playful and pleasant exchange might have seemed impossible just a few years prior. "From his faith came his foundation of how he lived, how he operated, how he treated people," Rush says.

Now, when opponents pushed or shoved him, Olajuwon would feel sorry for them instead of letting anger swell within. People would ask him how he could be religious in such a violent sport, and Olajuwon would respond that he knew that good and evil were always at odds in some form or another and that the Prophet Muhammad (PBUH) was part warrior, part peacemaker. He, too, had to figure out when to fight and when to speak. "I was in darkness," Olajuwon said at the time, "but now I'm in the light and know how to conduct myself."

He now had a focus, a perspective, he hadn't before. "I saw the transformation. . . . It gave reason and purpose for why he did everything and how he treated people and how he played the game," Smith says. "I thought prior to that, he was a superstar player, but it raised his level of focus and intensity. A level that became the greatest player in basketball."

He was still competitive and as relentless as ever on the court. He still wouldn't let anyone step on his toes, but his *reaction* was different. "What Islam gave him was a limit to his retaliation," Smith says, "whereas before, he had no limit to it."

• • • •

ISLAM ALSO HELPED HIM HANDLE THE ADVERSITY HE WAS EXPERIencing with the Rockets—and with his own health.

He had missed almost two weeks during the 1991–1992 season after an episode of atrial fibrillation: an irregular heartbeat. In a separate incident the year before, Jay Goldberg remembers receiving a call in the middle of the night that Olajuwon had to go to the hospital. "Talk about another scare," Goldberg says, referring to an incident in January 1991 when an elbow from the Bulls' Bill Cartwright caused a fracture to the bone around Olajuwon's right eye. Olajuwon had surgery and sat out for twenty-five games. "I think it finally dawned on him," Goldberg says. "He realized how short life can be, how short a career could be."

Although Olajuwon returned to the lineup after the atrial fibrillation scare, the Rockets spiraled further downward. Coach Don Chaney was fired in February 1992 after an overtime loss to the 10–40 Minnesota Timberwolves brought the Rockets back to .500 with a 26–26 record, and Tomjanovich was promoted to interim head coach. Tomjanovich had been with the organization for many years, not just as an assistant but also as a player, suiting up for the Rockets in the early 1970s when the organization looked as much like a traveling circus as a basketball team.

The Rockets didn't have a permanent home court then, sometimes playing in San Antonio, about two hundred miles from Houston. Once, during a game in El Paso, a windstorm blew through town, spraying sand all over the court. The Rockets continued to play, slipping and sliding everywhere; the referees agreed not to call traveling violations.

Another instance, at a Rockets appearance at the Sharpstown mall, an elderly woman asked Tomjanovich to take a picture with players. "I never knew you were that big," she marveled. "How do you fit in the spaceship?" (She thought the Rockets were astronauts from NASA. Who had ever heard of the NBA?)

When the Rockets offered him the head-coaching job, Tomjanovich hesitated. He cared deeply for the franchise but always saw himself as a minor part of the Rockets family, more of a helper, not the man in charge. He worried about time away from his family. "I'm not even a first assistant yet," he told Carroll Dawson, who had served in that role. "Suddenly I'm getting into this deal?"

However, Tomjanovich was the right person to turn the Rockets around. He was one of the smartest basketball minds in the business, having learned from Dawson's tutelage for years as a scout. Most importantly, Tomjanovich was a player's coach. He understood players were people; they had feelings. He was stern but sensitive. He lacked ego. He was, in many ways, the opposite of Bill Fitch's *my way or the highway* style. He had been close with Olajuwon; he was the one person who could use "Hakeem" and not "Dream" if he was upset with him.

Tomjanovich was a hard worker who came from humble beginnings. When he was growing up in the blue-collar town of Hamtramck, Michigan, money was tight. The family went on welfare. His dad worked a number of jobs, including as a shoemaker and as a garbage collector for the city. Sometimes he wasn't home at night, out drinking. Tomjanovich always felt that he had to prove himself, and that crossed over to his hoops career. Like Olajuwon, he was determined. He didn't just play to play; he had to be *great*.

He eventually accepted the Rockets' head-coaching gig after much coaxing from Dawson. Dawson told him he would help him in any way he could. Still, Tomjanovich knew his work was cut out for him. Houston went on to end its streak of four consecutive first-round eliminations, but only because it missed the playoffs in 1991–1992 altogether for the first time since Olajuwon had joined the roster.

Olajuwon began hearing whispers in the press: *What if Dream never wins a championship? What does that mean for his legacy?* Some critics were harsher: *If he doesn't win a championship, he's a failure. His career is incomplete.* In retrospect, Tomjanovich doesn't remember hearing much of that kind of chatter. "It might have been out there, but I didn't hear a big movement like that, or read articles like that, but you start feeling it yourself," Tomjanovich says. "You start saying, 'How many years have I been in the league, and I haven't got one of those?' And it's what everybody wants."

Like any competitive professional athlete, Olajuwon burned to win, and he wasn't giving up on that goal. But since returning from Mecca, his perspective had shifted. He started to question what it meant to be successful. He started to realize that winning isn't everything and that a career couldn't solely be judged on championships. "My championship is *Jannah*," he later said, referring to the proverbial garden of paradise. "This is what Allah promises to his servants who do righteous deeds and live according to his law. I don't get attached to championships set by man. In our faith you work hard, do the best you can—but this does not affect your life."

He focused on being grateful to be able to play a game he loved and make a living doing so. He vowed to continue trying his best to win but believed he could be happy even if he didn't. When it was time to retire, he told himself he'd ask one question: "Did you give it all you had?" He wanted to be able to say he gave his best every night. He believed that if he was destined to win a championship, then it would happen. If it didn't happen, then it wasn't his destiny. Happiness couldn't hinge on a trophy, he concluded.

"I want to be remembered as a great person," he said at the time, "not the greatest player in the world but a person who was honest and gracious and honorable, a man who did his best, a good Muslim. That's as good as I can be."

His ultracompetitiveness, though, sometimes overshadowed that perspective. He yearned to win it all, and he wasn't sure if this franchise was capable of delivering it.

• • • •

TOWARD THE END OF THE DISMAL 1991–1992 SEASON, OLAJUWON reevaluated his future. Without a sustainable lineup around him, he didn't see himself in Houston any longer. He also thought that his contract wasn't commensurate with his level of play. He earned $3,170,000 in 1991–1992, less than half of Larry Bird's $7,070,000 and behind six other players' earnings.

Steve Patterson, who had taken over as general manager, recalls Olajuwon constantly trying to renegotiate when discussing a new contract. Patterson says this happened about every six weeks during the season. "As time went on, it was difficult with Hakeem," Patterson says. "When you've got your best player constantly renegotiating, that makes it very, very difficult to the point of almost being impossible to manage the roster and manage the [salary] cap and build a winning team."

Tensions soared when Olajuwon suffered a left hamstring injury in March 1992. Rockets management publicly accused him of faking the injury and sitting out for leverage in his contract discussions. Olajuwon was insulted, thinking that they were questioning his integrity. A doctor *had* cleared him for play, but Olajuwon still felt injured and unable to compete, so he sat out the next game. Houston then suspended him for failing to play. "I don't think he thought we had the balls to suspend him, and we did," Patterson says. "I do think actually part of it was, nobody ever said *no* to him, until we did."

Olajuwon called team owner Charlie Thomas a "coward." And in Patterson's eyes, Olajuwon still had a ways to go in terms of maturity. But Olajuwon felt he wasn't being treated with the respect he deserved. "Through the period he would just say, 'It's not right for me to receive less than I'm entitled because of my skill level,' or something logical and understated," says Leonard Armato. "He never was like, 'Those motherfuckers!' Nothing like that. He was always very respectful. He's the most respectful person I've ever met who is a professional athlete."

Still, the feud grew ugly as it played out in the media. Some papers portrayed Olajuwon as selfish and hostile. Others were baldly racist: "Olajuwon wanted a new contract, and the people of Houston began wondering if he'd ever be happy. They said he was greedy, and some said he should go back to the jungle and see how much money he'd make there."

Olajuwon's heart was no longer in Houston. "It was a really bad situation," Armato says, "and it looked like they were going to part company." Olajuwon asked for a trade. He wouldn't even go near the Summit. "Summer of '92 was, to me, the crossroads for the franchise, the crossroads for him, in terms of leaving a legacy in Houston," says Robert Falkoff, the *Post*'s Rockets beat writer, adding later: "That summer was a cold war."

"It was getting ugly," says Matt Bullard, the former Rockets forward. "All of us players were like, 'Oh my God. I can't believe what's going on. *Please* don't let Dream go. Because that would be a huge mistake.'" Something precious had been broken, and Olajuwon felt it was beyond repair. He told management to call him when they knew where he'd be playing the following season.

Behind the scenes, Armato tried to reason with Thomas. "He's really unhappy. You're really unhappy. We need to figure this out. Either you have to give him a contract commensurate with his value so he's happy, or you need to get rid of him," Armato said. When it became clear that Thomas wouldn't budge on the contract, Armato says, trade talks began.

"We talked to a bunch of teams," Patterson says. The Miami Heat showed interest, allegedly putting together a trade package of Rony Seikaly, Brian Shaw, and Willie Burton for Olajuwon and Sleepy Floyd. The Lakers were allegedly also interested, offering a package of Vlade Divac, Elden Campbell, and likely James Worthy for Olajuwon and Floyd. Both offers fizzled, in some part because of salary-cap issues. However, the Clippers showed the most interest, especially from their owner, Donald Sterling. "[Sterling] would be like, 'I want him so badly,'" Armato says. "He was so demonstrative in how much he loved Hakeem."

The Clippers were an attractive suitor for the Rockets. They could offer more draft picks and assets and were a younger team; for Houston, trading Olajuwon would necessitate a full-scale rebuild. Armato says Thomas agreed to arrange a trade with the Clippers for Olajuwon in exchange for Charles Smith and a couple of first-round draft picks. But when Armato went back to Sterling, he couldn't get a straight answer. They appeared to be at an impasse. Patterson says the Clippers weren't willing to give up Smith. "We were close," Patterson says. "I'm not saying we were all the way there. I think we were like, one person going one way, [another person] the other way. . . . I think if we would have gotten another guy, we would have done it."

Olajuwon appeared to be stuck in Houston. There was so much bad blood between him and management that it wasn't obvious how the air could be cleared. More pressing was the question of whether Olajuwon would even *accept* any new contract offers from Houston.

It wasn't until the beginning of the following season, on a November 1992 trip to Japan for the season opener, that Thomas and Olajuwon moved toward reconciliation. Over fourteen long hours on American Airlines, the two began hashing out their differences before landing in Narita. Stepping off the plane, they were confident they could work out a deal and move forward. It took five more months before a new contract was finalized, but Olajuwon would stay a Rocket.

Still, that summer had reminded everyone: nothing is forever.

CHAPTER 16

CLUTCH

ALL SIGNS POINTED TOWARD OLAJUWON BEING NAMED MVP IN 1992–1993. He won Defensive Player of the Year. He led the NBA in blocks per game for the third time in four years. He was one of the few players in the league who could defend multiple positions. Offensively, he had also increased his range to around seventeen feet with the Dream Shake. But the MVP award went to Charles Barkley of the Suns. (Barkley got fifty-nine first-place votes, Olajuwon got twenty-two, Michael Jordan got thirteen, and Patrick Ewing got four.)

Upon hearing the news, Olajuwon said it didn't bother him. Neither did the fact that prior to 1992–1993 he had received only four first-place MVP votes. Awards, according to him, were worldly and unimportant. "I'm not fighting for exposure. That's insecurity, immaturity . . . ," he said in November 1993. "I just do my job for the people who appreciate the game."

These days, he focused on his teammates, averaging a career high in assists in 1992–1993. He was now willingly passing out of double-team situations, something he hadn't always done earlier in his career. Tomjanovich had reassured him: "If you give up the ball, we'll give it back to you." In a game against the Mavs in February 1993, Mavs guard Derek Harper hit a pair of jumpers to cut the

Rockets' lead to six with five minutes to go. Instead of trying to be the hero and win the game himself down the stretch, Olajuwon then hit forward Otis Thorpe with a laser pass in the paint. Thorpe converted the layup, and the two big men hugged each other after the play. It was an emotional moment.

Olajuwon wasn't just making his teammates better; he was listening to them, understanding them. He had finally embraced a critical lesson: he needed his teammates to help him win. He was still a private person and, in many ways, always would be. "He was very good at interviews because he said very little," says Craig Ehlo, former Rockets guard. Olajuwon kept his world *his*. But at the same time, he began opening up to his teammates more on a personal level, including a guard out of UC Irvine named Scott Brooks. They often sat next to each other on planes, talking about their childhood experiences. "He was always interested in *me*," says Brooks, a former NBA head coach and now an assistant coach for the Blazers. Brooks was in awe of Olajuwon, how dedicated he was to prayer, staying in while everyone went out for beers. "He was almost like a mythical figure," Brooks says. "I'm like, 'Wow, this guy is one of the best players in the world, but he acts like he's trying to make the team like I am.'"

Players now saw how down-to-earth Olajuwon was. He generally didn't sit in first class, preferring to sit with teammates or even total strangers, talking to them about philosophy, art, fashion, and, of course, basketball.

Teammates loved his youthful spirit. He'd master a move and run around the court giggling, screaming, "I did it! I did it!" His personality was infectious. Once, in the middle of the fourth quarter of a back-and-forth game, the Rockets called a time-out. The music at the Summit was blasting. Olajuwon turned to Brooks and said: "Scotty! Joan Jett and the Blackhearts, right?"

"What?!" Brooks said.

"That's Joan Jett! 'I Love Rock n' Roll'!"

Brooks started cracking up to see that a competitor as fierce as Olajuwon would blurt that out mid-game. Olajuwon's sense of humor charmed his teammates. Once, in practice, former Rockets forward Earl Cureton, who gave an interview for this book before passing away at age sixty-six in 2024, remembered Olajuwon Dream Shaking someone so successfully that he turned to the player and said, "You must not have cable! You never saw this before?"

On team buses he'd interrupt conversations with a running joke where he'd call out his teammates: "Who would be an athlete if he did not play basketball?" he'd say, explaining that there was a difference between a basketball player and an athlete. Each day he'd name someone else.

Olajuwon considered himself an *athlete*; he had destroyed people in table tennis without any formal training, and still does to this day. He could do the limbo, easily ducking under the bar with such fluidity that one might wonder if he had ever been in gymnastics. So each day on the Rockets team bus, Olajuwon would say there were only two athletes on the team. "Me and Vernon," he'd say one day, then another day: "Me and Kenny." He got the most laughs when telling one teammate, "If you didn't play basketball, you'd work in sales."

Once, Jay Namoc, former Rockets equipment manager, was stuck in traffic driving to the game. "I see this car, and it's Dream's car," Namoc says. "And he's driving on the shoulder literally the whole way. Passing me in traffic. I get upstairs, and I say, 'Dream, what were you doing driving on the shoulder illegally?' He goes: 'No risk, no reward.'" They both laughed, and the phrase "no risk, no reward" became their inside joke.

When Anthony Falsone took over as the Rockets' strength and conditioning coach in June 1995, after Robert Barr had moved into an executive role, he and Olajuwon became close. One afternoon, on a bus ride in New York, Olajuwon began telling Falsone about a famous cemetery nearby. Olajuwon described it in great detail: the statues, the style of architecture—*this part is from France; that one is from the tenth century.*

How does he know all of this history? Falsone thought as Olajuwon continued describing the cemetery. Thirty minutes later, they finally passed it. "Anthony," Olajuwon said, "do you know what you must do to get in that cemetery?"

"No. What?"

"Anthony. You must . . . die." Olajuwon burst into laughter. Falsone did, too. "I made up all the other stuff," Olajuwon said, proud of himself for holding character.

Most of all, his teammates admired his newfound focus. He was so locked in on his faith that he didn't have time for much else. If you asked him what was happening in the Super Bowl or the World Series, he wouldn't be able to tell you who was playing. Once, the team traveled to Denver, where Mile High Stadium used to be across from McNichols Sports Arena, the Nuggets home at the time. Snow was coming down furiously. Olajuwon turned to Tim Frank, the Rockets public relations man who had succeeded Jay Goldberg in that role.

"What is that?" Olajuwon said.

"What do you mean?" Frank said.

Olajuwon pointed to the football stadium.

"It's the football stadium."

"They play football *outdoors?*"

"He was so used to Houston, and he never watched football. . . . He just knew the [Houston] Oilers played at the Dome," Frank says. "Denver was in the Rockets' division, and he had been going to that arena twice a year, at least, sometimes three times, for ten years. Never even noticed it because he was just so focused on basketball and then the other parts of his life."

Another time, during a road game against Detroit, Olajuwon and Bullard walked over to the coolers in the locker room. There were two: one for soda, one for beer. Olajuwon, who, of course, no longer drank alcohol, pulled out a Mountain Dew from the soda cooler. "Hey, Bull," Olajuwon said, "what is Mountain Dew?"

"Dream. It's soda. But it's got a lot of caffeine in it, so maybe you don't want to drink it because it'll keep you up."

"No, this is beer! You're tricking me."

"Dream, you don't know what Mountain Dew is?" He laughed. "But that was just Dream."

. . . .

THE ROCKETS WERE DETERMINED TO FINALLY BREAK THROUGH IN 1992–1993, but the season ended in heartbreak. Houston had won the Midwest Division for the first time since 1986 and made it to the second round of the playoffs for the first time since 1987. But once again, they couldn't get past the Sonics. "That pain that we felt from that loss," Bullard says, "that airplane back from Seattle was the quietest airplane ride I've ever been on. And it was a long one."

"Our trauma," Bullard says, "we used as fuel," referring to the next season.

Looking back, Tomjanovich agrees. "I believe that the failures, that the hurts that you have along the way, they are necessary," Tomjanovich says.

Several key pieces were added to the 1993–1994 squad, including sharpshooter Mario Elie and a confident rookie named Sam Cassell, bolstering the backcourt behind starting guards Kenny Smith and Vernon Maxwell. Second-year forward Robert Horry was poised to take another big step, and Otis Thorpe held down the paint. Scott Brooks, Carl Herrera, and Matt Bullard anchored the bench. It wasn't a team of superstars, but everyone competed.

Tomjanovich instilled tough-nosed defense, telling his players during training camp that defense would be their identity. They'd regularly keep teams under a hundred points. But Tomjanovich also did something innovative on offense: he was one of the first coaches to implement a four-out, one-in offense, with four players outside, surrounding Olajuwon in the paint. It was the precursor to much of today's modern basketball in terms of floor spacing. "It fit our team perfectly," Tomjanovich says, "and it really made it easier for Hakeem to read the defense and make good passes out."

The league looked vastly different at that point. Michael Jordan had just retired (for the first time). Critics were dubbing the Knicks the title favorite. The Suns, behind Charles Barkley, were also a strong contender. The Sonics were always tough. In other words: the race was wide open and felt different than it had while Jordan was leading the Bulls to a three-peat from 1991 through 1993.

Few picked Houston, which entered the season with the seventh-best title odds, but the team began the season 15–0. In December 1993, after Maxwell drained a game winner against San Antonio on the road to move to 22–1, some Rockets staff gathered at a bar to watch highlights of Houston's comeback win. During the short walk back to the hotel, Tomjanovich looked at a river in the distance, glimmering in the dark. "This," he said, "is a special season."

· · · ·

PERHAPS HE HAD SPOKEN TOO SOON. IN JANUARY THE TEAM SUF-fered its first four-game losing streak in more than a year. Friction seemed to be building among some players. The team had a meeting that essentially came down to this: *We're either going to step up and play like we should play or call it a season.*

Olajuwon was a man of few words, but when he spoke, everyone listened. "He wasn't holding back," Brooks says. "He was saying, 'This is what we need to do. This is what we're going to do. And if we don't want to do this, you guys can basically leave now.'" In hindsight, Brooks thought the meeting was a turning point: "It changed the whole trajectory of our season. To me, that day pretty much gave us a chance to win a championship."

The team started clicking, taking to heart one of Olajuwon's oft-used phrases: "Keep it simple." Meaning: play hard defense, give him the ball on offense, and if he doesn't have a good look, he'll pass the ball out, and someone else will score.

Olajuwon's Dream Shake evolved into a complex set of counters no one could guard. "He showed some moves that we hadn't even seen," Elie says. "There were some games I just felt *bad* for some guys. I'm like, 'Why are these teams not double-teaming?' I mean, Dream used to *punish* guys on a nightly basis. All the elite players."

He had learned to face up. His ball-handling skills were tighter. He played with both urgency *and* patience, dominating the game but letting it come to him. Defenders were unsure whether to give him the shot or let him drive; either way, he'd destroy them.

But it was his defense, his shot blocking, that made him elite. "It was scary, I'm not going to lie," says Nick Van Exel, former Lakers guard, recalling that Olajuwon blocked his shot too many times to count. "How many times!" he says, laughing, remembering when teammate Sedale Threatt said to him: "How many times we gotta go into the paint and Hakeem is going to block our shot and send it out to the perimeter? When are we going to learn?!"

Those who know Olajuwon best say his recommitment to his faith enabled him to raise his game even higher. "He became an unbelievable player after that," says former Rockets assistant coach Carroll Dawson. "It wasn't a show. It was serious for him. But it

made him, I felt, the best player in the league." Usually, players slow
down as they age; Olajuwon, at thirty-one, was in his tenth year but
was somehow . . . better? He finally had the brute strength of Wilt
Chamberlain, the quickness of Bill Russell, and the scoring prowess
of Kareem Abdul-Jabbar.

During Game 2 of the Rockets' first-round playoff series against
the Blazers, Olajuwon, who scored forty-six that night, made an
errant pass to Smith. Portland guard Rod Strickland stole the ball
and charged down the other way, thinking he had an easy layup
ahead.

Olajuwon began sprinting down the court. "We're all thinking,
'There's no way he's going to catch that,'" Brooks says. Not only
did he catch up with Strickland at the other end of the court, but
he also swatted his shot down from behind with authority. It was
mind-blowing, watching a center accelerate that fast. "Not too many
players can do that. One, to have the physical ability to do that. But
two, the determination never to quit on the play, when you're almost
like, 'Nah, there's probably a five percent chance of getting that.'"

• • • •

AFTER BEATING PORTLAND, 3–1, IN THE FIRST ROUND OF THE 1993–
1994 playoffs, the Rockets faced their biggest test yet: the Suns. "We
always talked about the 'fire drill,'" Tomjanovich says. "It's pressure
time now. Everybody's got to go to the right places and all that.
We're not going to make mistakes. And we were very good at that,
but against that Phoenix team, they had our number. . . . Their confidence was soaring, and we were down."

The first two games were ugly for the second-seeded Rockets. In both games, they blew big fourth-quarter leads, eighteen-
and twenty-point margins, respectively, to find themselves down
0–2. Worse, both games were at *home*. Houston fans booed them,

holding up posters of chickens. Local newspapers called them "Choke City." Letters to the editor were scathing. "Dear Rudy T," one person wrote. "May I suggest that you rent *Wizard of Oz*. Sit all your players down and make them watch it. . . . Explain to them that—like the Tin Man, Scarecrow, and cowardly Lion— the heart, the brains, and the courage comes from within and not from some wizard."

The season seemed lost. After Game 2, the Rockets' locker room was silent. "It was like a morgue," Bullard says. Earl Cureton, the former Rockets forward, remembered hearing Suns players blasting MC Hammer's "It's All Good" through the walls, singing, dancing, celebrating. They partied like the series was over.

The Rockets' silence continued as they flew to Phoenix. Olajuwon was last to board. He paused at the front, looking at everyone. "Fellas, we led both games by twenty points. We are better than they are. We will win this series," Bill Worrell, the former Rockets broadcaster, recalls Olajuwon saying. Players took a collective breath. They believed. And they dug deep, motivated to shut up the talk of *Choke City*.

The Rockets bounced back to win Game 3, 118–102, focusing on defense. Olajuwon had six blocks and two steals, along with twenty-six points, fifteen rebounds, and six assists. The Rockets then won Game 4, 107–96, to tie the series at 2–2. They weren't giving up.

During one play in Game 4, Barkley took the ball strong to the hoop for a dunk, but Olajuwon came out of nowhere to stuff it down. It was a symbolic moment: Olajuwon rejecting Barkley, the Rockets swatting back anyone who counted them out. "It's not Choke City," said owner Leslie Alexander, who purchased the team from Charlie Thomas for $85 million in 1993, shouting as players ran into the locker room, "it's Clutch City!"

Echoing Alexander, the newspapers now called the Rockets "Clutch City." Tomjanovich was so amped he told reporters that "the Rockets aren't chokers; they are men with a hell of a lot of character." The Rockets followed with a Game 5 win back in Houston, 109–86. But then the Suns came back, winning Game 6 on their home court, 103–89.

In Houston for Game 7, the Rockets clawed and scratched their way to a series-winning 104–94 victory behind Olajuwon's thirty-seven-point, seventeen-rebound outburst. They advanced to the Western Conference Finals against the Utah Jazz. They had confidence, they supported one another, and they were ready to keep proving their doubters wrong.

· · · ·

THE ROCKETS CONTINUED TO ROLL IN GAME 1 AGAINST THE JAZZ, winning 100–88 behind Olajuwon's thirty-one points. And then, before Game 2, Olajuwon received word that he was finally being named league MVP.

It was undeniable. He was the best player in the league, in the world.

It wasn't just his numbers, which were astonishing; it was his commitment on both ends of the floor. He never sacrificed a possession.

On the night he was to receive the MVP award, ahead of the Game 2 tip-off, he asked his teammates and staff to accept the award with him. "Basketball is a team sport," Olajuwon said to his teammates. "The MVP trophy belongs to the whole team." Thorpe, the starting forward, ended up holding the trophy as Commissioner David Stern presented it to the group. Olajuwon seemed so far from the player who had openly feuded with teammates, who had asked to be traded. He was, as Stern said while presenting the award, the epitome of "grace and elegance."

Olajuwon didn't disappoint in the immediate aftermath, dominating Karl Malone in the post and showing off the finesse and physicality that had earned him the MVP trophy. With thirty-nine seconds remaining and his team leading by one, he hit an impossible running bank shot across the lane, over the outstretched arms of *three* defenders, leading to a 104–99 victory. He finished with forty-one points, thirteen rebounds, and six assists as the Rockets took a commanding 2–0 lead.

The Jazz fought back to win Game 3, 95–86, but it would be their only win of the series. The Rockets took Game 4 in Salt Lake City, 80–78, and won Game 5 at home, 94–83, to advance to the NBA Finals. They were set to play the Knicks. A title was on the line.

Finally.

CHAPTER 17

RING

BOTH THE ROCKETS AND THE KNICKS KNEW IT WAS GOING TO BE A physical series, for they were the league's top two defensive teams. The Knicks were particularly hard-nosed—a grind-it-out, half-court, disciplined team coached by Pat Riley.

Olajuwon would have his work cut out for him, going against a strong front line of Patrick Ewing, Charles Oakley, and Anthony Mason. "They were never the league's most skilled collection of players," journalist Chris Herring wrote in his book on the 1990s Knicks, *Blood in the Garden*. "But for what the Knicks lacked in finesse, they made up for with fight (often literally) and floor burns; grit that endeared them to countless New Yorkers."

Journalists were billing the series as *Olajuwon vs. Ewing*. Both players downplayed it, saying instead that it was *the Rockets vs. the Knicks*. They had a profound respect for each other dating back to their college days. "Patrick is my toughest opponent," Olajuwon said earlier in the season. Ewing said Olajuwon always brought the best out of him: "He's been a thorn in my side for many years."

"Hakeem, he had it all," Oakley says. He saw firsthand Olajuwon's arsenal of moves: "He can face you up and try to cross you over and shoot it," Oakley says. "He can get on the block. He had a little jump hook. He could go at the post. I mean he was a triple threat."

Olajuwon was productive in Game 1, scoring twenty-eight points and grabbing ten rebounds in the team's 85–78 win, but the Knicks weren't giving him any easy buckets. Mason, a six-foot-seven, 250-pound forward known for his brash play, stuck to him like Velcro. He and Oakley and Ewing shoved and pushed Olajuwon before he even received the ball. They were hoping to frustrate him and get him out of rhythm. It wasn't just the front line, though; there were times Kenny Smith couldn't bring the ball past half-court because Derek Harper was in his grille. "I thought every game [both teams] were going to fight," says Carroll Dawson. "Pat [Riley] had them really fighting. The hand-checking, the rubbing. They'd knock you down. We were giving it back to them."

The win was particularly special for Olajuwon, who finally played in front of his parents for the first time. Salam and Abike had traveled to Houston during the summers but had never seen him play live. In the early years, Olajuwon sent home VHS tapes of his games. His parents didn't know much about basketball then. Now, after the win over the Knicks, his parents talked about each player. It was a proud moment for them, seeing how far their son, the one they had to be persuaded to even *let* play basketball, had come.

The Knicks came back with a vengeance in Game 2, winning 91–83. After one practice, a journalist saw Olajuwon walking with a little bit of discomfort, courtesy of Mason's physical play. But Olajuwon scoffed at the idea that Mason was containing him. "I've been hearing and seeing all these things that he's my nightmare," Olajuwon said. "That's a joke. Just throw the ball to me."

It wasn't so simple. Olajuwon was expending so much effort fighting for position against multiple defenders that Tomjanovich had to find a way to preserve his energy. He came up with an alternative method for feeding Olajuwon the ball: running pick-and-rolls to the other side of the floor so whoever was guarding him had to rotate out of position. Still, there were bigger issues: Tomjanovich thought that his team looked disjointed in Game 2. He saw his players squabbling with one another. After the game, he sat on an ice chest in the locker room and gave them a pep talk: "If a team is going to behave the way we behaved to each other out there, I don't think we should be champions . . . ," he said. "The way we have to do it is by always staying together. Let's not let this opponent turn us against each other."

In Game 3 the two teams once again battled down to the final minute. With forty seconds to play and the Knicks up two, Olajuwon backed down Ewing on the block before spinning to find Cassell setting up beyond the three-point arc. The rookie hit the game winner, silencing the Madison Square Garden crowd for the eventual 93–89 victory. Olajuwon had trusted his teammates, who continued to step up night after night. "You look at a lot of the wins that we got, it was not [Olajuwon] making the shot," Tomjanovich says. "He was the guy that drew the defense and took the ball out."

Olajuwon was unstoppable. So much so that the world-famous Carnegie Deli in midtown Manhattan debuted a two-pound sandwich in honor of Olajuwon. For $15.95, the "Hakeem the Dream" sandwich had corned beef, pastrami, turkey, beef brisket, Swiss cheese, coleslaw, pickles, and a hot pepper: a little bit of everything, just like Olajuwon's game, according to Murray Trachtenberg, the deli's general manager.

During one play in Game 4, Olajuwon leaped over the bigger seven-foot-tall, 240-pound Ewing to grab the offensive rebound and dunk it home. "I'm from the East Coast, so I knew Patrick Ewing. He was a legend," Smith says. "Hakeem was the first person I saw to make Patrick look mortal." However, the Knicks came back strong to win, 91–82, behind a big night from Oakley. Critics called the series ugly because of the low-scoring games. But for people who appreciated a bucket-for-bucket, grind-it-out type of game, the series was that and more.

Game 5 was not only gritty but also . . . historic. Before the tip, criminal charges were filed against O. J. Simpson in the killing of his wife, Nicole Brown Simpson. During the game, Simpson led police on a car chase throughout Los Angeles in a white Ford Bronco as fans in Madison Square Garden watched on a split screen. NBC was broadcasting both the chase and the NBA Finals. Players, too, were rapt. "Everyone was huddled around the TV at halftime watching," says David Spangler, a former Rockets spokesperson. Tomjanovich tried to focus his players' attention, but the Rockets faded down the stretch as the Knicks took Game 5, 91–84.

The Rockets were a bit despondent heading back to Houston down 3–2 in the series. If they lost one more game, they'd lose the championship. That night, guard Mario Elie was feeling down and walked to Olajuwon's room because they were staying on the same floor of a hotel on Thirty-Third Street. The door was open. Olajuwon, dressed all in white, was with his friends. "Mario," Olajuwon said cheerfully. "What's going on?"

"Dream, man, we're down 3–2."

"Mario, we're going home for two games. We're going to be OK. Don't worry about it. We're going to be *OK*."

Something in Elie shifted. Olajuwon's confidence was palpable. He wasn't just saying things would be OK; he *believed* it. His calm in the moment was just what his teammates needed.

. . . .

But now, for the first time in the series, ahead of Game 6, Olajuwon really did feel the pressure. He knew how much was on the line, and that pressure only ratcheted up as the game, filled with runs by both teams as the Knicks fought back every time the Rockets threatened to pull away, came down to the wire once again.

With 5.5 seconds remaining and Houston up 86–84, Oakley inbounded the ball to shooting guard John Starks, who was hounded by Maxwell. Ewing set a screen near the top of the key, and Olajuwon was forced to switch onto Starks but stumbled for a brief second, trying to catch him.

Oh, Lord, Elie thought. Starks was wide open. He had already drained six shots in a row. "He was hot as fish grease that night," Elie says. Starks, too, thought his shot was going in. "I took two dribbles to my left, fired, and when it left my hand, it was money," Starks later said. But Olajuwon gathered himself, using every muscle in his body to leap toward Starks. Miraculously, Olajuwon grazed the ball with his fingertips, enough to deflect Starks's attempt with two seconds left, securing the Rockets' 86–84 win.

The series was now knotted at 3–3. It was an extraordinary play by Olajuwon, who recovered in a blink and had the length to pull off the block.

The win energized the Rockets. Players believed winning the ultimate trophy was just within reach. "Once we knew the series was tied, we knew we were going to win Game 7," Elie says. "The confidence level in that locker room after that—we were hugging, and everybody's fired up. We're hugging Rudy. Rudy's hugging Dream. It was an amazing moment for the squad."

Olajuwon couldn't sleep the night before Game 7. Tossing and turning, he again felt pressure. He tried to think only positive thoughts, seeing himself succeed, spinning, whirling, Dream Shaking. It was surreal for Rockets players, walking into the locker room the next morning. The room was already set with plastic that the players could use to cover their clothes to protect themselves from champagne—*if* they were so lucky to be the team popping champagne. Olajuwon reminded everyone of the *if* at shootaround.

On the sideline, media relations director Jay Goldberg mused to an NBA official in attendance: "How would you like to have the [championship] ceremony on the court?" Goldberg had been thinking about it for some time as it had never happened before: "[The official] says, 'Really? David Stern's been wanting to do that for years!'" Goldberg then huddled the Rockets at half-court, telling them an on-court ceremony might happen. "After we beat the Knicks," Goldberg said.

Olajuwon politely interrupted: "God willing. *If* we do beat the Knicks. God willing."

Inshallah.

Everyone was speechless and then began nodding. "Yeah, yeah," players said. "God willing. Dream's right."

• • • •

TOMJANOVICH FELT READY FOR GAME 7 AFTER HIS SUPERSTITIOUS playoff pregame meal: grouper, which he called his "lucky fish."

The Rockets set the tone early. On the first play, Olajuwon passed to Horry, who hammered home a two-handed dunk over Ewing that was so forceful the big man stumbled out of bounds.

The game flowed back and forth, neither team able to maintain an advantage. With just under two minutes remaining, and Houston with the ball up 80–75, Maxwell drained a three. The Rockets mobbed him, forcing a Knicks time-out. Starks, who had defended Maxwell, was *off.* After his scorching fourth quarter in Game 6, he'd gone ice-cold in Game 7, struggling to a two-of-eighteen shooting performance and missing all eleven of his three-point tries. Starks hadn't slept the night before Game 7 or the two nights prior. He had been haunted by the end of Game 6.

The Knicks were making Houston sweat, and a few plays later, Maxwell had to come up big again, sinking free throws with 4.2 seconds remaining to make it a six-point game. Houston began celebrating. The Knicks threw a long pass, which the Rockets intercepted, sealing the victory. Olajuwon dribbled as the clock expired, and Houston had won, 90–84.

They did it. They finally did it. They were World Champions.

Houston. World Champions. The city's first ever, not counting the Houston Oilers of the fledgling American Football League in 1960 and 1961 before the league merged with the NFL, or the Houston Aeros of the World Hockey Association in 1974 and 1975.

In that moment the failures of other Houston sports teams washed away, healing the trauma of a city that had grown accustomed to falling short. A city that had endured a laundry list of *almosts*: NC State's Lorenzo Charles dunking a game winner over Olajuwon's Phi Slama Jama Cougars in the 1983 NCAA Tournament's championship game; Mike Renfro making an epic touchdown catch during the 1980 AFC Championship in Pittsburgh only to have it discounted by an official; Nolan Ryan and Bob Knepper pitching gems in games 5 and 6 of the 1986 National League Championship Series against the New York Mets, only to lose both contests and a World Series bid in extra innings.

While Rockets players ran around the court, celebrating, crying, hugging, screaming, and dancing, Olajuwon took a seat at the scorer's table, cradling the ball, watching everyone rejoice. A tear streamed down his cheek. It was a striking image, everyone else moving while he was still and satisfied, confetti raining down on him.

He thought about everything he had been through to get to that point. He remembered how that morning, he had prayed that if it was God's will for the Rockets to win, it was His will; Olajuwon could live with the result, no matter what. So right after winning the title, he took the time to thank God, taking in every detail of the moment so he would never forget it. "I never realized that the burden was on his shoulders," Smith says. "We're all running around, and I'm looking for him, and he's reflecting and he's praying, sitting on the bench. It showed that there was a bigger weight on his shoulders than I realized."

Years of losses, of nearly leaving the city, and finally he had achieved the ultimate prize. "He looked like a man who was like, 'Man, I did it. The monkey's off my back,'" Elie says. It was no coincidence to those closest to him that his biggest achievement came when he was finally at peace within, when he was guided by a higher purpose than himself or even his sport.

"It took such a long time for me to get there . . . ," Olajuwon said afterward. "It took me all those years in college and in the NBA to do it, and I felt like I wanted it so badly many other times. I was so close, and I couldn't have it. But now, after 10 years in the league, I feel like I had the maturity that it took to get there, and that has enabled me to really appreciate the accomplishment more than I ever could have before."

The Rockets raised the trophy while fans cheered at the top of their lungs. "Houston," David Stern said into the microphone, "or should I say, Clutch City!" Rockets players then ran to the locker room, jumping, screaming, and crying. It was time to pop champagne for everyone except Olajuwon, whose Islamic beliefs prohibited him from drinking alcohol. Each player had a basket of expensive champagne and cheese at his locker. "Dream!" some teammates asked, "I know you don't drink, so can *I* have it?"

Olajuwon smiled. "In our faith we cannot drink it and we cannot give it or sell it. I can't give it to you to drink." Olajuwon ended up pouring his champagne into the sink. His teammates were stunned; he was emptying expensive bottles of champagne as if they were water. But it made them respect Olajuwon even more. Even on his biggest night of achievement, he wouldn't sacrifice his principles. "Wow," a player said to Olajuwon. "That is powerful."

Olajuwon left the arena a little earlier than some of his teammates, and on his way out he found Ewing in the loading dock near the Knicks' team bus. Ewing was, understandably, dispirited. Olajuwon told him that he knew the effort he put in, that he gave his best, and that he had to keep walking with his head held high. The two hugged, holding the embrace for a beat.

Olajuwon left in a limo as chaos ensued outside. It took fans hours to get home because the streets were filled with celebrations. "He [Olajuwon] said, 'If they knew that I was in that vehicle, they would've toppled it over,'" says Ibrahim Arch.

While his teammates partied that night, he went to pray at his local mosque. Yousuf Syed, a friend who happened to be at the mosque, was stunned. "That was the most amazing experience I've ever had in my life," Syed says. "I couldn't believe we were there after the game with him."

Olajuwon began to pray. Outside those walls, the sports world declared that he had cemented his place among the greats. But in that moment, Olajuwon's only concern was gratitude to God.

He let a tear fall. Without Allah, he felt, he would not have won that game. That ring.

This was his celebration.

• • • •

THE NEXT MORNING, GOLDBERG SPOTTED OLAJUWON AT THE hotel connected to the Summit. "Does this make up for 1983?" Goldberg asked him, referring to the Final Four loss to NC State they had both endured.

Olajuwon smiled and said, "It does."

Goldberg beamed at Olajuwon, who he had watched reach heights neither could have imagined. "I was so happy for him," Goldberg says. "It was like a dream. Did this really happen? Did we go to three Final Fours? Did we win the NBA Championship?"

Reality gradually set in as the Rockets celebrated throughout the week. Championship rings were customized. Olajuwon didn't get his championship ring made in gold like his teammates—14 karat gold with 14 diamonds totaling one karat—because Islam prohibits wearing gold. He had his ring made with platinum instead.

Similarly, two days later, the Rockets' parade in Houston was scheduled to start at the same time as his Friday *Jumu'ah* prayer service. He told everyone to go ahead without him as if a championship parade would be possible without him. The best player on the planet. "I will miss it," Olajuwon said. "No choice for me. I'm going to *Jumu'ah*."

Five hundred thousand Rockets fans jammed the streets of downtown Houston for the parade, standing and waiting patiently for about an hour while he prayed. An escort arrived at the mosque to pick him up. He was going to the parade, after all. Finally, when he arrived, riding on a fire truck along with his teammates, fans roared.

For so many Muslims around the country, the victory was especially sweet. They appreciated and admired that Olajuwon didn't give up his faith to succeed. To many, he proved that one could stay true to God—and to himself—and achieve at the highest levels of sport. In a world that was hardly kind to Muslims, Olajuwon inspired a generation to feel pride in themselves and in their religion.

CHAPTER 18

DISCIPLINE

Olajuwon had been contemplating whether he should fast on game days during Ramadan. In that month, commemorating the time when the Qur'an was revealed to the Prophet Muhammad (PBUH), adult Muslims, whose health permits, abstain completely from food, drink, and sexual activity from dawn to sunset. It's a time of spiritual discipline, reflection, and gratitude. One turns inward, trying to get as close as possible to the Divine. Ramadan also binds the community closer together, reminding all of the suffering and poverty that many of its members endure.

Olajuwon hadn't yet fasted during actual games. "I cannot do it on game days," he told reporters in February 1993. "So what I have to do is make up for the days I miss after the season." But a conversation with Denver guard Mahmoud Abdul-Rauf, another Muslim player, inspired him to contemplate fasting on game days. Olajuwon wasn't aware at first that Abdul-Rauf, with whom he had prayed before, had done it.

After a game in Denver in January 1995, the two caught up with each other. "I got to get something to eat. I've been fasting," Abdul-Rauf said.

"You fast?" Olajuwon asked.

"Yeah, man. I'll tell you. I can't explain it. My focus is on a whole 'nother level. You would think it would be down. It's like . . . *magnified*."

"Really?" Olajuwon responded, surprised. "Well, you fast. I'm going to fast."

"Alhamdulillah!" Abdul-Rauf said, which translates as "praise be to God."

"We're athletes," Abdul-Rauf says now, reflecting on that conversation, "but we're also competitive in terms of, if we see somebody that has some good qualities and it sounds good, well, shoot, I'm going to try it."

Hanif Khalil, Abdul-Rauf's manager and a Houstonian who had prayed alongside Olajuwon as well, explains the dynamic: "That's one of the things in Islam, is that in the sight of Allah, that we don't compete as far as bank accounts. We don't compete in worldly affairs or anything like that," Khalil says. "But if there *is* a healthy competition, it is in the deed of piety and good works. . . . Hakeem is a fierce competitor. If he sees that Mahmoud is [fasting], it's almost a competition in good deed . . . a healthy competition."

Olajuwon began to publicly discuss the idea because he decided he would fast during games throughout Ramadan. "When you are on the road, you are allowed to make it up. But to go all the way instead of delaying it to make it up [is exciting]," he said in February 1995. Olajuwon was referring to the stipulation that he was considered a traveler, and the Qur'an permits one to postpone fasting and make up the days at the end of Ramadan. "He didn't want to do that," says Rudy Tomjanovich, the Rockets coach. "He wanted to do it the proper way." Olajuwon believed that the traveler rule didn't apply to him because it was meant for ancient times when traveling by camel over difficult terrain. That didn't compare, he felt, to an NBA player's travel by airplane.

Olajuwon knew fasting on game days would be difficult, an extraordinary exercise of self-restraint. It would be a shock to his system. But it became a joyous time for him, something he looked forward to—albeit something that came with great sacrifice. "It is a way of purifying the body and the mind and it makes me feel good," he said at the time, adding that it requires discipline. "Yes, it is hard. But that is why it helps in the long run. You learn to appreciate the gifts God gives us, even something as simple as a glass of water. We take so much for granted. We ignore the value of so many blessings."

However, the Rockets staff members were concerned. They reasoned that players, especially centers as mobile as Olajuwon, expended a tremendous amount of energy running up and down the court. "You worry about dehydration as much as anything," says Bruce Moseley, Rockets team physician from 1993 to 2003. "Because they sweat so much. They exert themselves so much. It's pretty constantly for about two and a half hours. The normal NBA player will sweat an enormous amount of body fluid." Moseley and the rest of the Rockets staff monitored him more closely during Ramadan.

"Certainly, I had concerns," says Ray Melchiorre, former Rockets trainer. "But I knew he was eating good when he did eat. . . . He prepared for it." Olajuwon often ate a bowl of oatmeal and drank juice and water in the mornings before prayer. And he took such care of his body and his fitness that he knew he could sustain the fast.

The Rockets, despite their initial reservations, supported his decision. "We respected his personal choice," Tomjanovich says. "We wanted to let him know that we were 100 percent behind him." That was evident in other respects, too. Staff members scrambled to find prayer rooms for him on the road. Much of that duty fell on Jay Namoc, the equipment manager, who made sure Olajuwon had his prayer rug and compass, and would ask other teams for a private locker room or an auxiliary space. "He just needs it for a thirty-minute block of anywhere he can pray that's private," Namoc would say.

It wasn't always easy to find a space. "We had some rooms where he would be praying in these little closed closets," Namoc says. Often, there wasn't a clean room available. "He didn't care how bad it was inside," Namoc says, "as long as he had a place to put his rug down and pray."

Eventually, David Nordstrom, the equipment manager, spearheaded the construction of prayer rooms both in the Summit and in the team's practice facility. Rockets trainer Keith Jones was also instrumental in making sure Olajuwon had everything he needed to pray. But for the 1994–1995 season, he made do with whatever room he had.

His first game-day fast was on February 2, 1995, and Olajuwon played spectacularly. He dropped forty-one points in a win over the Utah Jazz, all the while being defended by the relentlessly physical Karl Malone. The next game, a nationally televised Sunday showdown against Charles Barkley and the Suns in Phoenix on February 5, he put up twenty-eight points, eleven rebounds, three assists, and three blocks in thirty-nine minutes. The Rockets won the game 124–100. "You do wonder how the heck he does it," Tomjanovich says. "He was *so* good. God. It's just amazing."

Olajuwon averaged 29.5 points, 10.1 rebounds, 3.8 assists, and 3.4 blocks during that month of Ramadan, winning NBA Player of the Month honors. "I saw it," Bullard says. "I don't believe it." Olajuwon also lost ten pounds in the process. "There are 48 minutes to a game," Robert Horry, former Rockets forward, later recalled, "and for you to play 42 minutes of that 48 and not even be able to take a sip of water? That is just phenomenal."

In the coming years he'd have some of his career-best performances during Ramadan. In 1997 he averaged 25.4 points, 8.3

rebounds, and 3.4 assists in 37.2 minutes a night. Against the Nuggets, he had 48 points and 10 rebounds in 43 minutes. Against the Bulls, he tallied 32 points, 16 rebounds, 5 blocks, 4 assists, and 4 steals in 39 minutes, snapping Chicago's nine-game win streak. "He's unsolvable," Michael Jordan said afterward. Barkley, who had joined the Rockets in 1996, agreed: "To be able to play like that without water for the whole game, it's one of the most amazing things I've seen in my life."

Not only did Olajuwon seem to play better during Ramadan, but he also seemed to *feel* better. "Your stomach begins to shrink up after a period of time," says Anthony Falsone, former Rockets strength coach. "But he got stronger. He was a guy who, the mental part of it was so strong. He would say, 'Anthony, I feel so good.' We'd be two weeks into it. In my mind, I'm going, *There's no way he feels stronger.* He's like, 'I'm stronger. I'm lighter. I'm quicker.'"

As Olajuwon said at the time, "Many people think playing basketball is more difficult because of the absence of food. But when they see the benefit and that it is the opposite, [they can see] that we have more energy, [are] much quicker, faster, more focused."

"If only they knew," Olajuwon said about NBA players and how good it felt to fast, "they would be fasting."

He was posting video-game stats on the order of forty points and fifteen rebounds on national television against some of the toughest in the league: Jordan, Ewing, Robinson. Name an elite player, and Olajuwon dismantled him—with nothing in his belly. "It was remarkable," Moseley says.

Perhaps that was because his ability to excel had as much to do with his inner drive, his spiritual sense, as any physical source of strength. His teammates asked him: "How do you do it? Where are you getting this energy?" He'd simply say: "Allah. Allah gives me the energy I need."

Olajuwon made himself believe he wasn't tired, wasn't thirsty. He focused on controlling his desire. He reminded himself of the purpose of his fast and how, although his body was being starved, his soul was being nourished. "He saw it as the fuel that gave him the determination to be the best," says Ameer Abuhalimeh, the director of Olajuwon's Islamic Da'wah Center. "He told me many times that in fasting . . . it made him move around the court much easier. Not thinking about food, or not having food in his stomach, made his thinking process much sharper and his focus much sharper, which translated into a better game and better numbers."

But the reality is that fasting during games is extraordinarily difficult—for anyone. At one point during his fantastic February 1995 Ramadan stretch, he shot just ten of twenty-one in a loss to the Knicks despite finishing with twenty-seven points, nine rebounds, four blocks, three steals, and three assists. He admitted that he felt drained of energy: "I had a burning in my chest all day from not being able to drink and didn't play the kind of game that would allow us to win."

Staff monitored the sun during games, constantly checking to see if it had gone down so Olajuwon could take a sip of water or eat a fresh date, which the Prophet Muhammad (PBUH) ate to break his fast. During time-outs, Olajuwon would ask: "What time is it? Is it time?"

"Not yet."

Some of the games in which he fasted began just before sunset, so he could break his fast at halftime. But many times the Rockets had afternoon games with a 1:30 p.m. or 2:30 p.m. tip-off, and he wouldn't be able to eat or drink until some time after the buzzer sounded. "We were concerned like, 'Dream, do you want some water?' even though you knew not to ask him," Namoc says. "Our concern was his health."

Sometimes they'd ask him if he wanted some Quench Gum, to generate saliva and give some moisture to his mouth. Bullard remembered seeing salt around the edges of Olajuwon's lips. "Dream, drink some water!" he said. "You're getting dehydrated! You have to drink!" Olajuwon calmly responded: "No."

Not a sip.

Not a drop.

"He refused," says Joel Blank, Rockets director of broadcasting from 1994 to 2016. "He would say: 'I can't go against the principles.'" It was almost as if he were in a trance, so driven toward his purpose. "Oh my gosh. This just adds *levels*, and layers upon layers of just being in awe," says Scott Brooks, the former Rockets guard. "There were times that I would say to myself, 'There's no way you're going to be able to do this,' but he did. . . . I'm like, 'Man, you are not *real*.'"

Yet Olajuwon didn't see himself as superhuman, even if everyone else did. He was simply satisfying his obligation as a Muslim, no different from any of his brothers and sisters at the mosque. "For him, the way he saw it, is that he wasn't doing anything special," Arch says. "He saw it as fulfilling his commitment." The only difference in his life, Olajuwon once mentioned jokingly, was that his hotel bills were far less expensive during Ramadan. No room service.

Many of his teammates didn't even know he was fasting until reporters mentioned it. "He didn't really talk about it," says Pete Chilcutt, former Rockets forward. "He just did it. When he came to work, he came to *work*."

After his magnificent performance against the Bulls during Ramadan in January 1997, reporters peppered him with questions about how thirsty he must be, how much he must *crave* a drink of water. He calmly answered their questions, telling them about controlling desire, about being grateful for the blessing of water. "Before, you take it for granted," he said. "You can have water at any time. Now, a glass of water becomes like a jewel."

But as many times as Olajuwon explained he felt revitalized by fasting and that Ramadan was a time of great spiritual *rejuvenation*, some in the press didn't seem to understand. The Associated Press, for one example, wrote one night that he led the team to victory despite being "depleted." Another time, after a loss to Orlando during Ramadan in 1997, one report claimed that Orlando's players said that the "reason for the defeat was Olajuwon's unwillingness to rehydrate himself." When asked about that claim, Olajuwon maintained it made him a better player; the final score just wasn't the outcome he had hoped for.

He became connected to Muslim leaders around the country by attending services during road trips. "When we travel, you don't know anybody. Then all of a sudden . . . the community [knew me]," Olajuwon later said. "So, life on the road, for a Muslim—I've never felt like I'm on the road. I'm always at home."

And in Houston, Olajuwon wouldn't just show up to an event here or there; he seemed to be ever present. Every Friday, kids would ask one another, "Are we going to see Hakeem?" He traveled without any security, as a "normal" person, but in a slick white Mercedes, only adding to his legend. Many everyday Muslims have their own "Hakeem stories." They met him at this mosque or that mosque.

Many appreciated how he publicly spoke about Ramadan, about Islam. "Hakeem presented it in a very beautiful way. It's powerful. It's very powerful," says Mohamed Naser, a Palestinian-Jordanian Muslim who immigrated to Houston in 1984. Naser was around nineteen when he began watching the Rockets. Some of Naser's happiest moments have been seeing Olajuwon play, huddled around the TV with his Muslim friends while drinking tea and coffee. After watching the Rockets win the 1994 championship, he took his kids outside. Hundreds of people were celebrating on the street, on top of their cars, including Naser and his family on their minivan. "My kids even dented the roof [of the car,] we were so excited," Naser says.

"You see somebody like Hakeem and he's fasting for example during Ramadan, and I'm fasting, too. That creates awareness," Naser says. "He gave a good example of Islam. The ideology. Because the media, or average man on the street or Americans, think we are dumb idiots, terrorists, all of these things."

Nauman Khan, a Muslim Rockets fan who grew up in Houston, recalls: "Pre–9/11, there just wasn't a lot of awareness about Muslim people." Olajuwon was his hero, and he'd see him at Houston mosques. "And then all of a sudden, that spotlight came, and then you finally had somebody to highlight what you looked like growing up. . . . It just meant a lot to us growing up, and being able to really kind of feel like he was one of our own."

Islamophobia began long before the terrorist attacks of September 11, 2001. Muslims had long faced bigotry and been portrayed negatively in popular culture and media, mostly as terrorists and "dangerous fanatics," as journalist Arun Kundnani wrote in *The Muslims Are Coming!*

According to Waleed Mahdi, an associate professor at the University of Oklahoma and an expert on US-Arab cultural politics who traces the history of Islamophobic images in the media, negative stereotypes of Muslims date back as early as the silent-cinema era around 1914. Films like *The Sheik* exoticized Muslims as fundamentally different, as the "other," a term coined by the cultural theorist Edward W. Said.

Those portrayals continued in the coming decades, and in the 1970s Muslims and Arabs were often seen on-screen as threats to national security. That concern was heightened in the early 1980s, amplified by media coverage of the Iranian Revolution. "Acute anti-Muslim bigotry began with the hostage crisis," journalist Roxanne Dunbar-Ortiz wrote in *Not a Nation of Immigrants*, referring to the 1979 Iranian storming of the US embassy in Tehran, trapping diplomatic hostages there for over a year.

Major prime-time broadcasters, including Walter Cronkite of CBS and Frank Reynolds of ABC, spoke of the "Muslim hatred of this country." Mainstream print publications seemed to follow suit. The January 6, 1980, *New York Times Sunday Magazine* titled one article: "Militant Islam: The Historic Whirlwind," feeding a fear of Islam, questioning its compatibility with the very notion of democracy.

Anti-Muslim sentiment spread over the next decade, heightened by the 1991 Gulf War against Iraq and the 1993 bombing of the World Trade Center. Some media continued to portray Islam as a threat. The *Boston Globe* ran a 1991 series on Islam titled "The Sword of Islam." The Sunday *New York Times* "Week in Review" headlined its January 21, 1996, issue with the title "The Red Menace Is Gone. But Here's Islam." Black Muslims, here in America, also faced their share of xenophobia in public media and discourse.

Olajuwon may have been fasting because he was fulfilling his religious obligations, but his actions nonetheless raised awareness about Islam with non-Muslims. For example, Tomjanovich would call a time-out for him when he needed to pray during a game because he was obligated to pray five times a day, and he'd head into the tunnel for a brief moment. Meanwhile, broadcasters would tell viewers that Olajuwon had briefly left to pray, and then explain why.

Olajuwon was, of course, aware of the influence of his voice, but for the most part he didn't concern himself with his impact or standing. He instead focused on Islam's emphasis on humility. "Hakeem is more concerned about his faith in living his life based on his conviction than he is about perception and the impact that he has on others," says Lynden Rose, his close friend from college. "His conviction is front and center in everything that he does."

Still, many times throughout his career, he acknowledged the impact of his reach. "My role is very important because Islam has been misunderstood, especially in America," he said in 1996. "You have to educate the people. Islam is a religion of peace . . . submission and obedience to the will of God."

After he retired, he became even more vocal: "When I was playing, I didn't realize how much of an impact I would make on people, Muslim or non-Muslim. We played a lot of games during Ramadan. On national TV, the announcers were commenting about Ramadan, and this raised the awareness to the general public, and we made all the Muslims very, very proud. . . . So, I feel so grateful to Allah for giving me that opportunity while I had that chance to make that impact. And thankfully it impacted all the people—more than I realized."

His games brought many Muslims closer together. Omar Usman, contributing writer to MuslimMatters.org, grew up in Houston, and he remembers many such moments. "It was a whole event where everyone's getting together," Usman says. "It became a mini community event almost."

Watching Olajuwon was something that connected the younger and older generations of Muslims, especially those who had immigrated to the United States and raised their kids in Houston. "He wasn't just The Dream," journalist Monis Khan wrote. "To many Muslim-Americans, he was the epitome of the American Dream."

· · · ·

Majid Syed was just ten years old when he watched the Rockets defeat the Lakers in the 1986 Western Conference Finals. He and about a dozen members of his family huddled around the TV after *iftar*, having just finished breaking the Ramadan fast. They were supposed to go pray *Tarawih* afterward. "But half the adults were like, 'We're watching this game!'" Syed says.

Syed, whose license plate reads "DRM34," now has a son of his own. The two often see Olajuwon at the mosque. "My son sees him at the *masjid* and thinks, 'He's just a guy that I pray next to.'" But for Syed, that accessibility is what made Olajuwon a hero for him, growing up in Houston in the 1990s. Olajuwon didn't just know people's names; he knew about their lives as well. Their families. He always asked how everyone was doing. "When you actually interact with him," Hanif Khalil, Mahmoud Abdul-Rauf's manager, says, "he almost makes you kind of look at yourself to say, 'OK. Am I humble enough? Am I generous enough?' It's so inspirational. It helped me in my journey."

At times, Olajuwon even shared vulnerable parts of himself with everyday people at the mosque. Syed remembers being around sixteen when Olajuwon feuded with management—when they accused him of faking an injury. Syed and his friends were devastated at the possibility of a trade. "Please don't leave us," they begged him at the mosque.

"No, no, no, I don't wanna leave you guys," he remembers Olajuwon saying. "I love you guys here in Houston." He explained how management had offended him. "He's expressing himself to a bunch of sixteen-year-olds," Syed says. "He goes, 'How could you play for someone that calls you a liar?' We're shell-shocked because we didn't expect it." Such an exchange would be virtually impossible today, in the era of social media and TMZ, where every moment in a superstar athlete's life could be caught on camera.

Syed and his friends had a profound respect for the way Olajuwon helped organize and sponsor local Muslim basketball tournaments in Houston, bringing the community even closer. Syed still has the tattered T-shirt Olajuwon signed for him from the 1991 Muslim basketball tournament. The event was deeply meaningful for Syed, seeing so many different Muslim communities and ethnicities playing together, feeling proud of who they were, how they prayed.

"The whole generation gap between maybe let's say our parents and us—he really was kind of like the beacon," Syed says. "I hate to say this, but maybe in the early '80s, we tried to assimilate a little too much because maybe that's what our parents wanted us to do. . . . Without losing your identity and your culture and your value systems—you try to fit in. . . . Being picked on and looking different and 'smelly foods,' things of that nature growing up. We now had a person to look up to, to say, 'Hey, it's OK to be *you*.' You could adapt without having to change your identity, your culture, and your belief systems.'"

Ahmed Mattoo, another Muslim basketball player who grew up in Houston during the 1990s, would watch Rockets games with his grandmother. Seeing Olajuwon not just dominate the court but also so openly discuss Islam gave Mattoo a boost of confidence. "During Ramadan, I wouldn't shy away from fasting because, hey, Hakeem did it, you know?" says Mattoo, who felt comfortable telling his coach that he was fasting. His coach would immediately understand, saying: "Oh, like Hakeem?"

Mattoo didn't always feel comfortable talking about his faith. "It's kind of embarrassing to say, 'Hey, I'm Muslim, and I'm fasting.' Or, you know, 'I have to go pray.' I wouldn't. I simply would just wait. Maybe when I got home, I'd do it behind closed doors," Mattoo says. "I wouldn't fast during Ramadan at school because I knew maybe the kids would make fun of me because maybe they don't understand. But then when Hakeem came out, and everybody sees Hakeem, and it's everybody's talking about, 'Hey, man, did you see Hakeem? You know he's not drinking water or eating anything? Can you believe that?' It just brought this joy from inside."

When he was in eighth grade, he remembers his friends saying to him as Ramadan approached: "Hakeem always balls during Ramadan! His numbers are higher." Then Mattoo shared that he would be fasting, too. "When did you become Muslim?" his friends asked.

"No, I've always been Muslim," he said. "I just didn't show it in front of you guys."

"[Hakeem] knew kids were watching. He knew this was bigger than himself," Mattoo says. "An entire generation of Muslims grew up being accepted in the community because of Hakeem."

He inspired female basketball players, too. Amina Chaudary, award-winning filmmaker, scholar, and journalist who founded the magazine the *Islamic Monthly* (*TIM*), grew up "obsessed with the NBA" and Olajuwon. She was captain of her high school basketball team. In the mid-1990s, Olajuwon happened to visit her school, and she took a risk, wearing her bright-red Olajuwon jersey instead of her white button-down shirt and green plaid skirt uniform. "I tried to hide it in the hallways," she says. It didn't work; the straight-A student was sent to the principal's office. "I'm not even going to tell you why you're here," the principal said.

"I know," Chaudary said. "But I love him so much. Please can I just wear it?"

"When he walks through the hallway," the principal replied, "you can put it on then."

Chaudary, carrying a red sharpie, eventually got Olajuwon's autograph and would interview him years later for *TIM*. "He wasn't the first [Muslim athlete]. Obviously there was Muhammad Ali . . . but it was something about that era, the '90s, that's the era I grew up in, and I was trying to figure out myself as a Muslim and an American. I grew up with immigrant parents. It was really impactful to have that time, seeing someone like Hakeem Olajuwon that was so loved."

. . . .

CLOSER TO HOME, MANY COLLEGE AND PROFESSIONAL BASKETBALL players were inspired by Olajuwon, especially those who'd go on to compete at the highest levels of the game. "He was so giving of his time," Abdul-Rauf says. Olajuwon always helped Abdul-Rauf find a place to pray, and the two would often pray together before games. Olajuwon would also invite him over to his home. "Every time we talk, you can just feel the genuineness and the brotherliness in it," Abdul-Rauf says. "As I'm talking about him [now], I'm sitting over here literally teary-eyed. He's really a special individual."

Abdul-Rauf is not the only one who felt that way. When Olajuwon began fasting during games in 1995, a freshman forward at Cal named Shareef Abdur-Rahim watched intently. Abdur-Rahim, who would jump to the NBA a year later as the number-three overall pick of the 1996 NBA draft, had been admiring Olajuwon for many years. He and his sister were often the only Muslim kids at their school in Marietta, Georgia. "Seeing even from a distance, seeing someone that had a funny name like mine, with a hard-to-pronounce name, what that meant to me," Abdur-Rahim says. "I'm like, 'If he can do it, maybe I can do it.' Islam wasn't something that was widely known about or understood. People didn't understand it. So having a person explain Islam, be mainstream, do things like fast during the season and during games . . . as a young person seeing that, it's inspiring."

Abdur-Rahim, now the president of the NBA G League after a successful twelve-year NBA career, saw Olajuwon's generosity up close while at Cal. He had a fancy awards banquet to attend but needed a proper suit. A good friend happened to be friends with Olajuwon and called him. Olajuwon didn't know Abdur-Rahim, who was around nineteen at the time, but he set up an appointment for the young man to get a tailored suit for the occasion. "That meant the world," Abdur-Rahim says. "I wanted to be able to follow that example."

The two eventually competed against each other in the NBA, during the tail end of Olajuwon's career. Olajuwon even invited him to pray with him before the game. Abdur-Rahim was moved by Olajuwon's kindness. "It's how he lived his life. It's what he represented," Abdur-Rahim says. "You couldn't just identify him as a basketball player. He was deeper than that."

As the G League's first Muslim president, Abdur-Rahim hopes to inspire young people in the same way Olajuwon did. "I know what it meant to me to have somebody I felt like representing me," he says. "I want to carry that forward."

Mahmoud Abdelfattah, a Rockets assistant coach in 2022–2023, became the first Palestinian and first Muslim to be named a head coach of an NBA or NBA G League franchise when he coached the G League's Rio Grande Valley Vipers from 2019 to 2022. He was named G League Coach of the Year in 2021–2022. He and Olajuwon prayed at the same mosque. Abdelfattah felt it was almost fated, getting his first NBA coaching opportunity in the same city as the NBA's most prominent Muslim player.

"There's no coincidence. Things happen for a reason," says Abdelfattah, former head coach of the Sydney Kings in the Australian NBL.

The first time they spoke at the mosque, the conversation lasted nearly two hours. Olajuwon would always check on Abdelfattah, wanting him to know he was there for him. The two participated in Rockets Muslim Family Night in March 2023, with Abdelfattah moderating a conversation. It was surreal for him, sitting onstage with his hero in front of so many Muslim kids.

Abdelfattah wants to provide inspiration for other Palestinians and Muslims the way Olajuwon has for so many around the world. He remembers Olajuwon telling him: "You can't do this for you. If you do this for you, you're going to be selfish. At the end of the day, you have to do it to please God."

CHAPTER 19

HEART

Although Olajuwon had played magnificently during Ramadan in February 1995, the Rockets struggled with consistency all season. The path to a second straight championship seemed uncertain. The Rockets began the 1994–1995 campaign with nine straight victories but then dropped eight of their next twelve. The team hit rock bottom with an embarrassing 100–81 loss to the Jordan-less Bulls on January 22, 1995, dropping its record to 23–14.

To make matters worse, in the middle of a February game, Vernon Maxwell ran up eleven rows in the stands and allegedly punched a fan. He said he was provoked into doing so because the man had allegedly uttered racist and defamatory comments directed at him. Maxwell was suspended for at least ten games and fined twenty thousand dollars.

The Rockets hardly resembled the championship team they had been the previous season. "We lost that hunger. And we weren't the same team," says Rudy Tomjanovich, the Rockets coach. "You don't want to think our guys are getting overconfident and not going out there with an edge. The guys admitted it later that they were getting interviews, they were getting endorsements. . . . It took away some of their hunger."

Houston needed a change. A trade. Tomjanovich had his eye on Clyde Drexler, Olajuwon's former teammate from college, who at that point had become Portland's all-time leader in scoring, steals, and rebounds.

"He was such a good player," Tomjanovich says, "but we also thought, 'How am I actually going to get a good player to come in here in the midseason and fit into another team?'" Robert Barr, then vice president of basketball affairs, spotted Olajuwon in the hallway. "What if we got Clyde?"

Olajuwon paused. "We get Clyde," he said, "we win the championship." Olajuwon and Drexler had long dreamed of it. They talked about the NC State loss many times. "All these years," Drexler later said, "we've talked about how we wanted to make things right and win a championship together." Finally, the trade went through on February 14, 1995, sending Otis Thorpe, the rights to Marcelo Nicola, and a 1995 first-round draft pick to the Blazers for Drexler and third-year forward Tracy Murray. Houston was sixth in the Western Conference at the time.

"In my wildest dreams," Olajuwon said, "this is too good to be true."

Some other teammates weren't exactly thrilled: the Rockets had traded away Thorpe, the heart and hustle of the team. Many also thought trading a "big" for a guard like Drexler, especially at age thirty-two, wasn't smart. How would he fit in? It took time to gel, and losses mounted heading into the playoffs.

Olajuwon was diagnosed with anemia in March 1995 and had been playing with a severe iron deficiency without even knowing it. "His blood count was like half of what it normally would be," says Bruce Moseley, the former Rockets team physician. It's unknown if he was suffering during his awesome Ramadan stretch, but if he had been, that would make the feat even more impressive. However, team officials at the time were convinced that the anemia had more to do with the anti-inflammatory medicine he was taking than with his fast.

He sat out for two weeks and returned with just six games left in the regular season. The Rockets were still the sixth seed in the Western Conference, hardly viewed as a contender. "Dream was *pissed*," Barr says. "He said, 'We gotta do something.'"

But even Tim Frank, Rockets public relations director, had booked a vacation; he assumed that the team wouldn't last long in the playoffs.

• • • •

THE ROCKETS EMBRACED THE UNDERDOG MENTALITY HEADING into their first-round series with the Jazz. But nothing came easy. Maxwell was given an indefinite leave of absence following a verbal altercation with Tomjanovich after a Game 1 loss. Olajuwon carried the team on his back, leading the Rockets to a Game 2 win. Trading wins, Utah then stole Game 3 in Houston, the Rockets took Game 4, and everything was on the line in Game 5.

Once again, the Rockets had to dig deep, trailing by twelve in the fourth quarter. When Olajuwon sank an impossible bank shot after spinning toward the left baseline, it seemed like he wasn't going to let his team lose. Drexler was unguardable down the stretch, coming up with big play after big play. "The championship spirit just came out of us," says Mario Elie, former Rockets guard.

Houston advanced to face the Suns, a stacked team led by Charles Barkley and Kevin Johnson. In true Houston fashion, it found itself in a hole, down 3–1 in the series after dropping the first two games in Phoenix, as well as losing Game 4 after blowing another big first-half lead.

Olajuwon kept his teammates mentally strong. "You must believe in something . . . ," he said at the time. "We are in a do-or-die situation." But Drexler was dealing with the flu ahead of Game 5, vomiting and receiving an IV before the tip-off. He somehow rallied to play, invigorating his teammates, especially as he knocked down critical free throws to help secure the win. The Rockets continued to roll at home, beating the Suns by double digits in Game 6.

Once again, it came down to Game 7.

The Suns didn't have an answer for Olajuwon. On one play, as Phoenix's Kevin Johnson charged down the open floor for a break-away dunk, Olajuwon chased him down and blocked his shot. "In every round, you never really got the sense that Hakeem was going to let us lose," Tim Frank says.

Still, the Rockets found themselves down by ten at halftime. Players were pissed. The Suns had been talking trash all game. But Olajuwon walked into the locker room, calming everyone down. "We got them right where we want them," he said without a trace of irony. It was as if the team collectively got its swagger back after that, clawing its way back as soon as the second half began.

The back-and-forth game came down to the final seconds as the Suns' Danny Ainge double-teamed off Elie. Robert Horry then found Elie in the corner behind the three-point line, the score tied 110–110 with under ten seconds to play. With Ainge not immedi-ately closing out on him, and Suns center Danny Schayes sticking to Olajuwon inside, Elie knew the shot was his. "Once I let the shot go," Elie says, "it felt *good*." The shot, which hit nothing but net, would be dubbed "The Kiss of Death" because Elie celebrated by blowing a kiss to the Suns Joe Kleine, who was on the bench and had been talking trash. Kleine was so angry he turned "red as an apple," Elie says.

The Rockets won, 115–114, to survive and advance, becoming the first team in twenty-seven years to win a Game 7 on the road after trailing 3–1, and just the second team to do so in league history.

"We were a resilient group of players," Elie says. "We always believed in each other. We always had each other's back."

. . . .

OLAJUWON WOULD FACE ONE OF HIS TOUGHEST FOES IN THE WESTern Conference Finals, the Spurs' David Robinson. Robinson was among the top centers in the league, one of the all-time best big men, but Olajuwon shook him, shimmied him, *dominated* him so badly that Barr can only describe it as "the worst, excuse my French, the *worst* ass kicking I have ever seen in the NBA. I mean it was horrible. He *killed* him."

Olajuwon was so unstoppable, Dream Shaking every which way, that journalists ran out of descriptors: *He mixed Robinson in a blender! He twisted Robinson into a pretzel!*

Olajuwon made one move look more extraordinary than the next, muscling his way to the paint with force, then fading away with elegance. His power and grace were on full display, always in harmony. Olajuwon even swished a rainbow-arc shot just above Robinson's fingertips. Robinson is seven feet one, giving him a clear height advantage, and was known for his shot-blocking prowess. Yet Olajuwon made it look easy, shooting over the moon. "The great ones, they do things under pressure," Tomjanovich says. "David Robinson is so quick, great defensively, but Dream in that series, he was just amazing. That's not some subpar player he's playing against. He's playing against the cream of the crop."

Olajuwon suffocated him on defense, too. In Game 1 alone, which the Rockets won on the road by a single point, Robinson went just five for seventeen. But as if Olajuwon needed any more motivation ahead of Game 2, he watched from the Houston bench in the Alamodome as David Stern presented Robinson with the regular-season MVP award. Olajuwon finished fifth. "Who in the hell does the

MVP voting?" guard Sam Cassell said at the time. "What are people thinking? . . . Fifth is ridiculous."

His teammates had never seen Olajuwon with the look he had on his face that night, watching Robinson hold the MVP trophy. Robinson thanked many other NBA stars but not Olajuwon, arguably his toughest foe. That riled up the Rockets players: "Dream! He didn't say your name! He didn't respect you!"

Olajuwon just stared straight ahead, silent. "I never really saw that look in his eye," Elie says. "I remember coming out for the introductions, I think he 'bout broke my hand when I went to slap him five. I knew he was razor locked-in." His teammates were waiting for him to explode or to show *some* kind of emotion. Kenny Smith stood next to him, scanning his face. "Man, that doesn't make you feel a *way*?" Smith said.

"No, no, no," Olajuwon said. "He deserves it."

Elie and Barr looked at Olajuwon and said: "Dream! Look at [Robinson]! Look at him smiling! He's got your trophy, Dream!" When Olajuwon's expression didn't change, a few other teammates asked: "Dream, are you OK?"

"It is OK," Olajuwon finally said. "Because it is not about the smaller trophy. It is about the fact that we will get the bigger trophy."

Everyone just looked at him in awe. "At that point," says Joel Blank, then the team's director of broadcasting, "the whole team was like ready to run through a wall." From the opening tip, Olajuwon went *off*. He could maintain he didn't care about the MVP all he wanted, that Robinson truly deserved it, as he would do in the coming decades. But on that court, before that 1995 playoff game, his teammates just *knew*—Olajuwon was *pissed*. Humility be damned; he was a competitor at heart, and when he was in that *mode*, no one could stop him.

Bill Worrell, the Rockets' longtime broadcaster, was at a loss for adjectives at one point in Game 2 when Olajuwon blocked Robinson. Olajuwon ran down court to the other end, then set up on the corner. With Robinson defending him, Olajuwon took a crossover dribble and drove baseline, then spun and pump-faked Robinson into the air, toying with Robinson, as if to say, *Is this what you were looking for?* before going back under—*Remember this?*—and gently laying the ball in uncontested. "Olajuwon has David Robinson just bamboozled!" Worrell said on the air in a now-iconic call. "Bamboozled was the only thing that came into my mind," Worrell now recalls. "David was so bewildered; everything he tried on Hakeem did not work. I mean, it was the most embarrassing performance I've ever seen. The most *dominating* performance I've ever seen by one great player over another."

Olajuwon finished with forty-one points and sixteen rebounds in his team's 106–96 win. After the game, he found Smith. "Kenny!" Olajuwon said. "I'm going to his house to get my trophy!"

"I *knew* it was bothering you!" Smith said, laughing. "It was bothering *me* that he didn't say your name!"

Olajuwon had profound respect for Robinson. He still does. It was precisely Robinson's quickness and shot-blocking prowess that forced Olajuwon to raise his game. But Olajuwon was too creative, too crafty, for Robinson. When reporters asked him about some of his Dream Shakes in the series, Olajuwon shrugged. "Oh, it's just a move," he said.

He preferred to let his play do the talking, scoring forty-three points in a Game 3 loss, 107–102. Robinson managed to "contain" him in Game 4, limiting him to . . . twenty points and fourteen rebounds. Reporters asked him after the 103–81 San Antonio victory how he could "solve Hakeem."

"You don't solve Hakeem," Robinson said. Olajuwon quickly proved him correct, exploding for forty-two points, nine rebounds, eight assists, and five blocks in a 111–90 Game 5 victory in San Antonio and then going for thirty-nine points, seventeen rebounds, and five blocks to win Game 6, 100–95, and advance to the NBA Finals.

Robinson had stepped to the free-throw line in the dwindling seconds of Game 6 with a chance to stave off elimination, but he missed both shots and ultimately went six of seventeen from the field. He sat at the podium afterward with a glazed look on his face. His voice was barely audible. He said he didn't want to seem as if he were joking, but "I actually thought I did a pretty good job covering him."

He wasn't wrong.

Olajuwon was simply on another plane. He was, in the words of Kareem Abdul-Jabbar, who had attended one of the games, sitting in the second row, "unreal." Olajuwon's game had evolved so much since he faced Abdul-Jabbar in the 1986 Western Conference Finals. Back then, defenders tried to force him to the middle, away from his automatic baseline jumper on the left side. But now he was just as lethal going into the lane.

Drexler was in disbelief after the series. "I've never seen anybody on this planet play as well as this guy," he said, pointing to Olajuwon at the locker next to him. "He's phenomenal."

Olajuwon looked uncomfortable. He gently grabbed Drexler's arm as if to stop the praise. "Is he embarrassing you?" a person nearby asked.

"Yeah, yeah, yeah," Olajuwon said, grinning, then deflecting: "When you play with the right team, it brings the best out of a player. That's what happened with my game. The team makes me play better."

Olajuwon went to shower. Meanwhile, Robinson came into the Rockets' locker room, wanting to offer his congratulations to Olajuwon. "Where's Hakeem?" Robinson said.

"He's in the shower," Drexler said.

Robinson told Drexler to pass on his message to Olajuwon. Drexler insisted he stay: "[Hakeem] really wants to see you. He's right there. In the shower."

Robinson paused. *In . . . the . . . shower?* "I don't know about that," Robinson replied. "I don't know if I want to climb in the shower with the man."

"He really wants to see you," Drexler said.

Robinson stuck around, offering Olajuwon his best. Robinson knew he had witnessed something special.

· · · ·

AS IF THAT DUEL WASN'T ENOUGH, OLAJUWON HAD TO BATTLE another top center next, Shaquille O'Neal, the Orlando Magic's larger-than-life center. The 1995 Finals was a duel of the big men, experience versus youth (O'Neal was just twenty-three). He had long admired Olajuwon. When O'Neal was sixteen, he snuck in the back door of the HemisFair Arena in San Antonio to get Olajuwon's autograph.

The two got to know each other as adults, sharing an agent in Leonard Armato. "When I first came in, he opened his arms to me," O'Neal says. "We would talk every now and then." The two had something in common that extended far beyond hoops: "We have the same religion," says O'Neal, who was "born and raised" Muslim. As they got to know each other in the NBA, O'Neal only admired Olajuwon more. "Shaq was *so* respectful of Hakeem," Armato says. The usually boisterous, charismatic

O'Neal had nothing but praise for Olajuwon. "Hakeem's the best center in the league. The best in the world," O'Neal said at the time. "Don't compare me to anybody else but him." When asked how he defended against Olajuwon, O'Neal once said: "I just put my hands up and hope he misses."

The Magic was a talented group, especially with O'Neal and guard Anfernee "Penny" Hardaway leading the way. "He was a ten and I was a nine, so I wasn't intimidated," O'Neal says. "I thought I was going to dominate, but he just showed me that in order to get a championship, you got to go to that next level. And I was still at a nine and he took it to eleven, twelve." Still, the Rockets found themselves down twenty points in Game 1. Orlando was trapping Olajuwon everywhere, but other Rockets players shouldered the offensive load and helped mount a comeback. Smith eventually sent the game to overtime on a three with 1.6 seconds remaining after the Magic's Nick Anderson missed four straight game-sealing attempts at the line. In overtime, Olajuwon tipped in a missed Drexler shot with three-tenths of a second left to lift the Rockets to an improbable 120–118 win.

The next day at shootaround, though, Tomjanovich sensed something was off. His players were going through the motions, resting on their laurels. "Happy feet," he called it. Tomjanovich gave them a stern talk; they would have to earn every win.

Horry responded with a fantastic Game 2, showcasing his elite defense; he had seven steals in that game alone. Tomjanovich's innovative offense thrived, switching Horry, often a small forward, to power forward to space the floor and complement Olajuwon. Cassell came up big, too, so confident he told Smith before the game: "Relax. I'm giving you the night off." He finished with thirty-one off the bench.

"I thought he was kidding," Smith said.

Olajuwon, who scored thirty-four, was dominant, despite Shaq being seven feet one and seventy pounds heavier. Olajuwon beat him with his quickness and creativity. On defense, Olajuwon couldn't guard O'Neal with a three-quarter front; instead, he took to heart Assistant Coach Carroll Dawson's words: "Just stay behind him. He doesn't have the moves that you've got. Let him get the ball, but guard him after he gets it."

Olajuwon realized, though, as he had throughout the playoff run, that responsibility was not all on him. The struggles of Rockets teams of the past were a distant memory; his current teammates weren't afraid of the moment. They had his back. But what allowed the Rockets to break through wasn't that Olajuwon finally trusted his teammates, as many would claim. It was that Tomjanovich had implemented a different system that catered to his strengths. And Olajuwon finally had the right personnel around him.

The Rockets won Game 3, 106–103, taking a commanding 3–0 series lead. Tomjanovich stuck with his superstitions, ordering his lucky grouper the night before Game 4. Emotions were high. The Rockets knew the Magic weren't just going to lie down and accept a 4–0 sweep. But they were prepared and responded to every Magic run. Horry had a thunderous dunk. Elie rained threes. Cassell made clutch plays. Cries of "Sweep! Sweep!" rang out. And every time the Magic went on a run, Olajuwon reassured his teammates: "We're OK. We're OK. Just keep playing. Play some defense. We'll keep chipping away. We'll get them."

And with ten seconds left, Olajuwon hit a three-pointer to seal the win. Yes, a *three*. Drexler raised his arms in disbelief, tilting his head back; he couldn't help but smile. As the clock wound down in the 113–101 win, Smith screamed at Drexler: "You got one! You got one!" After twelve years, Drexler finally had won a championship ring, and Houston was crowned back-to-back champions. "I have one thing to say to the nonbelievers," Tomjanovich said afterward. "Don't ever underestimate the heart of a champion!"

"I don't have the words in my vocabulary to describe how I feel about this team," Tomjanovich said. "Nobody ever had to do what this team did. To beat the No. 1, No. 2, No. 3, and No. 4 seeded teams, nobody's ever done that. I'm the proudest guy in the world."

The Rockets became the first sixth seed to beat four fifty-win teams and win a title. And they were just the sixth team to sweep the NBA Finals. Renowned journalist Scoop Jackson of *SLAM* thought that Olajuwon had ascended to a different level, putting fear into his opponents. He operated his very own "torture chamber . . . no place for the weak of heart, weak of mind, weak of defensive skills." Jackson had covered so many of the great centers from that era and remembers how they were pretty much all bruisers. Olajuwon, on the other hand, operated with "a sense of smoothness," Jackson says. "There's something unforced about the way he played basketball. And it coincided, to me, with the way he carried himself."

Olajuwon and Drexler embraced after the buzzer, too emotional to speak. They had finally won a championship together. No longer young men, mourning the loss to NC State—they were seasoned veterans with families of their own, their basketball journeys nearly completed.

Olajuwon later found O'Neal and hugged him. O'Neal seemed in a daze, almost as if he couldn't believe what had happened. Olajuwon, ever the mentor, encouraged him, telling him this was a valuable experience. "That's called paying your dues," Olajuwon told him. "If you win easily, you don't really value what you have. That's part of growing up."

"In order to be the best," Olajuwon said, "you have to beat the best." O'Neal says that Oajuwon wished him luck and added: "You're definitely going to win the championship." "He taught me that it's not over until it's over," O'Neal says. "I didn't know anything about raising it to that next level. . . . It just taught me as a professional that if I ever get back to the finals, I have to dominate, dominate, dominate."

"In that series, I showed him way more respect than I showed other guys just because he was just so nice," O'Neal says. "When I played against all my other centers, I really didn't like them, but he was just such a likeable guy. Even when I would hit him with a blow, I would try to get him mad, he would just say stuff like, 'Nice elbow, brother.'"

"I learned from him that it's okay to be nice," O'Neal says. "Just because NBA stands for Nothing But Actors, I wanted everybody to think I was mean, I was crazy. But I realized that off the court, you couldn't be like that." Even now, looking back, when Kenny Smith, his cobroadcaster on TNT's *Inside the NBA*, O'Neal is surprised at some of Smith's stories about Olajuwon's temper in his early days in the league. "Kenny told me stories: *he was very mean*. I find that hard to believe. He was always nice to me, very hospitable. Every time I see him, every time we see the family, we can go sit down and get drinks. . . . it was just all love." And, after that 1995 series, O'Neal had nothing but respect for Olajuwon, who was named Finals MVP for a second straight year, joining Michael Jordan as the only player to achieve the feat. "I'm not allowed to root, but I've become a Hakeem Olajuwon fan," David Stern said, handing Olajuwon the trophy. "Because of his grace and the seeming ease with which he does it, because of his extraordinary calm under fire and his all-around class and grace, it sometimes masks the determination, the grit, the resolve that allows great athletes to carry their team and to make the players around them both better and in their own way great, and literally carry their club to a championship by virtue of their own will. That is Hakeem Olajuwon."

• • • •

REPORTERS WERE WAITING TO HEAR FROM OLAJUWON AFTER THE celebration on the court. Bruce Bernstein, a former coordinating producer at ESPN, who was in charge of *SportsCenter*'s remote coverage of the NBA Finals during that time, remembers dozens packed into a room while he waited near a modest TV set up with just one camera. "In later years we had more resources," Bernstein says, "but in 1995, we were set up adjacent to an open area with no security other than those of us working on the live shots."

That meant he could see and hear conversations that otherwise might have been private. He saw then Rockets public relations director Tim Frank bring Olajuwon over to Dr. Jack Ramsay, the Hall of Fame coach who was ESPN's analyst at the time, to do a live *SportsCenter* hit before the rest of the media had a chance to ask questions. After the interview, Olajuwon pulled Ramsay aside. He deeply respected the coach and couldn't squander the moment.

Olajuwon had just cemented himself as a member of the NBA pantheon but began to go through his arsenal of low-post footwork for Ramsay, twisting this way, turning that way.

"Dr. Jack," Olajuwon said, "how did I do?"

Ramsay was floored, moved by the sincerity in the younger man's eyes, the humility.

"Hakeem," Ramsay said, smiling, "you did just fine."

• • • •

OLAJUWON WAS SOON PEPPERED WITH MANY QUESTIONS ABOUT HIS place in the NBA's hierarchy. *Who's the best player in the game? Is it you?* "I'm happy with myself," he said. "I like my moves. I like my game."

It was such a simple but profound thing to say, the core of who he was. True happiness, true peace, he often said, came from within.

True contentment meant he didn't need to compare himself to others or to want for more. And even if the Rockets hadn't repeated as champions, he could have walked out of the arena with his head high, his heart aligned.

He knew who he was.

CHAPTER 20

CITIZEN

Even though Olajuwon had ascended to the highest heights of basketball, he still had one more goal: winning an Olympic gold medal. He had his chance as a member of Team USA at the 1996 Olympics in Atlanta.

Olajuwon was originally declared ineligible to play for the United States because he had played in an international tournament as a seventeen-year-old for Nigeria's junior national team at the 1980 All-Africa Games. The International Basketball Federation's press secretary didn't mince words in his press release: "We cannot have people changing nationalities like trousers." Olajuwon appealed. He wasn't "changing nationalities"; he was proud to be from Nigeria but had also legally become a US citizen a few years earlier, in April 1993, and at that point had lived in Houston for twelve years. "It feels more like home to me than Nigeria," he said at the time.

It took Olajuwon, his representatives, and several NBA executives months of appealing to FIBA to allow him to play for Team USA at the Atlanta Olympics. He was finally cleared in 1995, receiving special permission.

"There's no place like home," Olajuwon said. "I will always be from Nigeria. But I'm happy to be a Nigerian-American." Still, at times it was a difficult, even painful, subject for him to navigate because he never wanted to be disrespectful toward Nigeria. He was, in some ways, a man in between two nations, not always fully embraced by either.

Part of what led him to apply for US citizenship was that he had been subject to extensive searching at airports a number of times over the years upon handing over his Nigerian passport. He said he had been taken out of immigration lines, had his luggage examined, and had even been subjected to body searches. He felt stereotyped. "Drug traffickers, smugglers, dishonest politicians. Unfortunately, that seemed to be the first thing that anybody thought of when you presented a Nigerian passport," he said in 1996.

He just wanted to travel the world and be treated with dignity. He also knew the privilege an American passport afforded. "Being an American citizen," he said, "gives you respect." But gaining American citizenship didn't stop all slights. "I have a different background. I talk different. Native-born Americans just have to look at me or listen to me and they are reminded of the differences," he said.

Some Nigerians from home viewed him as having betrayed the nation because he opted to play for Team USA instead of Nigeria in the Olympics. As journalist Joshua Akanji wrote in the Nigerian *National Interest,* "The decision [to play for Team USA] earned him respect and accolades back in the States but got him scathing remarks in Nigeria where he was derided for opting to play for the U.S. to their detriment." Some Nigerians asked Olajuwon if he was no longer proud of his Nigerian heritage or if he had lost his Nigerian identity. "I hear: *Hakeem doesn't like Nigerians. He tries to pretend that he has nothing to do with them anymore. . . . Hakeem doesn't like Black Americans. He thinks he is superior.* These things are said out of ignorance," Olajuwon responded. "They are said by people who don't know me or who have never tried to know me."

He occupied a tricky space, one where he was expected to model fealty to two countries. He would always be proud to be Nigerian but no longer recognized the country where he had grown up. Military officer Sani Abacha had taken over as head of state in 1993 and had executed nine dissenters, including acclaimed Nigerian author Ken Saro-Wiwa. As a child and teen, Olajuwon remembered a completely different atmosphere, one filled with optimism. "The potential was incredible," Olajuwon said in the lead-up to the Olympics. "And to see that the great potential like that never really materialized, and destroyed, out of greed, corruption. It is very sad."

Dikembe Mutombo, who dedicated himself to philanthropic work throughout Africa, building hospitals and organizing annual relief missions in his native country of Zaire (now the Democratic Republic of the Congo), said at the time he would never apply for US citizenship. He came up to Olajuwon in the Rockets' locker room after a game and chided him, pulling out his Zairean passport, saying that instead of playing for America, the two should lead an African squad. "There are only two of us, Hakeem and me, representing maybe one billion Africans. That's why it is so important that we retain our identity, not as men from separate countries but as Africans," Mutombo told reporters. "It is very important that we represent our continent."

"He is so busy being an American," Mutombo said, "he forgets his home." But Olajuwon thought they perceived *identity* and *home* differently. "This [America] is home now. It is where I have chosen to live. It is where I have made my life," Olajuwon said. "Why wouldn't I want to represent America?" And just because Olajuwon wasn't publicizing his philanthropic work in Nigeria didn't mean he wasn't helping his community. "My cause is not limited to Africa. Or America. It is universal," he said. "Allah is for humanity. It is beyond tribes."

"Being a good citizen doesn't mean taking pride in where you were born. It means being a good citizen of the world," he continued. "That is the basis of Islam. There are no nationalities. We are all different colors, all different races, but all brothers." And he would always have pride in his roots: "I would never deny Nigeria. It is where I am from. It is part of who I am. Some of the best times of my life were my childhood years in Lagos. . . . All of my golden memories are of those years."

But what did it mean to "become" American? To "become" a citizen? What does one owe one's native country?

"Hakeem was and still is very much the face of African basketball," Mutombo now says, reflecting back on that time, "but it quickly became clear that even though he played for the US Olympic team, he would be able to represent Nigeria and Africa on the biggest stage and in the most positive and inspiring way."

Many Nigerians who had also immigrated to Houston embraced Olajuwon, resonating with that feeling of being in between. Longtime basketball fan Francis Okupa was one of them. He was born in England but grew up in Lagos, Nigeria, where his family is from. He immigrated first to St. Louis and then moved to Houston. "I still felt in between," Okupa says. "I was living the American teenage experience." He had been watching Olajuwon with pride for many years, and seeing him succeed was meaningful. "He's one of us," Okupa says.

Many other people within the diaspora saw their experiences reflected in Olajuwon's. "For Nigerians—particularly the Nigerian community in Houston—there is special pleasure in watching Hakeem," wrote Nigerian journalist Chido Nwangwu in the *Houston Chronicle* in 1995. "He seems poised to transcend mere basketball statistics. . . . For millions of Nigerians, including thousands in Houston, his is already a story far beyond basketball."

In the early 1990s, Nigerians constituted Houston's largest African immigrant group—as many as ten thousand, by some estimates—making Houston one of the largest Nigerian communities in the United States. Thousands of Nigerian students immigrated to Houston in the 1970s and early 1980s, partially because of the familiar climate as well as the economic opportunities within the oil industry. And many of their Nigerian American children felt connected to Olajuwon, who served as a bridge between the older generation and the younger one.

Houston native Datubo MacHarry was five years old when Olajuwon won his second championship. His parents are Nigerian immigrants, and his father was, and still is, a Kalabari chief. "I had to actually pay attention [during games] in my household because everybody—my brother, my cousins, my aunts, my uncles, my parents—they were like, 'HAKEEM OLAJUWON!!!'" MacHarry says. "It wasn't 'The *Rockets* won.' It was '*Hakeem Olajuwon* won.'" Olajuwon inspired him to feel a deeper sense of pride in his Nigerian American identity. "I saw somebody who is from where my parents are from," MacHarry says. "For Hakeem to land *here*? It's almost like divine intervention."

Ike Diogu, team captain for Nigeria in the 2012 and 2016 Olympics, was born in Buffalo, New York, and raised in Garland, Texas, just outside Dallas. His parents had immigrated from Nigeria in 1980. He felt at home within the Nigerian community in Dallas, frequenting Nigerian churches, eating at Nigerian restaurants, and going to Nigerian weddings. "I always felt like I was growing up in Nigeria because that's just kind of what I was around," Diogu says. He first heard about Olajuwon as a third-grader: "All the Nigerians around the Dallas area, Texas area, we all wanted to be like Hakeem. . . . Hakeem was the first one to really open the eyes to the rest of the world that Africa does have [professional basketball] talent," Diogu says.

Obinna Ekezie, who played for the Nigerian national team in 1998, grew up in Lagos but came to America for college, playing for Maryland, before briefly playing in the NBA. "Hakeem Olajuwon was my sole inspiration for playing basketball. He was my mentor," Ekezie says. He asked his dad to install a hoop in their backyard so he could practice his Dream Shake. "I was obsessed with Hakeem."

Olajuwon's undeniable success influenced the shifting demographics of modern basketball, just as the NBA began morphing into a global brand.

• • • •

DAVID STERN, WHO TOOK OVER AS NBA COMMISSIONER DURING the summer after Olajuwon was drafted in 1984, began to set his sights abroad. About a year later, Stern met with a group of officials from Beijing, led by Mou Zuoyun, the 1936 Olympian known as the godfather of Chinese basketball. "I look forward to one day hosting the Chinese national team as my guest," Stern said to him. A couple of weeks later, the Chinese national team did in fact fly to America, and the 1985 NBA/China Friendship Tour was regarded as one of Stern's first efforts toward transforming the NBA into a global power.

Stern realized that to do so, he couldn't just focus on selling NBA merchandise or even securing foreign broadcast rights, although both were important: the NBA was a business, first and foremost. He also took a longer-range view, seeking to build infrastructure abroad to scout and develop talent that might one day compete in the NBA. Historian and journalist Lindsay Krasnoff, author of *Basketball Empire: France and the Making of a Global NBA and WNBA*, has also written an extensive oral history of basketball in Africa. She says that the NBA's original goal was "to grow the [NBA's] business and imprint [in Africa], but that evolved to use basketball beyond the court, which eventually led to its use as a prism for education, economic development, gender equality, and building the larger ecosystem around all of this."

Stern wasn't alone in his pursuit. Much less known is the role of Kim Bohuny, currently the NBA's vice president of international basketball. Working in tandem with Stern, she pioneered much of the NBA's expansion abroad, including founding the Basketball Without Borders Camps in 2001. When she joined the league in 1986, she was excited about the NBA's potential growth overseas. "You felt you were at the beginning of something that was going to be really big," Bohuny says. She viewed basketball not just as a sport but as a vehicle for human connection. "She's sort of the unheralded visionary," says Chris Ebersole, NBA associate vice president, head of international basketball development. "She has a really true passion for the power of basketball and the power of sport to bring people together."

Bohuny and Stern first began grassroots work mostly in Europe and Asia, arranging for NBA preseason games such as the Japan games in 1992. Only about a third of NBA teams had an international scout in the early 1990s, and these scouts were focusing mainly on Eastern Europeans following the collapse of the Soviet Union. Former Mavericks GM and assistant coach Donnie Nelson was one of the first NBA coaches to scout internationally. In addition, he also served as an assistant coach to the Lithuanian national team and advised the Chinese national team.

But given Olajuwon's dominance, the NBA knew it needed to expand into Africa as well. "There was always interest in doing more on the continent," Bohuny says. That dated back to the NBA and Kareem Abdul-Jabbar's initial trip to several African countries in 1971, when Olajuwon was just a child. But by the time he morphed into a back-to-back champion in 1995, that interest increased exponentially. "I keep telling people: 'If you went to Nigeria around that time [in the 1990s], I'm sure you could have found 20 Hakeems.' That's always been the case," says Joe Touomou, NBA Academy Africa associate technical director. Touomou grew up in Cameroon and eventually became the first Cameroonian to play Division I ball when he suited up for Georgetown.

"Nigeria was not a dominant basketball country, but was the most populous country in Africa," Touomou says, "and also had the best human potential in terms of basketball and athletics, period. . . . There were so many Hakeems . . . [who] never got a chance to come to the US."

Although talented teams were emerging all over the continent, especially in Angola, many countries didn't have access to widespread infrastructure such as courts and other basketball equipment. Soccer dominated. Still, Olajuwon, who was named an international spokesperson for the NBA in 1994, inspired other African-born players who later came to the United States and thrived in the NBA, including Dikembe Mutombo (Zaire, now the Democratic Republic of the Congo), Manute Bol (South Sudan), Yinka Dare (Nigeria), and Mamadou N'Diaye (Senegal).

N'Diaye stayed up until 3 a.m. to watch Houston's two championships. He wore number 34 because of Olajuwon, and the two became teammates in the NBA. "He was the role model for all of us to come behind," N'Diaye says.

Olajuwon was prescient in predicting an influx of international players. "Down through the years, there will probably be many players from other countries who will come along and be able to win the MVP award and win championships," he said in 1994. "But no matter what happens or how many times they do it, I will always be the first," he added. "As I continued to play basketball in school [in Nigeria,] I became confident in my ability. I knew that if I got the chance, I could play in the NBA. Now, after seeing me, I think there are a lot of others who believe that, too."

The number of international players began to increase—not just in the NBA but in the NCAA as well. In 1990 there were 154 international players from 35 countries playing college basketball—including 18 from Nigeria and 10 from Yugoslavia; that number had doubled from the previous decade. "I've had 15 Nigerian attorneys come in here and tell me they have the next [Hakeem] Olajuwon," said Pat Foster, who had succeeded Guy V. Lewis as the University of Houston's coach.

Many European-born players became focal players on NBA teams, most notably with the arrival of Vlade Divac in 1989, followed by Dražen Petrović, Arvydas Sabonis, Toni Kukoč, Dino Radja, and Šarūnas Marčiulionis, as well as such later stars as Pau Gasol, Dirk Nowitzki, Peja Stojaković, and Tony Parker.

The Rockets had signed Žan Tabak for the 1994–1995 season after drafting him in 1991, a Croatian player whom Olajuwon had taken under his wing. Tabak barely spoke English, but Olajuwon shot around with him every day, labored on moves with him, and offered wisdom about off-court matters. "During that time, when I was playing in the NBA, international player was not a common thing," says Tabak, now a professional coach in Croatia. "International player was not treated the way it is today. There were no stars like [Nikola] Jokić or [Luka] Dončić. . . . What made the transition easier was Hakeem."

Seismic change was on the horizon, mainly as a result of the 1992 Dream Team's gold medal at the Barcelona Olympics, which globalized the game immensely. For decades, international rules wouldn't allow NBA players to compete in the Olympics. The hope was for parity to balance out America's advantage in hoops. But that rule was dropped in April 1989 when it was clear that the United States, which had finished third at the previous Seoul Olympics, was falling behind as the rest of the world advanced.

Known as the greatest team ever assembled, the Dream Team, led by Michael Jordan, Larry Bird, Magic Johnson, Charles Barkley, and David Robinson, Olajuwon's former playoff foe, breezed through the tournament, winning games by an average of forty-four points. Opposing teams appeared more interested in taking photos with the players than playing against them. "They approached perfection," wrote Jack McCallum in his iconic book *Dream Team*. "They are history writ large."

The following year—specifically August 1993—was crucial in the NBA's expansion in Africa. NBA officials, including Stern and Bohuny, along with several players, including Mutombo, Alex English, and Bob McAdoo, and coaches Wes Unseld and Alvin Gentry, traveled to Johannesburg, South Africa, as well as to Kenya and Zambia, to conduct basketball clinics and build basketball courts. It was a watershed moment, officially ending the US sports boycott of South Africa's apartheid regime.

Soon-to-be president Nelson Mandela, head of the African National Congress, had spent twenty-seven years in prison before his release. He invited the NBA contingent to visit South Africa. He had asked Sam Ramsamy, the newly elected president of the South Africa Olympic Committee, to reach out to Richard Lapchick, the renowned human-rights activist who led the America sports boycott during apartheid, and ask him to speak to David Stern about the NBA coming to South Africa. "[Mandela] said that he wanted the NBA to be the first sports organization from America to come to his country," Bohuny says, "because he wanted the young people of South Africa to meet prominent African Americans from the most powerful country in the world."

Mandela hoped to use sports to help rebuild the nation and address wounds inflicted by apartheid. "Mandela placed a huge emphasis on the sports boycott of South Africa and its importance in him being freed as well as becoming president," Lapchick says. "I think that he was all geared up for using a sports example to bring his people together, in addition to other ways."

The NBA group was supposed to just have a cocktail with Mandela, a brief introduction; it was the year leading up to his historic presidential election. But Mandela enjoyed his time with the group so much he asked them to stay for dinner. They were in awe of this larger-than-life person, generous and kind as could be. "It was an emotional trip for everyone," Bohuny says. She remembers most "the warmth in his eyes. I just can't describe it. What an incredible human being, especially knowing what he had gone through. To have that much empathy and love in his eyes, it just really made me emotional when I saw the way he talked, the way he'd look at you."

After the NBA's first visit in 1993, Mandela asked Stern to have the NBA make regular visits to South Africa to help further develop basketball. "Whenever the league came to the country, if President Mandela was in town he would visit with the NBA delegation," Bohuny says.

The NBA would commit over the next three decades to working alongside existing African basketball federations and African leaders who had long been doing the work of growing the sport across the continent. The NBA returned to Africa the following year, 1994, when Mandela was finally named president. "When we did the clinics, the kids never wanted to stop," says Lenny Wilkens, the Hall of Fame coach who was on that trip. "I don't care what the weather was like. They never wanted to get off the court. They wanted to be there all the time. . . . They wanted to learn everything they could about the game of basketball."

Many hoped to become the next Olajuwon, including Masai Ujiri, now Toronto Raptors president, who grew up in Nigeria. "Because he's from our country, my country," Ujiri says. Ujiri's mother, who traveled overseas for work within the medical field, would bring him back basketball shoes or videotapes of Olajuwon's highlights. "She knew that would make me happy."

Ujiri eventually met Olajuwon after moving to America to attend college and play hoops, first at Bismarck State College in North Dakota and then at Montana State University Billings. He continued his playing career overseas before getting into coaching. Throughout, Olajuwon often offered advice and support. The two became closer as Ujiri climbed the NBA ladder, beginning as an unpaid scout for the Magic, sleeping on floors and couches, chasing his dream. He then became a paid scout for the Nuggets before leapfrogging to Toronto's director of global scouting, to general manager of the Nuggets, and to his current role as the Raptors' president. He kept Olajuwon in his thoughts as he began strategizing how he, too, could give back, not just to Nigeria but to Africa as a whole.

• • • •

OLAJUWON WAS THRILLED WHEN HE FIRST PUT ON HIS TEAM USA jersey, saying: "Look at this! This is great." He felt as if he were about to complete the last step in his journey. "I won't underestimate the effect of the '92, the original Dream Team," says Fran Blinebury, the former Rockets beat writer for the *Chronicle*, "and how being a Dream Team member elevates your status in the NBA pantheon. And so I think that became part of it. It was very important [to Olajuwon]."

Reggie Miller, one of Olajuwon's Team USA teammates, knew what the Games meant to him. "These are Hakeem's Olympics in a lot of ways," Miller said at the time. "He's the best player in the league who hasn't had the chance yet to wear USA on his chest. . . . I'm not sure anybody appreciates it more than he does."

Gary Payton, another member of Team USA, remembers how excited Olajuwon was to be on a team full of superstars. "He was like, 'Yo, this is great to play with twelve great basketball players.' Not just him and having one or two [stars]," Payton says. "He always talked about that when we was at practices. The practices were better than the games, and it was because we was always going at each other."

Olajuwon marveled at how many people attended the Olympics. He even got to meet Desmond Tutu, the South African archbishop and human-rights activist, when he came to Team USA's practice. He brought his awestruck grandson, Simon, who shook hands with Olajuwon. "He's lucky," Tutu said of Simon. Tutu then invited Olajuwon to come to South Africa. "We want you to come and inspire our guys," Tutu said.

The US team didn't automatically breeze through the competition. "We were challenged," says Bobby Cremins, assistant coach on the team.

"What they wanted to do was be as good as the first team," says Lenny Wilkens, the head coach of the 1996 team, who also served as an assistant coach of the 1992 Dream Team. "The world was challenging us in basketball, and we wanted to show the world. And that's what I would use as a motivational factor with the [1996] players: 'If you really want to show the world how good you are, here's your opportunity.'"

The United States eventually won gold, defeating Yugoslavia by a score of 95–69. Although Olajuwon played only about twelve minutes per game, contributing 5.0 points and 3.1 rebounds, he nonetheless enjoyed the experience. He and his Team USA teammates raised their arms in the air while the crowd cheered them on as they were about to receive their gold medals. Olajuwon was the final player to be presented with a medal. He bowed his head as the medal was draped around his neck. He smiled, clutching the medal for a second, before waving to the crowd.

When Olajuwon wasn't competing, he attended other countries' games, especially the African teams. He took special pleasure in watching team handball, his former love. He became animated, shouting out direction from the stands.

Earlier in the tournament, a few hours before his USA squad was to play Australia in the semifinals, Olajuwon heard someone call his name. "Hey, Hakeem, you probably don't remember me . . . but you punched me in college." It was Scott Fisher, the former UC Santa Barbara forward now playing for Australia. Olajuwon had gotten ejected in the final minutes of that college game in 1984. Olajuwon reached for Fisher's hand, held it for a second. "I remember," Olajuwon said, pausing, looking him in the eye. "And I'm sorry."

It meant a lot to Fisher. "It was absolutely sincere," he says.

Olajuwon was so far from the person he used to be. And he was still evolving.

CHAPTER 21

BUSINESS

EVEN AS HE BLAZED HIS OWN PATH ON THE BASKETBALL COURT, Olajuwon continued to do things differently off the court. Around this time, he signed a deal with Spalding to make more affordable sneakers called "Akeem the Dreams," a stripped-down, no-frills sneaker that sold for $34.99. Air Jordans and Nikes, at the time, dominated the market and often exceeded $200. Shaquille O'Neal had his own Reeboks, as did guard Grant Hill with Fila and Shawn Kemp with Reebok—the zebra-striped "Kamikazes."

"It was a revolutionary thing, the idea of tying one player to a shoe and making it a big deal," says Russ Bengtson, a former *SLAM* and *Complex* editor and author of the 2023 book *A History of Basketball in Fifteen Sneakers*. However, Olajuwon set off in his own direction, selling his shoes at discount stores such as Payless, Wal-Mart, and K-Mart without any major national advertising campaign. "How can a poor working mother with three boys buy Nikes or Reeboks that cost $120?" Olajuwon said at the time. "She can't. So kids steal these shoes from stores and from other kids. Sometimes they kill for them."

He had traveled to factories where some of the most expensive Nikes and Reeboks were made and saw that the shoes were significantly cheaper at wholesale, then sold for much higher prices at retail, so he went from the factory straight to the store without a middleman.

"The big companies did not like what I did because you expose [them]," Olajuwon said at the time. "Because you have the same [quality] shoe . . . one is $35 and one is $120. Which one is better? You can't tell the difference, but the price is like night and day."

Olajuwon had always chosen a different path than his NBA peers when it came to sneakers. When he first came into the league, he signed a deal with Etonic to make his signature high-top sneaker, "The Dream." But both the Etonic and the Spalding shoes never gained mainstream commercial success. It was said that the NBA may not have marketed him as much as other superstars. Bias, either implicit or explicit, may have also been a factor. No matter how successful he became, no matter how many years he spent in America, sustained major national endorsements eluded him, although he did at times represent Visa, Taco Bell, Uncle Ben's rice, and Frito-Lay, among others.

Olajuwon was at times positioned as an outsider even in his prime. As the *New York Times* pointed out in 1995, after Olajuwon won his second championship, "Where are his cheeseburger, sneaker, computer, soda, and car commercials? Despite projecting an image of class and reliability, the Nigerian-born Mr. Olajuwon is also a man who speaks English with a foreign accent and has a name that is hard to pronounce. . . . He plays in Houston, not New York or Chicago. He is not a flashy character, a trash-talker, a tattoo-wearer, or a backboard smasher." The article quoted Marty Blackman, a prominent athletic-advertising executive, who said, "Madison Avenue prefers an American guy. Is that a disadvantage? Yes. No question. It's not racial. It's just a fact."

The *Houston Chronicle* agreed: "After all his years in Houston, there is still a cultural gap that keeps Hakeem from being fully accepted into the mainstream. There is the heavy Nigerian accent and the fact he does not project a hip, MTV image."

Olajuwon had participated in an ad for Visa alongside Scottie Pippen ahead of the Olympics in which his Nigerian accent was the butt of a joke. It began with Olajuwon saying: "Me, Hakeem Olajuwon, and the rest of the American Dream Team are going to treat these guys for lunch." Pippen then whispered into Olajuwon's ear: "Hakeem, we said we were going to *eat* these guys for lunch!"

Olajuwon, however, didn't take issue with the ad. "It is my favorite of all the ads I have ever done," he said. "Somebody was finally not afraid to have fun with the way I talk. They used the accent as a positive, not a negative, and played to it. It made me feel finally like I was being accepted as one of the members of the American Dream Team, not an outsider from someplace else."

His sneakers, though, still weren't as commercially successful as those of some of his peers. Perhaps it had to do with his position. Big men struggled to sell shoes in general; O'Neal's shoes were not a top pick, either. But perhaps it had something to do with Olajuwon's reserved nature and his religious values. "With Hakeem being Muslim, he leaned more into his faith where you don't really honor yourself, you honor Allah and Islam more than you do your individual greatness," says Will Strickland, a Toronto-based cultural creator and curator who also played basketball for Rice University in Houston. "Your greatness is rooted in your relationship with Islam."

Indeed, one reader wrote a letter to the editor of the *New York Times* in response to the article questioning why major endorsements eluded Olajuwon. "You wonder why advertisers shy away from the best basketball player in the world," wrote Michael Myerson. "Gone unmentioned is that Olajuwon's religion is Islam, and he prays to Allah. We've had decades of demonizing and stereotyping of Muslims. Can anyone recall an instance of promoting a product by projecting a Muslim as a hero worthy of emulation?"

Olajuwon's dedication to his faith influenced other off-court decisions, too. Many other stars accepted statues of themselves outside of their arenas, for example, but Olajuwon would not. It would be a form of idolatry to have a bust of himself. So a twelve-foot-tall bronze monument of his jersey, number 34, weighing more than half a ton, was eventually erected outside the Toyota Center in Houston. The monument rests on a red granite foundation listing his career milestones.

And in 1997, when Nike created a logo on a pair of sneakers that resembled the word "Allah" in Arabic script, maintaining that the logo was meant to look like "flames for a new line of shoes with the names Air Bakin', Air Melt, Air Grill, and Air B-Que," Olajuwon, along with the Council on American-Islamic Relations, demanded an apology. "To Muslims who live an Islamic life, the name of God is sacred," wrote Olajuwon in a two-page letter to Nike. "His name should not be taken in vain, or used lightly or frivolously."

Olajuwon brought those same values to his own signature sneakers. Olajuwon and his marketing team argued that these sneakers were a success, maintaining the importance of making shoes affordable to everyone. However, Foot Locker, a prominent shoe outlet, opted against selling Olajuwon's Spalding shoes. Many didn't want to risk displaying what was seen as an inferior sneaker. Kids would be mocked, Foot Locker's reasoning went, if they were seen wearing the far-less-cool Spaldings over Jordans. "How do you define *cool*?" Olajuwon said at the time. "What's cool is doing the right thing at the right time, being proper, displaying manners, representing your family very well."

Olajuwon wasn't preoccupied with being popular or even wealthy. He would eventually launch a successful real estate career and would ultimately make as much, if not more, money in real estate as he did during his NBA career. He was a savvy businessman, a long way from watching his mother conduct deals at the Lagos wharf. So even if mainstream outlets didn't embrace his sneakers, he was proud of what he had done.

"I am at a different point in my career," he said in 1997. "I get all of the same enjoyment out of the game and from winning. But I would like to do it all very quietly. I don't need the recognition. I don't need the attention. As an individual, I have nothing left to prove. I am just enjoying my career and the fruits of all the years."

His body, however, began to feel the weight of those years.

• • • •

TIM FRANK'S PHONE RANG AT ABOUT 3 A.M. CARROLL DAWSON, who had recently become the Rockets general manager, was calling: "I need you to fly back to Houston." It was late November 1996, near the beginning of the 1996–1997 season, in the early hours after a road win against the then-Washington Bullets.

"Why?" said Frank, the Rockets public relations director, barely awake. The team was supposed to fly to Toronto the next day to face the Raptors.

"Hakeem is having his atrial fibrillation. We need you to go home with him. You can come back and join us in Toronto. We don't want him traveling alone."

Olajuwon, who had previously experienced atrial fibrillation in 1991 and had experienced a similar episode about two weeks before the Bullets game, met Frank downstairs to take a cab to the airport. It was pouring rain, and the driver was driving erratically. "[Hakeem] was already nervous," Frank says. Much felt out of his control. The car, his heart.

Upon their arrival at check-in, the agent took her time with Olajuwon's license, mispronouncing his name: "So where is Mr. O-Lu-Ju-Wa-Won?" Her colleague leaned in: "Not much of a basketball

fan, huh?" She looked up at Olajuwon, then back down at the
license. "It's Hakeem Olajuwon!" she said, finally putting it together.
They started laughing, but Olajuwon was too on edge to join in. It
was one of the first times Frank saw any fear in him. "All right, let's
go through security," Frank said.

"OK. But I need to pray."

"Excuse me?"

"Well . . . it's sunrise. I have to pray."

"Dream, we're at an airport. How am I going to get you a place
to pray?"

"I don't know but I have to, Tim. I'm not *not* doing it."

Frank looked around. Nothing was open. And then, as if by
divine intervention, a Continental Airlines worker came up to them
and said, "Hey, Hakeem, we were wondering if you could sign a few
things for us?"

"I'd be happy to," Olajuwon said, reaching for the gear.

"No," Frank said, "we need a room. And then he'll sign whatever
you want."

The worker said: "You need a room?"

"Yes," Frank said. "I just need a room—privacy for him for ten
minutes. He has to pray as part of his faith."

The worker escorted them back to the airline's ticket office and
kicked out all the employees, giving Olajuwon the space to pray.
"Even when his heart's out of whack and we're flying back at six in
the morning, he wasn't going to let it go," Frank says. "He *had* to
do it."

The prayer fortified Olajuwon, but he still seemed off. "He was
scared," Frank says. The two chatted the entire flight. Usually, Olajuwon would be reading the Qur'an, but he was asking Frank about
his own life. His family, his background. "He didn't want to *not* be
talking to somebody," Frank says. Although Olajuwon didn't say so,

"he wanted to have a conversation going, make sure that somebody was awake with him."

Back in Houston, Olajuwon was treated at the hospital, where the doctors shocked his heart back into rhythm. He would eventually be cleared to play, but the ordeal was frightening, especially because it seemed it could happen again at any moment as it had years before. But he knew he couldn't live with fear.

He carried himself with the mentality he once shared with Kevin Willis before Willis had joined the Rockets. Willis was on the Warriors the previous season when he stepped onto the court to warm up for a game against the Rockets. Olajuwon came out of the tunnel and noticed that Willis had an intense look on his face, hard as stone.

"Hey," Olajuwon called out to him. "What's going on, man?"

The two had never spoken before. Willis had long admired Olajuwon but was so startled he couldn't get out any words.

"How is everything?" Olajuwon said.

"Going pretty good, man. Just doing my thing."

The two talked a bit, and Olajuwon complimented him on his game. And then: "Can I give you some advice?"

Willis nodded.

"Remember," Olajuwon said, "this is just a game. It's just a basketball game. And we do it because we love to compete. We love the game. But when you compare it to life? It's really nothing. You know you come out, you're aggressive, and you play that way, but just relax. Enjoy it. Smile more. Have *fun*. It's just a game."

• • • •

OLAJUWON, FAR FROM THE PLAYER WHO USED TO CHASTISE HIS teammates by telling them, "You do not love the game," was now the elder statesman of the new-look Rockets team, which now included

Charles Barkley, who had arrived in an August 1996 trade that sent
Chucky Brown, Mark Bryant, Sam Cassell, and Robert Horry to
the Suns. "He's a teacher," says Tracy Murray, former Rockets forward. "He's taught all of us that came underneath him how to be a
professional. How to have patience, poise." Olajuwon would often
tell players what books he was reading, offering recommendations to
anyone who inquired.

Olajuwon mentored teammates, including Eldridge Recasner,
who joined the Rockets in 1995–1956 after spending his rookie season with the Nuggets. During one game, Recasner, affectionately
called "Little Warrior," came down the court and shot a fifteen-foot
jumper. "What are you doing?" Olajuwon said. "That's a bad shot."

"That's a bad shot? I been making this shot my whole life," Recasner said.

"Well, not on this team."

Olajuwon didn't speak to him for two weeks because, as Recasner
surmises, speaking up for himself was "disrespecting him." Later,
after the two patched things up, Olajuwon saw Recasner walking
onto the team plane. "You need to take $10,000 and buy a new
wardrobe. I'll hook you up with my tailor," Olajuwon said. Clyde
Drexler started laughing. He knew, of course, that Recasner couldn't
afford that with his modest salary. He had only one suit. "Don't pay
no attention to him, man," Recasner remembers Drexler saying. "He
doesn't understand. He's making $6 million a year."

But Olajuwon wasn't talking about a price tag. Dress, to him,
meant something else entirely. "You need to look like a professional,"
Olajuwon said.

Later, Olajuwon would relay that idea to high-flying rookie guard
Steve Francis during the 1999–2000 season. The two couldn't have
been more different. Francis was a ball of energy, just waiting to
break loose. Once, on a plane to Seattle, the two sat next to each

BUSINESS   293

other. Francis was listening to Jay-Z while Olajuwon was reading the Qur'an. Then Olajuwon gave him a *look*. Francis knew he was about to receive something important. "Every word that comes out of the man's mouth is like it's coming straight from God Almighty," Francis said.

"Steve, you walk around dressed like a bus driver."

"Come on, Dream."

"What are these construction shoes you have on?"

"These are *Timberlands*, man. Come on."

"Steve, let me help you. Come to my tailor with me, and we'll get you 10 suits. Custom-made. Cashmere."

Not exactly words for the ages, but still important coming from Olajuwon. Francis had tried to emulate Olajuwon as a teenager, especially Olajuwon's footwork and crossover. Yes, his crossover—as a six-foot-three *guard*—came from the big man.

That Olajuwon modeled professionalism stuck with Francis and many other players. "He was one of the best teammates I've ever had," says Eddie Johnson, former Rockets forward who shared a locker next to Olajuwon. "It was just all straightforwardness and honesty with him."

Sam Mack, another former Rockets teammate, felt the same way. "A lot of times superstar athletes are hard to communicate with and I get it, they're superstars, they're guarded people," Mack says, "but Dream wasn't that way." The first time the two met, Olajuwon asked him what his goal was in the NBA, and then offered some wisdom: "In life, there are opportunities. This is an opportunity. Seize the moment."

Even though Olajuwon was in his midthirties, considered "old" in basketball years, he hadn't lost his own drive or skill. Some of his best Ramadan performances came during this period. And about midway through the 1996–1997 season, he was named to the 50

Greatest Players in NBA History by a panel of media members, former players, former coaches, and team executives, both former and current. It was hard to process. Wilt Chamberlain, Julius Erving, George Mikan, and Bill Russell congratulated him on the achievement after Commissioner David Stern finished announcing the honorees. To be in a room with them—to be mentioned on the same list as *them*—was something Olajuwon couldn't fathom. The former teen who had to be convinced to leave handball was now considered one of the greatest basketball players of all time.

Yet when he returned to Rockets practice, he still competed as if he were trying to make the team. Charles Jones, his backup center, was a thorn in his side every practice. He'd go without playing for a stretch of games, but he always challenged Olajuwon in practice.

During a scrimmage one day, Jones blocked Olajuwon's shot. Not once, not twice, but several times. "He wanted to fight Charles," Recasner says, even though Olajuwon's prime fighting days had been over for quite some time. "Rudy [Tomjanovich] had to call practice because Dream was pissed. Oh, he was *fuming*." He didn't fight Jones, but he came back the next day, out for blood. Olajuwon, even with deteriorating knees, couldn't stomach anyone beating him.

He suffered a left knee injury in 1997–1998 and had arthroscopic surgery, missing thirty-five games that season, the longest stretch in his career. He heard his critics: *Dream's really getting up there. Is it finally time for Dream to retire? Does Dream still have it?* Olajuwon wouldn't entertain those thoughts. "Nothing was going to stop him," says Robert Barr, then the Rockets vice president of basketball affairs. "No injury, no *nothing*."

He averaged 16.9 points per game upon his return, but it was the first season he dipped below 20 a night, finishing at 16.4. He was getting older. He couldn't stop time. Drexler retired after the season, which culminated in a first-round loss to Utah. It was a disappointing way to end things, and uncertainty loomed as Olajuwon had both of his knees examined in the off-season. He was in a great deal of pain, but he wasn't ready to call it quits.

That summer, Frank Rutherford, one of his closest friends from college, offered to help. He was a former track star at the University of Houston and a three-time Olympian (he won bronze in the triple jump in Barcelona). He saw how much Olajuwon struggled to run up and down the court. Worse, he struggled to jump or spin, the very things that made him so brilliant.

Rutherford thought Olajuwon needed to relearn running technique. The two worked all summer in scorching heat on the track as Rutherford taught him to stand straighter when he ran, as well as to use the balls of his feet and heels, rather than his toes, to alleviate pressure on the knees. On the first day, Olajuwon couldn't run half a lap, an eighth of a mile, without stopping because of pain. "I don't know if I can make it through a season," he told Rutherford.

But he kept working, not discouraged by the fact that, at thirty-five years old, he was learning how to run again. How to stave off the inevitable for as long as possible, to avoid that point where one is merely a shell of the athlete he used to be.

Slowly, he began to feel better and run faster. He came back pain free for the 1998–1999 season, ready to compete, even if others doubted him.

Can he still play? Does he still have the drive after two championships? Hakeem isn't hungry anymore. He has his two championships and is satisfied. "Doubt me," Olajuwon told reporters ahead of the season. "Go ahead. People have been wrong about me before."

Although the season was shortened to fifty games because of a lockout, Olajuwon performed as well as he could for a Rockets team that had added Scottie Pippen to the roster in January 1999. He'd have sequences where he looked every bit like classic Dream, rotating over for an incredible block out of nowhere, but he was more of a role player than a star. After a game in May 1999, Olajuwon slowly made his way to his locker, sitting down as a trainer strapped ice packs to his knees. "Looking old, Dream," someone in the locker room shouted. But before Olajuwon could answer, Barkley said, "That's 25,000 points right there. Twenty-five thousand points on those knees."

How quickly time had flown; Olajuwon remembered how, during his first few years in the league, he'd see veterans using ice and think, *Wow. That guy is finished.* But he knew now that postgame recovery was as important as performance. It was the key to his ability to perform, fifteen years into his NBA journey.

When he saw younger opponents do the Dream Shake, he'd think: *That is my move.* When reporters joked to him about it, how so many players were using it *except* for him as he was still regaining his mobility, Olajuwon offered a smile. "I have not lost it," he said. "Oh, no, you have to polish it. It's just rusty."

• • • •

THE ROCKETS, HOWEVER, COULDN'T GET BACK ON TRACK. AFTER suffering a second straight first-round exit in 1998–1999, this time to the Jazz, they missed the playoffs entirely the following season. Olajuwon suffered a hernia and had surgery. Now thirty-seven years old, he also dealt with respiratory issues and was diagnosed with a disease that restricted the flow of air through his bronchial passages during heavy exercise, causing spasms in his lungs. He began to take medication, but doctors hinted at retirement, advising he shouldn't play "for a while."

He played less following the diagnosis, about thirteen minutes below his career average, struggling to breathe. "You just knew it wasn't the same Dream," says Walt Williams, former Rockets forward. Even though his health issues were known, the chatter about him continued:

Dream lacks the same fire.

Dream's looking for the easy way out.

Olajuwon knew neither was true, but it bothered him that critics also claimed he lacked the desire to compete because of his religion, that he was so devoted to Islam he became too passive to handle the physicality of the NBA. That couldn't have been further from the truth. "I was deep into Islam when we won two championships. It gives you strength," he said. His religion, if anything, made him a *better* player. It also made him compete harder because it would not be permissible to take his full salary and not give full effort; Islam pushed him to always give more. "If I care so much about Islam, about God, then that is exactly the thing that would not let me give up. In that way, I am my own safety-check," he said.

But unbeknownst to him, the Rockets were discussing a deal to trade him to the Raptors to begin a full rebuild. At first, the Rockets reportedly turned down the deal, which Olajuwon would learn about by reading the local papers, the contemporary equivalent of a player today reading a tweet and discovering he was part of trade discussions. It was surprising, and hurtful, for him to find out that way. "Common courtesy," Olajuwon said. "I think they owed me not to find out that way."

"I can't picture myself playing anywhere else," he said. "If anything, a trade would have speeded up my plans for retirement. I don't know what the people making those decisions were thinking. When I look at my career, it is not just the Rockets or the University of Houston or the city of Houston. It is all together as part of one picture."

"There is a rhythm, a right way it should go to the end of the story," he continued. "I had always thought that my career would end like so many of the great players of the past in the NBA—Larry Bird, Magic Johnson, Michael Jordan. One team. One city. One identity. That means a great deal to me. . . . It is from that attitude that I feel betrayal. You want to get something for me? Haven't I been giving for years?"

"I guess," he said, "that is the business."

However, the deal wouldn't go through just yet. Olajuwon spent two more difficult seasons in Houston as his role became more and more diminished. His knee continued to pester him, and by the end of the 2000–2001 season, the thirty-eight-year-old suffered from a blood clot in his lower left leg that threatened to end his career. "We were kind of worried about him at that point," Barr says, "and I think he may have been a little worried, too."

It had finally caught up with him: the limitations of an aging athlete. He could not pirouette at the speed he used to, could not leap as high as he used to. At times it was painful to watch, a former star succumbing to time, just as it was when thirty-eight-year-old Muhammad Ali lost to Larry Holmes in "The Last Hurrah" of 1980, or when thirty-four-year-old Joe Namath spent his final season as a backup quarterback on the Rams, hampered by numerous leg ailments. By the ghost of who he used to be. "Sometimes [it] was a bit melancholy," Namath said in 1978, "looking around and knowing I wouldn't be playing football anymore."

It's just a game.

It was.

It wasn't.

Olajuwon had given so much to basketball, and he wasn't yet ready to leave it behind. This wasn't how he wanted to go out; the competitor in him still wanted to prove he had juice left.

The Rockets began trade talks again, not just with the Raptors but also with the Pacers. Olajuwon was ready for a fresh start but wrestled with the decision. A source close to him at the time told journalists that "this has really torn [Olajuwon] apart. . . . He has something to prove. Everybody believed he was done. But he is not done."

Houston was still interested in keeping him, but Olajuwon eventually turned down Houston's final offer of $13 million guaranteed over three years and was traded to the Raptors. It was a difficult decision, but he felt he could help them contend for a championship. He said he had no ill will toward the Rockets, but when asked if he felt Houston's interest in retaining him was genuine, he said, "Toronto realized I have value to their organization. This is a team that has a chance of winning an NBA championship."

The move was shocking. No one ever thought they'd see Olajuwon in anything other than a red Houston uniform.

Tomjanovich wasn't sure how Olajuwon felt about him even years later, in 2008, when Olajuwon was inducted into the Hall of Fame in Springfield, Massachusetts. Olajuwon called him. "Coach, this is for us," Olajuwon said. "You're a part of this, too." Tomjanovich was so overcome with emotion he had no words. "I sat down and I was numb for half an hour after he hung up," Tomjanovich says.

In the midst of the trade, though, Olajuwon's departure was painful. For the first time in his career, he was leaving the only US city he had truly called home. The only *team* he had called home. For seventeen seasons, he gave everything he had to the franchise. And now he was starting over in a new city, a new country.

CHAPTER 22

TORONTO

OLAJUWON TURNED ON HIS TV, HORRIFIED AT WHAT HE SAW. Planes crashing. Towers falling. People leaping out of buildings, clasping hands. Smoke. So much smoke. He prayed for those who had lost their lives. He prayed for those fighting to save lives. And he thought about who might be responsible for the horrific attacks he was seeing.

"Please," Olajuwon said to himself, "don't let them be Muslims."

September 11, 2001. He had been in Toronto for only about a month when the terrorist attacks occurred, when hijacked airliners struck the twin towers of the World Trade Center, the Pentagon, and rural Pennsylvania. There were nearly three thousand lives lost that day.

Fran Blinebury, the former *Houston Chronicle* writer, called Olajuwon for comment. "He was just devastated," Blinebury says.

"Of all the conversations I've had with him," Blinebury says, "that was probably as poignant a one [as any]."

In Blinebury's column, Olajuwon said: "My reaction, beyond the sadness for the lives that were lost, is that this is a very big setback for us. The Muslims in America are now the images of the crime, and this fulfills the stereotype. It puts us in a very bad position, all the way back to almost the beginning, to having to explain to a country where we are still in the great minority that the actions of a few cannot be allowed to represent all Muslims."

"Please, don't put us all together with them," he continued. "Not only is it unfair, but it would be incorrect. Look at the [April 1995] bombing in Oklahoma City. It was committed by someone who would represent himself to be a Christian. But we do not blame that act on Christianity. We are part of the same community. We have been exposed to the same danger. There were Muslims who were killed inside the World Trade Center. There were Muslim firefighters who died trying to save people."

He watched a memorial prayer service on TV, listening to an interfaith group that included a Muslim imam, a Jewish rabbi, and a Catholic priest. "I heard the same message," Olajuwon said. "We are in this together."

• • • •

IN THE COMING DAYS, AMERICAN MUSLIMS WERE TARGETED, harassed, and assaulted. Women were stripped of their *hijab* (headscarves). Businesses were burned down or vandalized, as were mosques. Sikh men who wore turbans were frequently mistaken for Muslims and thus were also targeted. Hate crimes against Muslims spiked, accounting for 27 percent of all religious-bias crimes in 2001.

Immediately after the attacks, 1,200 Muslim citizens and noncitizens, most of them Arab and South Asian, were rounded up, arrested, and questioned by various national and local law-enforcement agencies, including the FBI and the Immigration and Naturalization Service. They were also detained for periods of time, sometimes in solitary confinement.

"Arab" and "Middle Eastern" became synonymous with "terrorist." Nadine Naber, author of seminal essays and books on anti-Muslim and anti-Arab racism in the post–9/11 era, wrote about the pervasiveness of stereotyping in the aftermath of the attacks: "The arbitrary, open-ended scope of the domestic 'war on terror' emerged through the association between a wide range of signifiers such as particular names (Mohammed), dark skin, particular forms of dress (e.g., a headscarf or a beard) and particular notions of origin (e.g., Iraq or Pakistan) as signifiers of an imagined 'Arab/Middle Eastern/Muslim' enemy."

As President George W. Bush launched the "War on Terror," a process of "racing religion," as Moustafa Bayoumi put it, was intensified. But as Deepa Kumar noted in *Islamophobia and the Politics of Empire*, "To be sure, the racial Muslim was not a new project of racialization, but one that was expanded and amplified in the aftermath of 9/11."

This was also true for Muslims in Canada, where Olajuwon now lived. In Montreal, then home to Canada's largest Arab community, a mosque in the city's north end was firebombed the night of the attacks. A fire also engulfed Samaj Temple, which served eight hundred Hindus in Hamilton, Ontario. A mosque in Oshawa, Ontario, had its windows shattered, and a Molotov cocktail was tossed onto its front parking lot.

Five students described as having "Arabic-sounding names" were assaulted in Oakville, Ontario. A Muslim boy was beaten at a bus stop in Edmonton, Alberta. And a Muslim woman in Toronto's Union Station was approached by a stranger who said: "If I had a gun, I would shoot you right now . . . because you are Arabic." A similar message was left on the answering machine of a mosque in Waterloo, Ontario: "I hope you Muslims are happy . . . you better not walk out in the streets. You are going to pay for this."

Many Canadian Muslim leaders described this period as the worst-ever outbreak of hostility toward their communities, much worse than the Gulf War, which was "nowhere near the levels we're experiencing now," said Faisal Kutty, general counsel of the Canadian Muslim Civil Liberties Association. Canada's Bill-36, passed after the attacks, gave unprecedented power to police and government agencies, including the right to hold persons without a charge and freeze the financial assets of what they deemed "suspicious organizations."

John Asfour, a Montreal poet and president of the Canadian Arab Federation, who was born in Lebanon and had lived in Canada for more than three decades, said at the time: "Is tolerance which we stand for in this country only skin deep?" he said. "Eventually, you have to ask, what is my identity? Am I Canadian or will that always be questionable?"

Olajuwon spoke out in many Muslim venues in Toronto during this time. In front of a Ryerson University audience (the university was renamed Toronto Metropolitan University in 2022) packed with more than a thousand members of Toronto's Muslim communities, he urged that Muslims remain united: "Each one of us has a responsibility to represent Islam in our own way. We can't follow leaders that have no knowledge of our religion. So we have to take the lead."

He continued to speak up as the Raptors' 2001–2002 season began. "Speaking for the Muslim community, it was a big setback," Olajuwon said during training camp. "You have to make yourself comfortable, talk to the people, tell them what Islam really is, that this is against what Islam is. This is against the faith; this is not what it teaches. It's a religion of peace. [The terrorist attacks] are exactly against what Islam teaches."

It meant a lot to young Muslims to see him not just use his voice during this time but also physically show up to mosques. "There was some assurance that at least you have people who are in high society or who's very, very known, that are still able to come to the mosque, because a lot of people stopped coming to the mosque because of

9/11, and [because of] being targeted," says Azeem Ziodean, who saw Olajuwon often at the Salaheddin Islamic Centre. "Seeing this figure being there was like, if he can be here, why can't somebody else, you know?"

Shaffni Nalir, who grew up in Toronto, was about ten when he first met Olajuwon at Masjid Omar Bin Khattab. He was awestruck, watching Olajuwon in the *wudu* area, washing himself before prayer, so tall he could barely fit. He and his friend weren't sure if it was appropriate to ask him for an autograph. "We were very scared," Nalir says. But the two tore off a paper towel and respectfully asked for his signature. Olajuwon, with water still dripping from his face, obliged. Then: "All of these kids just lined up one by one," Nalir says. "He signed them all. He was so cool about it. He was that Muslim, that individual that you identified with. I was still a kid, but it's one of those things that was almost like a sense of pride for us."

Olajuwon continued to use his privilege and status to help others behind the scenes. In December 2001, Muslim students at Ryerson struggled to find a space to pray, using student lounges and halls. The university had the Multifaith Centre, but it was too small to accommodate the four hundred Muslim students for Friday prayers, which would have been a fire-code violation. One student approached Olajuwon at a mosque, asking for his help. Olajuwon wrote a letter to Ryerson administrators, asking them to provide students with a larger prayer room. He wrote that Friday prayer is a sacred part of the faith and that the university had an obligation to "assist [students] in fulfilling their religious obligations."

Olajuwon felt, as many Muslims did at the time, the need to defend his religion, the need to explain that it was peaceful. "You feel like you have to convince the people, *That's not Islam*," he later said. "You have to justify your position as a Muslim, being, all of a sudden, the enemy." Laila Lalami, a Moroccan American and Muslim author and professor, described that dynamic in her aptly titled book *Conditional Citizens* when sharing her own experiences after 9/11: "The demand to prove one's allegiance—even, at times, one's humanity—was made constantly of Arabs and Muslims. . . . We are, in other words, always on trial."

Anti-Muslim sentiment affected many Muslim businesses in the coming months. There had been a growing number of young Muslim professionals in the downtown Toronto area who needed a mosque. They usually rented different places for Friday prayers. "The joke was that they [were] the mobile, moving congregation," says Abdussalam Nakua, a senior executive within the Muslim Association of Canada (MAC). When a property nearby, a former bank, became available, the group decided to pursue it. But suddenly the building was no longer for sale. "Because," Nakua says, "I believe in 9/11, when it came, the bank changed their mind and didn't want to sell it to this school of Muslims. . . . That was the type of environment we were operating in back then."

About a year later, Nakua says, the space became available again, and MAC intervened to help secure funding. Olajuwon also assisted. Nakua declined to reveal the amount of Olajuwon's donation or other details because Olajuwon prefers not to be public about his charitable giving for religious reasons. However, Nakua says his help was instrumental in the group being able to secure the building. "It meant a lot," Nakua says.

"It's just incredibly powerful," he continues, "because there's so much to lose. He has so much to lose. If any bad stories, or any bad press came. Like you don't know, right? Nobody knows at that time, I remember. Nobody knows anything, and everybody wanted to be on the same side. . . . Some people would shy away. He didn't. That boosted the morale of the congregation."

That example also meant a lot to younger Muslims, those who weren't yet around to see him play during his NBA peak. Amir Ali, a basketball fan who grew up in Boston, was inspired by Olajuwon. Ali founded the New England Muslim Basketball League in 2022, naming the Defensive Player of the Year award after Olajuwon. "He never wavered. It's so easy to become a different person when you're more accepted," Ali says. "It's so difficult to stay the same person you are and to actually exude that with a sense of dignity. I don't think he was trying to be brave. I don't think he was trying to be a trailblazer, trying to be a leader. He was just simply being sincere."

* * * *

MAMADOU N'DIAYE WAS A SECOND-YEAR CENTER FOR THE RAPtors when thirty-eight-year-old Olajuwon joined the team. N'Diaye, who is Muslim and from Senegal, had long admired Olajuwon. When N'Diaye was growing up, Olajuwon was his hero. Now as NBA teammates, they began praying together. "Hakeem is one of those very few I know I can put my life in his hands," N'Diaye says.

The two played one-on-one every day. "The paint is your living room," Olajuwon would tell him. "You have to dominate it. Nobody comes in here. If anybody comes in here, they need to understand there's a landlord here." N'Diaye saw how hard Olajuwon competed, even though in the eyes of many he was past his prime. Olajuwon was convinced he could be a key player, and Vince Carter, the star of the team, thought so, too. He was instrumental in recruiting him. "Coming here gives him new life," Carter said before the season. "We get a chance to utilize his talent, and we give him a chance to win another championship."

Lenny Wilkens, Toronto's coach, looked forward to coaching Olajuwon again after their brief time together at the 1996 Olympics. "You just want to maximize whatever talent that he had," Wilkens says. "If you've been around the league long enough, the players long enough, you know when someone is towards the twilight of their career. You try to get the most you can out of it."

Olajuwon became a mentor to many of his younger teammates. "The best player or the worst player on the team, he still treated you as an equal," says Jerome Williams, former Raptors forward. He remembered how Olajuwon would support him during Raptors games. "J-Y-D!" he'd say, referring to Williams' nickname, "Junkyard Dog." "I can't even describe it," Williams says. "To have Hakeem Olajuwon encouraging you, cheering you on, hyping you up. I was always saying, 'Man. This is *crazy*.'"

Eric Montross, former Raptors center, gave an interview for this book before he died at age fifty-two in 2023. He remembered being excited to work with Olajuwon. Before Olajuwon joined the Raptors, every time Montross had played against him and the Rockets, he'd jot down a few things in his notebook about what Olajuwon had done well so that he could study him. Now he had the chance to guard him every day in practice in Toronto. "He carried around a bag of tricks," Montross said. "All he had to do was reach inside and figure out which one he was going to use that day."

Olajuwon's body, though, continued to betray him. He missed a quarter of the season with a back injury and averaged just 7.1 points and 6.0 rebounds per game. "The Dream Shake wasn't shaking people as much as it used to," says Tracy Murray, his former Rockets teammate who joined him on the Raptors that year. "It's tough to see an aging superstar. Somebody that you grew up watching. You end up being his teammate, you saw amazing things. It's hard to see that fall from grace, because you still hold him to that high standard, still with that utmost respect for him."

Olajuwon was playing in his eighteenth season but would not tolerate limping toward the finish line; he still had to spin and dance.

Somehow. He wouldn't let anyone see him wince, see him struggle. There were glimmers of his younger self, such as his nine-block outburst against San Antonio. And he always brought positive energy, although his decline was palpable and sometimes painful—the slow walk to the end.

The Raptors underperformed, losing to the Pistons in the first round of the playoffs, and the *Toronto Star* declared during the off-season that "the Olajuwon experiment will be considered one of the biggest busts in Raptors history."

Rather than undergo a back surgery and a lengthy rehabilitation, Olajuwon decided to retire in November 2002, announcing his decision formally in front of a Rockets crowd that watched as his 34 jersey was retired and lifted into the rafters of the Compaq Center. There wasn't a trace of regret in his voice when he made the announcement. "I don't look at this as the end," he said. "It is the beginning of the next phase of my life."

Many professional athletes struggle with leaving sports behind; it can trigger an identity crisis or a profound feeling of loss. But Olajuwon didn't feel that way. He was excited, more than ready to retire and embrace other parts of his life. "He realizes everything has an end," N'Diaye says. "Everything passes. You do it as long as you do it, then you do something else. He's at peace because of his relationship with God."

He considered himself blessed to love something as much as he did basketball, to give it all he had, for so many years. To meet lifelong friends, to travel the world, because of that orange-leather ball. But basketball was only a piece of his life. He knew its proper place.

It's just a game.

Unlike many of his peers, who turned to broadcasting or coaching or management—Kenny Smith, Charles Barkley, and Shaquille O'Neal became an award-winning broadcasting crew on TNT

while Michael Jordan became majority owner of the Charlotte Hor-
nets and owner of the billion-dollar brand Jordan—Olajuwon left
basketball behind.

He left North America behind, too. He moved to Amman, Jordan,
with his family, designing a home for them on top of a mountain.

CHAPTER 23

AMBASSADOR

OLAJUWON HAD BEEN TRAVELING TO JORDAN IN THE SUMMERS during the last few years of his career, spending about two to three weeks there each time. He had enjoyed himself so much in Jordan he resolved to eventually move there after he retired.

He was convinced of this while having lunch at a friend's house in Jordan one off-season. He was moved by "the simplicity of life" there, he later recalled. He heard the Call, the *Adhan*, from a mosque in the mountain. It was refreshing. Then they walked to the mosque for prayer. It was a beautiful experience, he recalled.

He loved the weather in Jordan and wanted to raise his family there. Olajuwon had married Dalia Asafi in a prearranged marriage late in the summer of 1996. Her father had worshipped at the same mosque as Olajuwon for years. Although Olajuwon was thirty-three at the time and Asafi was eighteen, Olajuwon explained that it was customary for women in their culture to marry younger. Because men and women are separated when praying, he didn't meet Asafi or her mother until a meeting was arranged in Houston.

Because of her background, beliefs, and religious understanding, he said, she possessed a maturity, knowledge, and wisdom beyond her years. They began building a life together. They'd eventually have five children together, three boys and two girls.

Olajuwon also remained close with Abi, his daughter with Lita Spencer. Hakeem and Lita continued to have an amicable relationship as coparents, devoted to taking care of Abi. She eventually played basketball at the University of Oklahoma and in the WNBA.

Olajuwon tried to instill in his children the same values his own parents, Abike and Salam, had instilled in him. Abike and Salam both lived into their nineties, passing away peacefully. Olajuwon often remembered a lesson from his mother, a lesson fundamental to Islam. "If you believe in Allah and do good deeds," Olajuwon recalled, "and you wish well for others, there's nothing to fear."

Olajuwon wanted to raise his own kids in an Islamic country and to devote himself to studying Arabic in order to recite the Qur'an in its most original form. He wanted his children to have the opportunity to learn Arabic, too, enough to become fluent. "My children can pick up the [language] earlier in their life," he later said. "That was my driving force: that I have the opportunity to take my children and give them that education."

Olajuwon had studied Arabic a bit before he moved to Jordan, taking a class at Rice University. But now in Amman, he enrolled at the University of Jordan to further his Arabic studies. It wasn't enough for him to study on his own; he needed to challenge himself at the university level, approaching his study the way he did basketball: all in.

Ameer Abuhalimeh, the director of Olajuwon's Islamic Da'wah Center in Houston, is Jordanian, and over the years the two would often talk about the pleasant weather in Amman. Toward the end of his time with the Rockets, Olajuwon would tell his teammates how he was in the process of designing a future home in Amman, buying a plot of land on top of a mountain. "I remember when he first bought it, he was showing me pictures, how excited he was. 'I'm going to put my house here!'" says Matt Bullard, the former Rockets forward. He showed Eddie Johnson, another former teammate, the actual blueprints of the place, gushing about each room. "He was like a little kid," Johnson says. "I mean this was his baby."

He cared about each detail. "He literally studies it," says John Ballis, his longtime real estate partner. "And he's good at it. He can design and do things just because of his passion."

The Jordan home sat in a quiet neighborhood, surrounded by olive trees. Some parts of his home were made of stone, and green tiles lined the roof, an innovative touch: nearby homes had only red clay tiles. Given his status, he could have bought land in Amman's most exclusive neighborhoods, but he chose a more secluded area, one where he could be at peace with his family.

When Olajuwon, Asafi, and their children moved to Amman, he also developed something for the community. In the front of his private compound, Olajuwon built a public mosque for his neighbors. "A beautiful thing," says Ibrahim Arch, his friend and former vice president of DR34M, who lived in Jordan for a period of time. Arch laughs at how many neighbors didn't recognize Olajuwon at first. He was able to keep a low profile the first few weeks at the university, too, carrying a backpack slung over one shoulder around campus. But it was not easy, at forty years old and almost seven feet tall, to blend in among the hundreds of twenty-somethings.

A steady chorus of whispers began to grow. "A lot of people, in that part of the world, the only name they know is Michael Jordan," Arch says. "So, it was kind of a joke: people thought it was Michael Jordan that was living at the top of the mountain."

· · · ·

WORD SPREAD; THAT WAS *NOT* MICHAEL JORDAN AT THE TOP OF the mountain. Many students were excited to see Olajuwon. "The novelty of it," says Dalia Qubbaj, then a student at the University of Jordan, "this giant, one of the best basketball players of all time, is in Jordan, and taking Arabic classes?!" At the time, Qubbaj, who grew up in Jordan, thought *Nobody is going to believe this*. One day she and a friend decided to approach him. Qubbaj was amazed that he didn't have any security with him; he just went to his classes and went home. "This idea that this guy made it to what he was—that he was so proud of his faith—that's a really big deal back home [in Jordan]," Qubbaj says. "That you could make it, be this successful, you have everything, and you're here in Jordan, of all places, learning, specifically to advance your faith. That's something a lot of people back there were amazed by. You don't hear or see many Muslim athletes connecting in that way or immersing themselves in that way."

Students made him feel as if he were at home. "They took 'Olajuwon' and made it Arabic. So, they'd call him, 'Hakeem Al'elewan,'" Qubbaj says, "to make it sound familiar, make it more relatable. In an endearing way, like, 'Oh, he's one of us.'"

Another student named Jawad El-Anis, who had long admired Olajuwon, waited until after Olajuwon's class ended to try to approach him. "Hi, Mr. Olajuwon," he said. "I'm your biggest fan." They spoke for a few minutes, and Olajuwon even allowed him to walk with him to the cafeteria, where he was about to eat lunch. "He was really humble and gracious, and thanking me for the support," El-Anis says.

But generally, Olajuwon kept to himself during the next few years. He wasn't interested in the limelight. He was hardly on social media. One day, he received a call from Fran Blinebury, the *Houston Chronicle* writer. They had traveled many places together over Olajuwon's nineteen-year career. *Why not go to Amman?* Blinebury thought.

"I want to come to Jordan and see you there," Blinebury said. But every time Blinebury followed up, Olajuwon would never give a firm answer. When Olajuwon returned to Houston briefly for a retirement ceremony and formal retirement announcement in November 2002, Blinebury broached the subject again. "Here is the last request I have for you," he said. "You've never let me go to Jordan. You've never let me come visit you there."

"Yes, I know. We are friends," he remembers Olajuwon saying. "Can we just have one place that's just . . . *mine*? It's not *you*. But you want to come here and write a story."

"Well, yeah," Blinebury said. "Of course."

"That's a part of me that I just don't . . . can I just have that, just for me and my family? It's not a story and I don't have to let everybody into that part."

He wanted to live his life, not be *Retired Basketball Star Hakeem Olajuwon*. He was a father. A husband. A servant of God. And that was more than enough for him.

• • • •

MEANWHILE, IN THE EARLY 2000S, AMADOU GALLO FALL, FOUNDER of SEED (Sports for Education and Economic Development) and current president of the historic Basketball Africa League (BAL), the first pan-continental professional league in Africa, had begun developing a vision for the NBA's African expansion. SEED is a global nonprofit organization that was established in 1998 with the mission of using sport to support and empower African youth in all facets of life.

Along with David Stern and Kim Bohuny, Fall was a critical member of the league's brain trust in building basketball infrastructure throughout the continent, having previously served as vice president and managing director of NBA Africa, where he coordinated with local federations, corporations, and nongovernmental organizations to help grow hoops across Africa.

Fall had grown up in Senegal, falling in love with hoops by following the Senegalese women's national basketball team. He knew all the names of the players from listening to radio broadcasts of the games. He eventually received a scholarship to the University of the District of Columbia to study biology and play basketball. He joined the NBA shortly thereafter, working as a scout for the Mavericks, noticing the grassroots programs and camps developing throughout Europe. "I always felt like if we ever get those types of structures in Africa, then the floodgates will be open," Fall says, "because there's no doubt that the talent is all over the place."

In 2002 he traveled to Senegal with NBA player Tariq Abdul-Wahad, who then played for the Mavericks. "I was telling him about the vision that I was thinking," Fall says as they began conducting camps. "We started to see that the talent is everywhere, and you cannot help everybody to go abroad. We shouldn't be looking to ship everybody abroad. So, it's always been, for me, how can we set up the system *here*?"

In other words, finding the next Olajuwon wasn't just about playing in the NBA; it was about finding talent and creating opportunities *within* Africa that would allow elite players to develop their game and perhaps even stay on the continent to play professionally. The trip was an inflection point, helping put ideas to action, effectively launching the SEED Academy, and providing a financial commitment. Abdul-Wahad was instrumental in enabling the SEED foundation's flagship program: the SEED Academy, launched in October 2002.

The NBA was becoming more international than ever, too. In 2003 a record sixty-five players from thirty-four countries and territories outside the United States suited up, accounting for 16 percent of all players—compared to only 6 percent in the prior decade. "The Foreign Invasion of the American Game" was the headline of one prominent 2003 story highlighting the demographic changes. Stars emerged in Dirk Nowitzki (Germany), Tim Duncan (US Virgin Islands), Peja Stojaković (Serbia), Manu Ginóbili (Argentina), Tony Parker (France), Yao Ming (China), Andrei Kirilenko (Russia), and more. "The talent just kept skyrocketing," says Terry Lyons, former vice president of international communications for the NBA from 1980 to 2008. "They were quicker and more agile. The game itself started to change."

The NBA established Basketball Without Borders (BWB) in Europe in 2001 and had its first BWB camp in Africa in 2003, also known then as the Top 100 Camp. Held in Johannesburg, in conjunction with FIBA and Basketball South Africa, it was the first camp that included the entire African continent. There were more than a hundred participants from nineteen African countries. The NBA donated balls, uniforms, sneakers, and socks, and it began working with African federations to build basketball courts.

Former NBA veteran Luc Mbah a Moute, who grew up in Yaoundé, Cameroon, was a teenager when he attended that camp. "Today there's so many camps," says Mbah a Moute, who became the first BWB Africa alumnus to reach the NBA after getting drafted by the Bucks in 2008. He also attended UCLA from 2005 to 2008 and now works as an NBA agent. Mbah a Moute has played a critical role in helping grow the game throughout Africa, mentoring many future NBA players and conducting annual clinics and camps. He has seen the growth firsthand. "[The younger generation] doesn't realize how hard it was," Mbah a Moute says.

When Mbah a Moute was a camper, NBA Africa was in its infancy. Travel to the camp was somewhat chaotic. Some kids had to fly out of the continent to get back in, often connecting through France. The NBA created grassroots basketball-development programs, such as the Jr. NBA, aimed at teaching the fundamentals and core values of the game. There are currently Jr. NBA programs in fifteen African countries. The hope is that as players develop, they can progress from the Jr. NBA (youth) to Basketball Without Borders Africa (BWB) and NBA Academy Africa (elite) and ultimately to the pro league BAL, as well as the NCAA, NBA, WNBA, G League, or other professional leagues around the world. "We wanted to have an ecosystem there that worked to grow the game," Bohuny says.

Africa has fifty-four countries, each with its own preexisting basketball structure, each with its own unique resources. Meeting the continent-wide facility needs would take hundreds of people— people newly dedicated to spreading hoops across the continent, in addition to people who had already been doing that work, including Senegalese men's coach Mamadou Sow and women's coach Bonaventure Carvalho, and Angolan coaches Victorino Cunha and Mario Palma.

Many others have contributed critical work. Opeyemi Babalola, CEO and founder of Webber Engineering, a basketball-facilities manufacturing company that has refurbished courts all over the continent, has been instrumental. Dikembe Mutombo, Manute Bol, and Luol Deng have played a critical role in helping spread hoops across Africa, particularly in South Sudan. Coach OBJ, former coach to Olajuwon and Raptors president Masai Ujiri, founded the "PEACE" Initiative, which continues to grow the game. "We teach more than just basketball," Coach OBJ says. "We teach the youth how to interact with other people that might have a different outlook than them."

Ujiri, following in Coach OBJ's footsteps, founded Giants of Africa, holding its first camp in 2003. Giants of Africa helps create academic, economic, and athletic opportunities for kids, and it might one day find the next Olajuwon. "We're doing it for those that come after us," Ujiri says. "And I came after him and he set that path well. The example was excellence. One day, there's going to be a generational guy like that."

Nowadays, Ujiri is friends with Olajuwon. "Keep persevering," Olajuwon often encourages him. "Keep going." When asked if he could have reached his level of success without Olajuwon's example, Ujiri became emotional: "No. He created a path for us, and I'm so proud of that."

To this day, Giants of Africa provides camps for both boys and girls, teaching not just basketball but also values: being on time, respecting others, setting goals. Ujiri has also built courts through-out Africa and is dedicated to building even more infrastructure. He believed that the powers that be needed a mentality shift: to "stop thinking of Africa as a charity and start thinking of it as an investment."

Whenever people ask Ujiri about the pride he feels in being the first African general manager of a North American professional team, he doesn't bask in the glory. He insists there must be a second, a third. A next and a next. He feels an urgency to help others reach even higher than he has: "We are representing a *continent*. You are representing people, you know? I cannot fail. I cannot afford to fail. Failure is not even an option. I need to give more opportunity for those coming behind. . . . I have that huge responsibility on my shoulder."

Many others feel that way, too, including Obinna Ekezie, the for-mer Maryland and Nigeria national team player. He moved back to Lagos to start his own basketball academy dedicated to develop-ing players' skills and helping them have a better chance at earning academic and athletic scholarships. "Hakeem is part of the reason I came back to do what I'm doing now," Ekezie says. "It all comes down to one thing: infrastructure. That's my main focus."

Joe Touomou, the NBA Academy Africa associate technical director and the first Division I Cameroonian basketball player, has also played a critical role. So have Roland Houston, NBA Academy Africa technical director; Franck Traore, NBA Africa head of basketball operations; and Ruben Boumtje-Boumtje, BAL's head of league operations and a former Georgetown star who in 2001 became the first Cameroonian to be drafted to the NBA.

The NBA set up its first office in Africa in Johannesburg in 2010. In May 2017 the NBA and SEED Project opened NBA Academy Africa, a first-of-its-kind elite basketball-training center in Africa for the top male and female prospects from across the continent. "In the past, we used to have kids going to the States, going to Europe, that's where they were getting prepared," Touomou says. "Now with this Academy, with [NBA commissioner] Adam Silver giving us a chance to have this kind of facility on the continent, people like myself, that's why we came back. Because we felt like we could get the job done here and the kids can live here and make it to the next level."

NBA Academy Africa has come a long way. It didn't have a gym at first, necessitating a two-hour drive every weekend to a local gym to practice. During the week, basketball drills were held on soccer fields. But in November 2018, NBA Academy Africa opened a new state-of-the-art facility in Saly, Senegal, that serves as the primary training location.

The hope was to start developing kids younger so that the next Olajuwon doesn't have to begin playing at age sixteen. "I keep telling people: If we get this kid to start playing younger—they can actually be ten times better than Hakeem Olajuwon, because now they learn the basics and how to play the game at a younger age, so by the time they are [sixteen], they already have the foundation," Touomou says. "Once we do that, this continent will have the best players in the world, I believe."

· · · ·

OLAJUWON CONTINUED HIS ADVOCACY WORK ON BEHALF OF THE NBA and was named NBA ambassador to Africa. He wound up moving to Birmingham, England, for a few years because one of his daughters attended school there. He helped coach camps and clinics with the Birmingham Basketball Club.

He often traveled back to Houston for Rockets events, including a party for the arrival of center Dwight Howard in 2013.

Sama'an Ashrawi, a Houston native and writer and producer, found himself at the party, held at the Toyota Center. He was excited. Olajuwon was his favorite player. Ashrawi is Palestinian. Although his family is Christian, he felt a kinship with Olajuwon when he learned that Olajuwon had been studying Arabic. Walking around the party, Ashrawi found a practice court and spotted Olajuwon sitting down on the far end. Ashrawi sat down next to him.

Ashrawi explained that his father is from Palestine. Olajuwon started to tell him about his time in Amman learning Arabic. It meant a lot to Ashrawi. "Jordan is not only our neighboring country to Palestine," he says, "but the majority of Jordan's population is Palestinian, so it was so special for me to know that my favorite player learned Arabic from my people."

Olajuwon soon returned to Houston for longer stretches of time. He continued on as a businessman and was thoughtful about how he approached his budding real estate career. He had the foresight to see that Houston's downtown was in need of revitalization. That became his focus, but he first needed to learn the ropes. He approached real estate as he did basketball, with an open, curious mind, hungry to learn more. "Hakeem was just like a sponge when he got through with basketball," says John Ballis, his real estate partner. "He wanted a new career and he wanted to know everything there was to know about real estate. . . . He was as good a student as he was in basketball."

The more fascinated he became with different properties, the more he tapped into his longtime passion for architecture and design. "He was all in," Ballis says. He'd study satellite views of buildings, maps, building valuations, and traffic patterns to make the best possible investment. He approached each project as if it were a mathematical exercise, studying the details down to the parking lot. "He's the most disciplined person I've ever met," Ballis says.

It took Olajuwon time, though, to find his footing. "He would say he was afraid to take a shot. He wouldn't go out on his own and buy a piece of real estate," Ballis says. "He didn't have the confidence in that." But one downtown purchase turned into two, two into three. And more and more.

He first spotted the downtown Franklin Bank Building, a three-story structure vacant for nearly twenty years, built in 1929 by future Texas governor Ross Sterling. He'd eventually turn it into the Islamic Da'wah Center, but in that initial moment he was quiet, just staring at the property, boarded up and not exactly looking like a steal of a purchase. Ballis thought Olajuwon's silence meant he wasn't interested. Until a short while later: "He just starts jumping up and down," Ballis says. "He couldn't wait." It was his first real estate project, and he poured himself into the floor plans, brainstorming detail after detail. "He fell in love with it," says Ameer Abuhalimeh, director of the Islamic Da'wah Center. "And he thought this is the best place [to] give other communities, Muslims and non-Muslims, the opportunity to learn about Islam."

Remarkably, Olajuwon made, and still makes, cash-only transactions because it's against Islamic law to charge or pay interest. Thus, he never sought outside loans. And because he wasn't beholden to lenders, he had a sense of agency and power. And because he didn't have to worry about lining up financing, that made him attractive to Houston's real estate community, and his contracts came together quickly. "He kept us from being billionaires," Ballis says, laughing. "Hakeem, he strictly will not borrow money. These rules were kind of new to me, because real estate is all about leverage. If you had to pay for everything in real estate, you'd never get anything done. . . . I just didn't believe it at first."

But Olajuwon was serious. And he made a point of not short-changing a business partner to profit unduly. There had to be a non-zero-sum quality to the transaction. Former *Sports Illustrated* journalist Alexander Wolff profiled Olajuwon and his real estate career after he had retired. "We talked very little about basketball," Wolff says. "It was about his business career, and about how he did all this investing but by strict, non-greed-driven Islamic principles." In Wolff's article, Olajuwon said, "Islam is about balance, doing things in moderation. You still do business, but you don't do greed."

To this day, Olajuwon has stuck to his mantra. He refuses to stretch his principles. He often jokes to Ballis: "You can't get this by Allah! You can't fool Allah!"

But with each purchase, he also thought about how it could potentially benefit others. "He lives his life that way: what can [his projects] do for him in the sense of his family, the community? That's what he looks at. That's what he strives for," Arch says. "It's not about accumulating wealth, because right now he invests in a lot of things. It's not that he needs to, he enjoys it, but he sees the big picture: to create wealth for his family after he's gone, and to be able to continue to fuel the different projects that he's growing in the community."

He never really left basketball either. He invested in turning a barn into a basketball court to be used as a training ground for current NBA players. He devoted himself to something many artists aren't willing to do: sharing the secrets of how their art is made.

CHAPTER 24

MENTOR

OLAJUWON BEGAN TRAINING THE NEXT GENERATION AT HIS secluded ranch in Texas. He decorated a foyer outside the gym with a small display of memorabilia in a couple of glass cases and a plaque with some of his favorite Qur'an verses. There were also modest locker rooms. "The ranch is very minimalistic," says Ibrahim Arch. "His trophies, rings, sometimes he doesn't even know where it is. Honestly, he puts it away. . . . You'll never see him wearing his championship rings. I mean, forget it. It's not going to happen."

Olajuwon first held a camp for big men in 2006, which included stars of African descent, including Emeka Okafor, Ndudi Ebi, DeSagana Diop, D. J. Mbenga, Ike Diogu, Luol Deng, and Mamadou N'Diaye. Olajuwon's lessons, of course, were vastly different than what centers were usually taught; he focused on quickness, speed, flexibility. Fakes and shakes. He made them aware of little details that make a big difference, such as pivoting on the balls of their feet rather than moving with flat feet. That helped with explosion, he explained, putting less overall strain on the foot.

He taught mentality, too. He'd tell his protégés: *Keep it simple.* He'd share some of his favorite phrases: "Do your own thing. Don't go for the fluff. Don't go for the hype." Or: "Your works matter." In other words, don't talk about it. Do it.

He'd break down the intricacies of the move, explaining that the first fake was to clear space, and the second move was to get the defender off his feet. That, he said, is where the fun began. He'd tell players that the paint was theirs to own, but they'd have to handle the ball tightly like a guard, shielding the ball from smaller players swiping for it every which way.

Professor Olajuwon was in his element, elated, not teaching concepts from afar but actually getting onto the court himself. He kept himself in top shape; why talk about the Shake when he could simply rock anyone in his midst? Even with "salt in his goatee," wrote former *Sports Illustrated* journalist Lee Jenkins when attending some of Olajuwon's sessions, Olajuwon "could still spin [a player] into a 7-foot pretzel."

Olajuwon enjoyed giving back but also loved continuing to learn the game himself. He never stopped being curious. "You always have to improve," he once said toward the end of his career. "But, unfortunately, by the time you master the game, it's time to retire."

. . . .

LEGENDARY PLAYERS STARTED SEEKING OUT OLAJUWON'S TUTORING, including the late Kobe Bryant in summer 2009. Bryant realized that as he aged, he had to find more creative, efficient ways to score. With bigger defenders crowding tighter spaces on the floor, he needed to spend more time in the post. "I was curious to see what else I could learn," Bryant said in 2011, "so I went to the best."

At first, Olajuwon thought Bryant's call was a prank. "Kobe, come on. You're the master," Olajuwon told him. "You don't need me. You've got all the moves already." Bryant could have sought out anyone in the world but insisted he needed Olajuwon's help. Bryant's reaching out was remarkable for another reason: the two men played completely different positions. It was a testament not just to the profound respect that Bryant and guards of his generation had for Olajuwon but also to his versatility.

All those years that he had studied guards—memorizing how they moved, how they faked—paid off. Basketball was changing into a more fluid, positionless game, and traditional big men were fading. Olajuwon was the rare player from the previous generation whose toolbox translated. Bryant had come to consider himself more of a post player, estimating he spent nearly 80 percent of his time in the post, and knew Dream would be an ideal mentor.

Naturally, Bryant thought they'd work out at some exclusive, fancy gym. But when he realized they were going to a barn, near a chicken coop and bundles of hay, his eyes lit up. He loved it. "[Kobe] was so appreciative when he came to work out," Arch says. Olajuwon soon realized that Bryant was the fastest learner he ever coached. "Kobe was brilliant," Arch says. "He was seeking out the master. He was seeking out the guru just to help him refine his game a little bit."

Olajuwon drilled him on footwork in the post, laboring over the same, simple moves again and again. He taught Bryant how to recognize a double-team situation and how to play with his back to the basket. They worked on changing direction quickly without wasting movement or losing balance. Bryant took to it quickly; he had long been studying Olajuwon's film, so he had many of the moves already, but Olajuwon helped him with intricacies he struggled to master. At one point, Bryant spent hours just working on the same pivot, over and over, without the ball.

Olajuwon provided videotapes of every workout, not just for Kobe but for all his protégés in the coming years, in which he'd break down instruction into four steps: theory of a move, demonstration, imitation and criticism, and repetition.

It was gratifying for Olajuwon, seeing Bryant's hunger to get better. How he *listened*. The two men had much in common. They were both ultracompetitive and obsessed with details. And they had genuine admiration for those who came before them.

Olajuwon admired how much Bryant coveted the post, how he'd even beat big men to the paint. "Kobe is a genius," Olajuwon said in 2013. "He told me, 'You big guys have it easy because you have the post. I would never leave the post.' If he could stay there all day, he would stay in the post." Bryant's footwork vastly improved after Olajuwon's sessions. He increased his number of post-ups, which helped him as he battled a knee injury later in his career. And he helped the Lakers win yet another championship in 2010.

"When I watch the Lakers," Olajuwon said in 2011, "I see [Lakers center] Pau Gasol doing things I taught Kobe."

. . . .

OLAJUWON FELT THE SAME PRIDE WATCHING LEBRON JAMES AFTER working out with him in the summer of 2011 and seeing how becoming more comfortable in the post helped turn him into an NBA champion.

Olajuwon also worked with Dwight Howard, beginning in 2010. (Howard would later sign with the Rockets in 2013.) Olajuwon had always been excited to work with him because the two had much in common. Height was never Howard's advantage. Like Olajuwon, he stood around six feet ten. He had to use his speed, face up against defenders, and elude them by outsmarting them.

The first time Howard came to Olajuwon's ranch, the two didn't even pick up a basketball. Focusing on Howard's feet, Olajuwon walked him through each step, showing him the myriad ways a defender might react before showing him *how* to counter in each situation. Olajuwon's teachings were as intellectual as they were physical, and after many sessions together, finally incorporating the ball and live one-on-one play, it was clear that Howard had improved.

He moved more efficiently and showed more fluidity from the post, first during the later stages of his Orlando tenure and then in Houston before continuing his career with the Lakers and eventually winning a championship there in 2020.

Olajuwon also mentored former Knicks players Amar'e Stoudemire, Carmelo Anthony, and Tyson Chandler. Mike Woodson, Olajuwon's former Rockets teammate, was the Knicks' head coach, and he knew Olajuwon could help his frontcourt. Once again, Olajuwon demonstrated the intricacies of the Dream Shake. "It was just a beautiful experience," Woodson says.

At one of those sessions, fifty-year-old Olajuwon played Stoudemire in a few full-speed games of one-on-one. "Coach," Stoudemire said, walking over to Woodson after losing three straight games, "I can't beat this guy."

"Son, don't feel bad," Woodson said. "He's a top-50 Hall of Famer."

Many more sought Olajuwon's help, including Rashard Lewis, Brook and Robin Lopez, Rudy Gay, JaVale McGee, Kenneth Faried, and, most recently, 2019 and 2020 MVP and world champion Giannis Antetokounmpo. Olajuwon didn't try to publicize these sessions. He was touched that the players thought of him, and he relished being on the court again.

. . . .

PERHAPS HIS CLOSEST MENTORSHIP WAS WITH THEN ROCKETS BIG man Yao Ming, the seven-foot-six center from China. Yao asked him for help in 2007.

Yao had long admired Olajuwon, for he was the inspiration for even thinking that it was possible to play in the NBA. Yao remembered watching the first live broadcast of the NBA Finals in China on June 8, 1994, between the Knicks and the Rockets. Growing up in Shanghai, Yao was thirteen years old and had just started playing basketball. He wasn't yet skilled, or even passionate about the game, but he and his teammates were given time off from training to watch the series.

He was mesmerized by Olajuwon's grace and athleticism; it was the first time he saw a man anywhere near his size move that fluidly. Something in Yao shifted; *maybe one day he could play in the NBA,* he thought, *and perhaps even represent Chinese people the way Olajuwon had Nigerians.*

By the time Yao reached the NBA as the number-one overall draft pick in 2002, Olajuwon had comfortably settled in Jordan. But when he returned more frequently to Houston, maintaining two homes, he'd become regularly present at the Rockets' practice facility. He would tutor the younger center. He even warmed up with Yao before one session, both in gray shirts, jogging up and back, then backpedaling and sliding laterally. "Come on, Dream!" a staffer shouted as Olajuwon trailed a half-step behind Yao.

"Aw, *man,*" Olajuwon said, struggling to catch his breath.

"You gonna make him wanna play again!" another staffer said.

Then Olajuwon took Yao aside at half-court, explaining the mentality for the day: use your height. "That's your advantage," he told Yao. They began with defense. Olajuwon asked Yao to bring his hands straight up so that he could see how intimidating merely even *standing* at full length would be for a defender.

Olajuwon had to use his quickness because he didn't have the height advantage Yao did, and he wanted Yao to know that it's OK to be big. It's OK to be powerful. Just like Lagos State coach Ganiyu Otenigbade had taught him all those years ago. No layups should ever come inside Yao's area, Olajuwon said. "All this area," Olajuwon said, walking around the paint, "*you* cover that. You cover here, here, *here.*"

Olajuwon then demonstrated his moves, beginning with a shake into a jump hook. "Your first move has to set up your next move," Olajuwon told him. "One bounce." Olajuwon took the ball, bounced it hard, and finished strong. Then Yao tried the move. Then Olajuwon again, then Yao. The pair kept going, one after the other, only breaking briefly as Olajuwon stopped him to correct subtle details in Yao's pivots and fakes.

A large sweat stain ran down Olajuwon's back as he was running through each repetition at game speed. "Feel me!" Olajuwon said, playing defense on him. Yao had been trying to execute the move *before* understanding what Olajuwon had given him. Olajuwon stopped play and explained that one had to feel the way the defender was guarding him before he made a move; which way one spun depended on where the defender was. "No, you spin *out*. You're gonna spin *in*," Olajuwon said. Demonstrating again, he explained, "Once I feel, I'm gonna spin."

Olajuwon told him to keep the ball high above his head at all times, explaining how legendary center Jack Sikma used to do that, not letting guards steal the ball from him. Yao struggled, losing the ball during a few possessions. Watching the workout, Jim Petersen, former Rockets teammate and current television analyst for the Timberwolves, recalls: "It must have been like if Fred Astaire tried teaching a normal person how to dance. He could try to teach you, but you were going to have a hard time copying it."

Slowly, Yao began catching on, spinning baseline for a dunk. The next play, when he spun to the baseline and saw Olajuwon had cut him off, Yao then spun back to the middle and finished with a buttery jump hook. "That's it! That's it! You see?" Olajuwon said, breaking into a wide smile. "Your spin move set up *this* move, your second move."

Toward the end of the workout, the two paused near the left wing. "Quickness, quickness is part of this," Yao told him. "But what I learned most from watching you is timing."

"Timing!" Olajuwon said, lighting up, realizing that his protégé finally understood. "Timing, that's everything, you know? It's about anticipating. . . . You don't want to play a big man's game. You want to play a cat's game of timing, quickness." Yao had received elite instruction and individual attention from a legend for nearly an hour and fifteen minutes, but it was *Olajuwon* who then said to him, "Thank you so much," before giving him a hug.

What a gift Olajuwon had, able to feel gratitude even as the giver.

EPILOGUE

OLAJUWON'S LEGACY CONTINUES TO INSPIRE THE NEXT GENERA-
tion of NBA stars.

A young man named Joel Embiid, growing up in Yaoundé, Cameroon, was far from a basketball prodigy and the 2023 NBA MVP
he would become. As a teenager, Embiid loved volleyball, given his
athleticism and height, and aspired to play professionally. However,
Embiid's uncle thought basketball would be a good sport for him to
try because of that height. His father, a colonel in the military, and
his mother weren't too keen on the idea. "They didn't want him to
play basketball. . . . They felt like that could have an effect on his
academics," says Joe Touomou, the NBA Academy Africa associate
technical director. But Touomou, who had grown up with Embiid's
uncle in Yaoundé, convinced the family to let Embiid give hoops a
shot, telling them that he and other Cameroonian players had used
basketball as a tool to further their education. He had studied at
Georgetown and related that Luc Mbah a Moute studied at UCLA
and played in the NBA, and that Ruben Boumtje-Boumtje studied
at Georgetown, where he was a double major in mathematics and
biology on a premed trajectory before becoming the first Cameroonian drafted into the NBA, in 2001.

Touomou then introduced Embiid's family to Guy Moudio,
head coach of the Kossengwe Basketball Club, and Roger Dassi, his
assistant. The first day of practice, Embiid, fifteen years old, arrived
wearing a jersey of Sacramento Kings point guard Mike Bibby. A

nickname was born. "I was not calling him Joel," Dassi says, "I was calling him Bibby."

Moudio and Dassi saw potential in Embiid, thinking he was a late bloomer like Olajuwon. "I see something different in this kid," Moudio said to Dassi. "I believe he is different from others. I want you to stay after practice every day and show him everything."

Dassi and Embiid trained for hours in the sun on an outdoor court. Embiid was a quick learner, adopting moves easily despite lacking physical strength. "He could not even make three pushups," Dassi says. They used to practice with a female player, and she used to cross him over and score on him. "Joel was so angry because he didn't know how to play," Dassi says. "People were laughing."

It dawned on Dassi that there was a player Embiid could learn from: Olajuwon. Soon, Dassi, who worked security at a gas station, was watching YouTube videos of Olajuwon late into the night, trying to figure out how to teach Olajuwon's moves to Embiid. Thinking similarly, Touomou gave Embiid a DVD of Olajuwon highlights in 2011. He instructed Embiid: "Study *Hakeem*. He is the model."

Touomou told Embiid to focus on the highlights. "It's going to be your breakfast, your lunch, your dinner," Touomou said. Dassi and Moudio agreed, telling Embiid: "This is a player that has taken Africa to the top. You have the same type of body language as Hakeem. Learn from him."

After the first night with the DVD, Embiid told his coaches "I want to be Olajuwon." And, as he continued to watch the highlights, he dreamed of more. "I know he wanted to be better than Hakeem," Dassi says, "because I said [to him], 'You can be better than him.' And with a smile, he said: 'Coach, I think I can be better than him.'"

Dassi and Moudio continued to teach him the fundamentals of the post. He was a novice but would throw a no-look pass or dunk on someone using hops he developed from playing volleyball. "If I tell you that I knew he was going to be this good, that's the biggest lie . . . ," Touomou says. "*No one* could tell you for sure that he was going to the NBA MVP candidate, the All-Star player that he is today."

One day, Mbah a Moute, the Cameroonian NBA player, spotted Embiid while on a trip to Cameroon for a basketball camp and, based solely on Embiid's then six-foot-ten frame, invited him to compete in the NBA's Basketball Without Borders camp. There he saw Embiid play for the first time. Mbah a Moute also called his former coaches at Montverde Academy in Florida, where he had studied before attending UCLA. "I've always seen something special in Joel," Mbah a Moute says. "He had only been playing for six months. And I remember some of the stuff that he was doing on the court—and it wasn't a lot—it was like here and there, you see things. I know guys who have played ten years who couldn't even do that. And for someone who had just been playing to just kind of understand and have that feel for the game to me was very impressive."

It was a no-brainer for Mbah a Moute to help Embiid. His father was a chief of their village, and he learned from him the value of helping the next man. "He's always had that mindset," Mbah a Moute says of his father. Mbah a Moute knew his own legacy had to be bigger than himself. He hoped to help the next Cameroonian basketball player, the next African player, succeed.

It's the same mentality that Amadou Gallo Fall, the president of the Basketball Africa League, had when he began working to grow hoops across Africa. "It's a fundamental African concept, something in the culture that is based on the whole notion of *Ubuntu*," Fall says, referencing the same concept Doc Rivers made famous to an American audience when advocating for Ubuntu with his title-winning Boston Celtics in 2007–2008.

I am because we are.

"You give back. That's what our whole belief system is based on," Fall says, adding later: "You take the lift to go down, send it back up, to pick up the next person. Or you take it to go up, then send it back down, to bring up the next one."

Embiid came back from the BWB camp even more determined. There was a path for him to play basketball in America, a path that didn't exist for Olajuwon, who by hard work, mentorship, and some luck made his way to the States. Embiid, on the other hand, had access to camps, academies, and clinics in Africa, benefiting from Olajuwon's success.

Embiid played at Montverde Academy before starring for Kansas as a freshman in 2013–2014. Kansas coach Bill Self couldn't help but make the comparison: "I'm not predicting Jo will have the same career that Olajuwon did," Self said in 2014. "I'm saying there's no way you can't think of Olajuwon."

• • • •

MORE AND MORE AFRICAN PLAYERS HAVE SINCE BENEFITED FROM BWB Africa camps and other NBA Africa clinics and academies. Sixteen BWB Africa alums, including Pascal Siakam, a Cameroonian star, former Raptor, now Pacer, have advanced to the NBA.

The NBA features more international players than ever before, both role players and superstars. The top three finishers for the 2023 MVP award were international players, two of whom are of African descent: Embiid (Cameroon), Nikola Jokić (Serbia), and Giannis Antetokounmpo (Nigeria and Greece).

"The thing that I like for the modern-day African athlete is that the narrative is changing," says Roland Houston, NBA Academy Africa technical director. "And it should have changed because *Hakeem* changed it. As far as just being big, strong, and athletic.

The narrative now is a skilled, cerebral player who *happens to be* big, strong, and athletic . . . because that's what Hakeem was."

The NBA Academy Africa has grown by leaps and bounds, producing top players who have gone on to play collegiately and professionally. There have been twenty-six former NBA Academy Africa and NBA Academy Women's Program participants who have committed to or gone on to attend NCAA Division I schools, and two former NBA Academy Africa players have signed with NBA G League Ignite, including Efe Abogidi from Nigeria, who also played for Washington State. "I'm doing this for my country, my continent," Abogidi says. "It's not just me."

In 2018 the first NBA Academy Africa Women's Camp was held at the Marius Ndiaye Stadium in Dakar, Senegal. Nearly 120 female prospects from fifteen African countries have participated in four NBA Academy Africa women's camps.

The NBA Academy Africa training center in Senegal features players from many different countries and many different cultures. "It's the language of love," Touomou says. "They cheer for one another. And they support each other. It's amazing. . . . It's beautiful. I always say, I wish reporters could come and see: this is what Africa should be about. People talk about identity, people talk about countries coming together. This is what it's all about. These kids are great ambassadors of their respective countries." Touomou often tells them about Olajuwon: "It's important that they know. . . . These kids [need] to see who Hakeem was."

The NBA opened an office in Nigeria in early 2022, its third office on the continent, further committing its resources to Nigeria. "It's strategic because we're not just thinking about basketball today. We're thinking about where will basketball be ten years from now," says Gbemisola Abudu, NBA Africa's vice president and country head of Nigeria. "How do we ensure that the kids with talent have the opportunity to maximize the opportunity that basketball presents to them?"

The talent will only continue to increase, given Nigeria's booming population: 225 million people. The median age on the African continent is nineteen, compared to thirty-eight in both the United States and China, and forty-eight in Japan. More than a third of the world's young people will live in Africa by 2050 estimates the *New York Times*.

"We're at this tipping point," says Chris Ebersole, NBA associate vice president, head of international basketball development. "We're scratching the surface still in a lot of ways. I think there's a very good chance that the number of players from Africa and the diaspora doubles, triples, quadruples over the next five to ten years. I don't think that's out of the realm of possibility."

Up-and-comers across Africa can now dream of not just playing in the NBA but also in the Basketball Africa League—the NBA's first collaboration to operate a league outside North America. The league launched on May 16, 2021, an emotional night for many watching the first game's tip-off in Kigali, Rwanda. "That was probably the best feeling," says Fall, president of the BAL. "My shoulders became so much lighter, because we were *there*. *We* were making history." Zamalek (Egypt) defeated US Monastir (Tunisia) to win the inaugural BAL Championship.

In July 2021 the NBA announced that former president Barack Obama had joined NBA Africa as a strategic partner. "There's so much more that we are going to achieve," Fall says. Fall, who oversees the BAL's business and basketball operations, leading its efforts to build a comprehensive basketball ecosystem in Africa, sees the BAL as an economic growth engine, using basketball to spur infrastructure development. "It is a gift for Africa. Many boys want to play in the BAL now," says Alphonse Bilé, FIBA Africa president.

"It took a long time, but now we are trying to see slowly the future. We are trying to see what basketball in Africa can be. All of this, Hakeem Olajuwon doesn't know but . . . he was the one."

• • • •

IN 2015, WHEN THE NBA WAS HOLDING ITS FIRST-EVER NBA Africa game on the African continent at Ellis Park Arena in Johannesburg, South Africa, Olajuwon hardly told anyone he was coming. The NBA wanted his entrance to be a surprise.

Current NBA players were divided into two teams, Team Africa versus Team World. Giannis Antetokounmpo, then a young, lanky, still-developing player, had just come onto the scene for Team Africa.

Tickets sold out, and the crowd roared as the game got underway. A time-out was called late in the game. Then, as players returned to the court, out of nowhere came fifty-two-year-old Olajuwon and forty-nine-year-old Dikembe Mutombo, ready to compete. The crowd exploded as Olajuwon pulled off a Dream Shake and drained a shot. "It meant everything. It was incredible," says Masai Ujiri. "If this was today, the internet would have broken. People went crazy everywhere."

It was beautiful, the past and present embracing, laughing, hugging, running, sharing their love for the game. "I thought it sort of completed the story," says Tim Frank, who worked with NBA public relations and attended the game. "Hakeem got to play. . . . People got to see him. It may not have been in Lagos, but it was in Africa. He made a shot, and I thought that was a really awesome moment."

Around 6 a.m. the next day, Olajuwon held the first of a few informal clinics to work on post moves. The first player to show up?

Antetokounmpo. And he'd show up every morning thereafter, *before* 6 a.m., already warmed up. Like Olajuwon, he prided himself on work ethic. His family is also Yoruba, and he grew up in a

Nigerian-Greek home that stressed discipline, humility, hard work, and selflessness. And like Olajuwon, Antetokounmpo, who also wore number 34, let his game do the talking.

Antetokounmpo had long admired Olajuwon, this Nigerian player who paved the way for people like him. And Olajuwon couldn't help but smile while helping Antetokounmpo, throwing him the ball in the post, which might as well have been a symbolic torch being passed.

In his element as a teacher, Olajuwon showed Antetokounmpo the Dream Shake, beginning with the footwork. Back and forth, again and again. Keep it simple. Don't waste movement. Fake, shake, explode. Think like a guard. Be creative. Let your art come from your heart.

I am because we are.

ACKNOWLEDGMENTS

THANK YOU TO MY WONDERFUL TEAM AT HACHETTE WHO HELPED bring this book to life, especially my editor, Brant Rumble. Thank you for supporting this book through all of its stages. I'm grateful to have worked with you.

Thank you to Amina Iro, whose thoughtful and detailed authenticity read of this book was so insightful. Thank you to Mike Giarratano, Kara Brammer, and Mollie Weisenfeld for your support in marketing and publicity.

Thank you to Anthony Mattero at CAA, my brilliant and awesome agent. You have always believed in my work, and I'm so thankful for you.

There are so many others who were instrumental in bringing this book to light. Special thanks to Matt Wong, whose reading and editing of early drafts of this book were critical. Your keen eye for detail and for big-picture structural changes was much appreciated. Thank you to my excellent fact-checker Adam Fromal for your diligence and willingness to find every last detail, and for the effort and care you give to each page.

Thank you to Oluwafemi Adefeso for helping me secure interviews with Olajuwon's former teammates and coaches from his youth in Lagos. I am deeply grateful for your passion for this project, and your unwavering kindness. Thank you to Mark Pozin, senior director, NBA Communications, for help in securing interviews with many NBA International leaders and pioneers. Thank you to everyone involved within NBA Africa, NBA Academy Africa, and the Basketball Africa League who took the time to speak with me and share your experiences.

Throughout my reporting, I met so many people who were instrumental in illuminating Olajuwon's story, and I am deeply grateful for the time that you all spent with me. Thank you especially to Henri de Ybarrondo Jr. for introducing me to your father, for supporting this project, and for opening your home to me. I will always remember Henri Sr.'s kindness and loving spirit.

Thank you to Ameer Abuhalimeh for welcoming me to Olajuwon's Islamic Da'wah Center and for helping me get in touch with other sources for this book. Thank you to Amina Chaudary for sharing transcripts of your wonderful interviews with Olajuwon over the years. As a reporter and as a person, you provided insights that were very helpful. Thank you to Anicet Lavodrama for the time spent talking to me about your recollection of hoops during your youth and during your teenage and collegiate years. It was crucial to my understanding of basketball throughout Africa and Olajuwon's early days in Lagos, and I appreciate your efforts to connect me to other sources. Thank you to Jay Goldberg for so many conversations about Olajuwon's early time at the University of Houston and with the Rockets. Thank you for letting me relive this era of hoops with you.

Thank you to Coach OBJ (Oliver B. Johnson) for your willingness to help with this project and for graciously sending me newspaper articles from Olajuwon's youth. Those primary sources were crucial to my understanding of Olajuwon's upbringing and Nigeria's basketball ecosystem at the time. Special thanks also to Sama'an Ashrawi, Ibrahim Arch, Matt Bullard, Morgan O'Brien, Tim Frank, Parker Ainsworth, Kevin Robbins, Nauman Khan, Imam Suhaib Webb, Peter May, James Mueller, Fran Fraschilla, Amir Ali, Hanif Khalil, Jim Perry, Silva Candembo, Jeff Conrad, Barry Warner, Fisayo

Omilana, Jim Petersen, Reggie Berry, Masai Ujiri, Brad Buchholz, Robert Falkoff, Jeff Twiss, Ed Bona, Jenny Dial Creech, Joe Touomou, Lindsay Krasnoff, Carmine Calzonetti, Bob Rathbun, and Adam Ryan.

As always, I remain grateful for the insights and wisdom of mentors and friends, including Jeff Pearlman, Matt Dollinger, Marcus Vanderberg, and Chris Herring, over the many months of writing this book.

There are not enough words to express my gratitude to my family and other close friends throughout this process. Thank you for being there for me, for laughing with me, for reminding me of what truly matters. You know who you are.

Mom, Dad, Lainna, Uncle Sidney, and the rest of my family: I love you. Everything I write is for you. Thank you for everything.

NOTES

I walked humbly into this project, wanting to explore the mystique behind the man known as Dream, a person whose story transcends basketball. My first book, a biography of Giannis Antetokounmpo, described not just Antetokounmpo's own journey but also how he was part of a larger, shifting hoops landscape, one that was growing more international and more diverse by the day. The more I thought about Antetokounmpo, the more I thought about Olajuwon, the first true international superstar in the NBA, who blazed the trail for Antetokounmpo and so many other international players to come.

To better understand the present moment, I had to visit the past.

In doing so, I wondered why Dream's story seemed to have been obscured over time: how someone so accomplished, and so beloved, is today less commonly mentioned by pundits in discussions concerning the all-time greats. It seemed to me that Olajuwon doesn't quite get the mainstream credit he deserves. Yet the more I worked on this book, the more I realized "credit" wasn't a currency Olajuwon sought or cared for. His mission was deeper than that. He inspired generations of Muslim people to embrace Islam, to build connection and community in the spirit of generosity and grace.

This book is about transformation: athletically, spiritually, globally. I made several trips to Houston in my reporting, including visiting the downtown Islamic Da'wah Center, the mosque that

Olajuwon founded and restored in the mid-1990s. Ameer Abu-halimeh, director of the center and longtime friend of Olajuwon's, kindly welcomed me to spend time at the mosque and helped me gain an appreciation for Olajuwon's deeply rooted impact on Muslim communities, both in Houston and around the world. Before I left the mosque, Abuhalimeh gave me a book about Islam to further my study, as well as a beautiful magenta prayer rug interwoven with silver thread. "When a Muslim gives you a prayer rug," he told me, "it is from the heart."

Olajuwon *is* Houston. You can find him at the local mosques or at local AAU tournaments, cheering in the stands as if he were an "ordinary" person. Hoopers at Fonde Rec Center, the spot Olajuwon first honed his game against Moses Malone, share stories of how Olajuwon, to this day, will leave signed sneakers on the bleachers for anyone to pick up.

On one of my reporting trips, I found my way to the home of Olajuwon's close friend, Henri de Ybarrondo. Ybarrondo's son, Henri Jr., arranged an interview with his father after gaining permission from Olajuwon. Serendipitously, I briefly met Olajuwon there that evening. Although he preferred to not grant a formal interview for the book—those in his circle emphasized that for religious reasons he prefers to stay out of the limelight and focus on his faith and his family—Olajuwon (via Abuhalimeh) steered me to others in his orbit who could shed light on his journey.

The reporting for this book included 266 interviews with close friends, former teammates, coaches, mentors, NBA opponents, NBA executives, and everyday Houstonians, many active within Houston's Muslim communities. I interviewed central figures in Olajuwon's life, both from Nigeria and from the United States, beginning with his youth in Lagos, thanks to the gracious assistance of Oluwafemi

Adefeso, a prominent Nigerian sports journalist. I also interviewed teammates and coaches from Olajuwon's college days at the University of Houston and his pro career with the Houston Rockets and briefly the Toronto Raptors, as well as those who have connected with him in his role as an ambassador for the NBA in Africa in the decades since.

In passages where I detail scenes, I interviewed at least one person who was present or had firsthand knowledge of what transpired. Where I've included dialogue, I interviewed at least one person who was present for the conversation, and I often note whose memory the anecdote came from. If the dialogue came from a secondary source, I cite that source directly in the notes that follow. When someone is said to have "thought" or "felt" or "believed" something, I obtained that assertion directly from the individual, from a source with direct knowledge of the individual's thinking, or from a secondary source cited in the notes, including the valuable insights gained from Olajuwon's own 1996 memoir, *Living the Dream*.

In my research, I also relied on primary sources from the late 1970s and early 1980s from Nigerian newspapers such as *Punch*. Olajuwon's former coach, Oliver B. Johnson (Coach OBJ), saved newspaper articles from that time and kindly shared them with me for this project. It was invaluable because many of those newspapers have been lost because of political instability and poor funding. Fantastic Nigerian journalists such as Fu'ad Lawal, who founded archivi.ng, are doing incredible work to digitize and preserve this integral journalism and history.

I've also included an extended bibliography for the books I cited in this book, as well as books that, though not cited directly, furthered my understanding of Nigeria, Africa, sports and race, Islam, and Islamophobia.

Epigraph

Ben Okri, *A Way of Being Free* (London: Head of Zeus, 2014), 22.

Prologue

10 a.m.: Mike Berardino, "What 'Bron Owes Hakeem: Priceless," *South Florida Sun Sentinel*, September 23, 2012.

"I feel like": Audio of group call between LeBron James and his team, Hakeem Olajuwon and his team, and Reggie Berry, who provided the audio of the call for this book.

cracked driveway, four-hundred-acre ranch: Chris Ballard, "Post Play Is a Lost Art in the NBA: What Happens to Those Who Still Believe in It?," *Sports Illustrated*, January 18, 2023.

how much pressure, "He was so determined": Berardino, "What 'Bron Owes."

thinks the host is talking about somebody else: Amina Chaudary, interview with Hakeem Olajuwon for the *Islamic Monthly*, May 27, 2014, held at Olajuwon's home, transcript provided to the author by Chaudary on November 8, 2023.

"wakes up": Hannah Storm interview with Hakeem Olajuwon, NBC, 1996.

"Indeed, Allah loves . . . ": Al-Hakim, Al-Mustadrak, 3:270 (Hadith 2001).

Chapter 1: King

Sometimes he'd get nervous: Hakeem Olajuwon, *Living the Dream* (Boston: Little, Brown, 1996), 47.

weekly telecasts of British football: Phil Hersh, "Nigeria Closing In on 1st World Cup Soccer Berth," *Chicago Tribune*, October 8, 1993.

siblings were not competitive: Amina Chaudary, interview with Hakeem Olajuwon for the *Islamic Monthly*, May 27, 2014, held at Olajuwon's home, transcript provided to the author by Chaudary on November 8, 2023.

19 Bank Olemoh: Curry Kirkpatrick, "The Liege Lord of Noxzema," *Sports Illustrated*, November 28, 1983.

trendsetters: Joy Sewing, "Dream Fashion: Olajuwon Hopes to Score with New Clothing Line," *Houston Chronicle*, January 6, 2011.

plucking fruit: Olajuwon, *Living the Dream*, 25.

Parents could watch: Chaudary, 2014 Olajuwon interview.

a hundred thousand people: Marilyn Nance, *Last Day in Lagos*, ed. Oluremi C. Onabanjo (Johannesburg, South Africa: Fourthwall, 2022), 124.

"For the first time": "29 Days That Shook the Black World," *Ebony*, May 1977.

"peak of Pan-Africanist expression": Nance, *Last Day in Lagos*, inside cover.

"For me": Nance, 51.

Things Fall Apart: Olajuwon, *Living the Dream*, 24.

five hundred ships: "Nigeria Expands Bustling Ports," *New York Times*, August 30, 1980.

business cards: Remer Tyson, "Akeem: He's Living His Parents' Dream," *Detroit Free Press*, January 2, 1984.

"Nigerians can revel": "Nigeria: Wielding Africa's Oil Weapon," *Time*, October 6, 1980.

Europe, Italy: Mark Heisler, "Taking Center Stage; Akeem," *Los Angeles Times*, May 18, 1986.

"We struggled": Tyson, "Akeem."

One photograph: Olajuwon, *Living the Dream*, 23.

thinking they were rich: Olajuwon, *Living the Dream*, 20.

"Our wealth": Tyson, "Akeem."

"Face your studies": Kirkpatrick, "Liege Lord."

"You're not serious": Olajuwon, *Living the Dream*, 15.

more than a thousand: Chinua Achebe, *There Was a Country: A Memoir* (New York: Penguin, 2012), 210.

one million: Karl Maier, *The House Has Fallen: Nigeria in Crisis* (London: Penguin, 2000), 53.

being fearful: Kevin Sherrington, "Recent Coup 'Nice,'" *Houston Post*, January 8, 1984.

"The possibilities": Achebe, *There Was a Country*, 40.

"Speaking vernacular": Olajuwon, *Living the Dream*, 24.

Students were charged: Roy S. Johnson, "Olajuwon Charms and Dominates," *New York Times*, March 29, 1983.

"enforce Islam": Chaudary, 2014 Olajuwon interview.

kneeling on her prayer mat: Olajuwon, *Living the Dream*, 28.

challenge, acknowledging their efforts: Cecile S. Holmes, "Olajuwon Goes One-on-One, Interfaith Style," *Houston Chronicle*, June 21, 1997.

stop and wait to hear: Olajuwon, *Living the Dream*, 27.

slink to his seat, dreaded lining up: Mike Littwin, "A Dream Is Coming True for Akeem," *Los Angeles Times*, March 11, 1984.

nervous: Olajuwon, *Living the Dream*, 25.

troublemaker: Chaudary, 2014 Olajuwon interview.

"dongo," *Why am I such a freak*: Jeff Denberg, "Akeem: Living an NBA Dream," *Atlanta Constitution*, May 29, 1986.

fights: Dave Anderson, "Basketball's New Force," *New York Times*, April 4, 1983.

"I was so out of place": Bob Sakamoto, "Olajuwon New Power Center: Rockets' Star Eclipses Abdul-Jabbar in the West," *Chicago Tribune*, May 22, 1986.

slouching near the doorway, leader: Olajuwon, *Living the Dream*, 35.

Chapter 2: Center

green, white, green: Kavwam Pokyes, *The Man 80–80 @ Eighty: An Adventurous Life* (Jos, Nigeria: Nyango, 2020), 90.

"They just want to use you," the ball came to him: Kevin Sherrington, "Soccer's Loss Is Coogs' Gain," *Houston Post*, March 23, 1983.

"I had no choice": Remer Tyson, "Akeem: He's Living His Parents' Dream," *Detroit Free Press*, January 2, 1984.

Chuck Taylor: Hakeem Olajuwon, *Living the Dream* (Boston: Little, Brown, 1996), 42.

***How can they do that*:** Terry Gross, "Hakeem Olajuwon Discusses 'Living the Dream,'" *Fresh Air*, April 29, 1996.

"This is an American game": Olajuwon, *Living the Dream*, 40.

Cairo, missionaries, "The future of basketball": Sal "Red" Verderame, *Basketball in Africa* (New York: Pyramid, 1967), 11–12.

a crowd of fifty thousand: "Africa Games Begin," *Washington Post*, January 8, 1973.

three thousand athletes, forty African nations, "essential product": "Africa Games Start Today in Nigeria," *Washington Post*, January 7, 1973.

Emmanuel Chagu, Alabi Adelanwa: Akinbode Oguntuyi, "Hakeem Olajuwon Heads List of 5 Greatest Nigerian Basketball Players," ESPN.com, April 25, 2017.

Prevented at times from playing: George Vecsey, *Harlem Globetrotters* (New York: Scholastic, 1970), 9.

"the game's most": Robert W. Minton, "Miles and Miles of Basketball," *Esquire*, April 1948.

"the most enthusiastic": Drew Pearson, "Africans Wowed by Globetrotters," *Washington Post*, December 28, 1957.

promoting a skewed image: Kevin B. Witherspoon, "'An Outstanding Representative of America': Mal Whitfield and America's Black Sports Ambassadors in Africa," in *Defending the American Way of Life: Sport, Culture, and the Cold War*, eds. Toby C. Rider and Kevin B. Witherspoon (Fayetteville: University of Arkansas Press, 2018), 131.

"I found": Gilbert Rogin, "'We Are Grown Men Playing a Child's Game,'" *Sports Illustrated*, November 18, 1963.

fifty-thousand-acre, "an America without discrimination": Arthur Siegel, "Celtics' Bill Russell to Live in Liberia," *Boston Globe*, November 20, 1960.

"I came here," wept: Bill Russell, *Go Up for Glory* (New York: Coward-McCann, 1966), 152.

"Basketball is the fastest," "return to the fountainhead": Terence Smith, "Biggest Name in N.B.A: Jabbar," *New York Times*, June 4, 1971.

"enthusiastic": "Jabbar, Robertson and Costello Find Trip to Africa Very Tiring," United Press International, July 1, 1971.

Shouldn't be interpreted, "opposed U.S.," decline an invitation: "Alcindor Rejects Role as Ambassador," Associated Press, June 23, 1971.

"Now that I am going overseas": Theresa Runstedtler, "Kareem Abdul-Jabbar Changed the Rules for Black Athletes," *Humanities*, March 22, 2023.

"I have been kind of quiet": Tom Seppy, "Bucks' Lew Alcindor Is Kareem Jabbar," Associated Press, June 4, 1971.

"In a lot of ways," "the betterment": "Alcindor's Trip to Africa to Be 'Like Going Home,'" *Washington Post*, May 7, 1971.

seven thousand, "roared every": "Bucks Big Hit in Africa Trip," United Press International, June 16, 1971.

"It is very lucky": "Bucks Are Smash Hit on Teaching Tour of Africa," Associated Press, June 16, 1971.

"Look . . . !" . . . ashamed: Kevin Sherrington, "Crowd-Pleasing Defense," *Houston Post*, March 16, 1984.

photo: Robert Ndabai, "Lagos, Kano Are Gold Favourites," *Intervals*, 1985.

kept newspaper: Olajuwon, *Living the Dream*, 51.

"our golden boy": Curry Kirkpatrick, "The Liege Lord of Noxzema," *Sports Illustrated*, November 28, 1983.

loved that feeling: Olajuwon, *Living the Dream*, 46.

Chapter 3: Yommy

"Hakeem, you've earned your basketball": Jerry Wizig, "Coogs' Olajuwon Is Something Special," *Houston Chronicle*, February 26, 1984.

simply bouncing: Hakeem Olajuwon, *Living the Dream* (Boston: Little, Brown, 1996), 57.

so nervous, "To me": Olajuwon, *Living the Dream*, 54.

master the footwork: Peter King, "Akeem's Dream Is Nightmare of Triple Teaming," *Cincinnati Enquirer*, January 22, 1984.

shoved and elbowed: Curry Kirkpatrick, "The Liege Lord of Noxzema," *Sports Illustrated*, November 28, 1983.

controversial decision, "I was not good enough": Amina Chaudary, interview with Hakeem Olajuwon for the *Islamic Monthly*, May 27, 2014, held at Olajuwon's home, transcript provided to the author by Chaudary on November 8, 2023.

confidence evaporated, afraid: Olajuwon, *Living the Dream*, 58.

Shocked, didn't feel ready, morning assembly: Chaudary, 2014 Olajuwon interview.

"Dan Blockers": Jonnie Isebor, "Hakeem Olajuwon: A Dream Story from Africa," USA Africa, Hyattsville, MD, 1994.

"They say if you don't": Fran Blinebury, "King Akeem," *Houston Chronicle*, April 1, 1983.

Ebony magazine: Chris Jenkins, "Keeping Up with Kareem; Still a Dream for Akeem?," *San Diego Union-Tribune*, May 13, 1986.

"I dare you": Norman O. Unger, "The Magic of 'Magic Johnson,'" *Ebony*, May 1980.

Angolan basketball players and coaches left: Alexander Wolff, *Big Game, Small World: A Basketball Adventure*, 20th anniversary ed. (Durham, NC: Duke University Press, 2022), 334.

one million people: Zoe Eisenstein, "Africa's Time Will Come," *Sports Illustrated*, August 2, 2004.

"This was [his] break": Ben Edokpayi, "The Million Dollar Dream," *Quality*, July 1987.

Chapter 4: Ticket

list of American universities: Evan Smith, "Hakeem Olajuwon: On His Hall of Fame Career," *Texas Monthly*, September 2008; Hakeem Olajuwon, *Living the Dream* (Boston: Little, Brown, 1996), 65, 67, 70, 88.

Houston, Providence, and Georgia: George Vecsey, "Changing Planes to the Final Four," *New York Times*, March 26, 1982.

Providence: Dick Joyce, "Olajuwon Big Key for No. 1 Houston," Associated Press, March 8, 1983; Alan Goldstein, "'World's Tallest Soccer Goalie: Awed by Status in U.S.,'" *Baltimore Sun*, April 3, 1984.

Georgia: Goldstein, "'World's Tallest Soccer Goalie'"; Jere Longman, "Akeem Is the Dream in Houston," *Philadelphia Inquirer*, March 23, 1983.

arranged visits: Dave Anderson, "Basketball's New Force," *New York Times*, April 4, 1983; Ray Buck, "For Akeem, It's a Dream Come True," *Sporting News*, November 28, 1983; Olajuwon, *Living the Dream*, 65, 70.

He gave him numbers, two days earlier: Amina Chaudary, interview with Hakeem Olajuwon for the *Islamic Monthly*, May 27, 2014, held at Olajuwon's home, transcript provided to the author by Chaudary on November 8, 2023.

"Akeem is the dream": Longman, "Akeem Is the Dream in Houston."

"It was October 10": Walter Leavy, "Akeem the Dream," *Ebony*, March 1984.

"Olajuwon's life": Jill Becker and Sheri Fowler, "Center of Attention," *Texas Monthly*, May 1995.

"poked his head": Vecsey, "Changing Planes."

pronunciation of "Houston": Goldstein, "'World's Tallest Soccer Goalie.'"

"I had all these kids": Gary Taylor, "Pack Just Missed Akeem," United Press International, April 4, 1983.

"employee": Dave Dorr, "Manchild Leads Houston to Promised Land," *St. Louis Post Dispatch*, March 31, 1983; Danny Robbins, "Out of Africa: Pond Gives His Side of the Story About Hakeem's Arrival," *Houston Chronicle*, March 4, 1996.

"works with the US State Department": Fran Blinebury, "King Akeem," *Houston Chronicle*, April 1, 1983.

"State Department official": Vecsey, "Changing Planes"; Alan Goldstein, "'Akeem the Dream' Molds Tall Tales at Houston," *Baltimore Sun*, March 29, 1983.

"No responsive," "A review": FOIA request submitted by Mirin Fader on August 16, 2022; FOIA response to Fader on January 24, 2023.

"Did St. John's": Adam Zagoria, "Did St. John's Miss Out on Hakeem Olajuwon?" *Zags Blog*, October 18, 2016.

"Hakeem lands": *Phi Slama Jama*, season 3, episode 11, ESPN Films, "30 for 30," October 18, 2016.

Pond had given him the St. John's coach's number: Chaudary, 2014 Olajuwon interview.

Georgia Tech: Vecsey, "Changing Planes"; Anderson, "Basketball's New Force"; Longman, "Akeem Is the Dream"; Goldstein, "'World's Tallest Soccer Goalie.'"

Oregon State: Anderson, "Basketball's New Force"; Goldstein, "'World's Tallest Soccer Goalie.'"

Illinois State: Longman, "Akeem Is the Dream"; Goldstein, "'World's Tallest Soccer Goalie.'"

"thought about sending": Fran Blinebury, "Eye for Talent Helped UH Land Young Olajuwon," *Houston Chronicle*, September 3, 2008.

flipped a coin: Gary Taylor, "North Carolina State Blew a Chance to Land Olajuwon," United Press International, April 4, 1983; Blinebury, "Eye for Talent."

"wanted to send," "would dominate": Chaudary, 2014 Olajuwon interview.

would have liked Olajuwon to play there, "Pack just missed": Taylor, "Pack Just Missed Akeem."

"You will like Houston": Jeff Balke, "Outtakes from Our Hakeem Olajuwon Interview," *Houstonia*, part 2, April 3, 2013.

"Houston was where": Fran Blinebury, "Naismith Basketball Hall of Fame: The Making of a Legend," *Houston Chronicle*, September 5, 2008.

Louisville, Houston, and Providence: *Phi Slama Jama*.

"old Army buddy": Fred Kerber, "Akeem Is Ready This Time Around," *New York Daily News*, April 1, 1983.

"close friends": Leavy, "Akeem the Dream."

"running in and out": Blinebury, "Eye for Talent."

"I didn't know," parents weren't sure: Chaudary, 2014 Olajuwon interview.

"Just how Akeem": Remer Tyson, "Akeem: He's Living His Parents' Dream," *Detroit Free Press*, January 2, 1984.

a little scared: Jackie MacMullan, Rafe Bartholomew, and Dan Klores, *Basketball: A Love Story* (New York: Crown Archetype, 2018), 366.

His parents gave him some: Chaudary, 2014 Olajuwon interview.

Chapter 5: Akeem

"I never dreamed": Jere Longman, "Akeem Is the Dream in Houston," *Philadelphia Inquirer*, March 23, 1983.

two more days, imagine how he would compete: Amina Chaudary, interview with Hakeem Olajuwon for the *Islamic Monthly*, May 27, 2014, held at Olajuwon's home, transcript provided to the author by Chaudary on November 8, 2023.

cowboy boots: Olajuwon, as told to Bob McSpadden, "Akeem: Playing Basketball for Houston," *Daily Cougar*, February 14, 1984.

took off running: Fran Blinebury, "Olajuwon Quick to Dazzle Teammates—Even Center's Early Days at UH Revealed Potential," *Houston Chronicle*, September 5, 2008.

goaltending: Clyde Drexler and Kerry Eggers, *Clyde the Glide: My Life in Basketball* (New York: Sports Publishing, 2004), 60.

"I don't care how you slice it": Curry Kirkpatrick, "The Liege Lord of Noxzema," *Sports Illustrated*, November 28, 1983.

outsider: "Akeem Eager to join NBA," *Houston Chronicle*, June 17, 1984.

"All I knew: Fran Blinebury, "Naismith Basketball Hall of Fame: The Making of a Legend," *Houston Chronicle*, September 5, 2008.

"I guarantee": "Akeem Turns to 'The Dream,'" United Press International, February 13, 1983.

laughed: "Akeem Flunks Dunks for Coogs," *Houston Post*, March 2, 1982.

"If he can do that": Blinebury, "Olajuwon Quick to Dazzle Teammates."

hypnotist: Jerry Wizig, "A Tribute to the Southwest Conference," *Houston Chronicle*, March 10, 1996.

bringing his own practice gear: Hal Lundgren, "I Don't Ever Remember Playing a Game That I Didn't Think I Could Win," *Houston Chronicle*, March 7, 1983.

"Akeem Abdul Olajuowa": Gary Taylor, "The University of Houston's Athletic Director Says the Southwest," United Press International, June 19, 1981.

"train of syllables": Thomas Bonk, "There's More to Coogs Than Meets the Press," *Houston Post*, March 23, 1982.

studying for his SAT: Chaudary, 2014 Olajuwon interview.

"Lewis has sequestered": David Moore, "Cougars' Dream of Stardom for Akeem," *Fort Worth Star-Telegram*, November 2, 1981.

"None had made it": Jere Longman, "Akeem Is the Dream."

"Lagos . . . as in Nigeria": "SWC Looks for Spirited Race," *El Paso Times*, November 11, 1981.

"The center": Moore, "Cougars' Dream."

didn't remember how the name started, "look like": Ben Edokpayi, "The Million Dollar Dream," *Quality*, July 1987.

"You got to win": Kirkpatrick, "Liege Lord."

35 pounds: Gary Taylor, "'Akeem the Dream' Grows Toward Stardom," United Press International, May 28, 1981.

no additional weights: Hakeem Olajuwon, *Living the Dream* (Boston: Little, Brown, 1996), 224.

having a car until age twenty-seven: Jeff Denberg, "Akeem: Living an NBA Dream," *Atlanta Constitution*, May 29, 1986.

"You'd say, 'What's happenin'?'": Longman, "Akeem Is the Dream."

"Now I am going to rock": Kirkpatrick, "Liege Lord."

often calling, Bisquick: Ray Buck, "For Akeem, It's a Dream Come True," *Sporting News*, November 28, 1983; Olajuwon, *Living the Dream*, 65, 70.

politics and racism in the South: Frank Andre Guridy, *The Sports Revolution: How Texas Changed the Culture of American Athletics* (Austin: University of Texas Press, 2021), 315.

"Akeem tried to tell us": Curry Kirkpatrick, "The Big Brothers of Phi Slamma Jamma," *Sports Illustrated*, March 7, 1983.

still prayed: Terry Blount, "Dream Come True: Reawakened Olajuwon Comes Full Circle in a Year Likely to End in MVP Honors," *Houston Chronicle*, May 22, 1994.

"didn't understand": Chaudary, 2014 Olajuwon interview.

"I'm not really religious": Dave Dorr, "Manchild Leads Houston to Promised Land," *St. Louis Post Dispatch*, March 31, 1983.

Chapter 6: Moses

"He was scared": "Morning Briefing: This Bo Gets Rave Reviews," *Los Angeles Times*, April 28, 1986.

Maserati, Frenchy's: Frank Andre Guridy, *The Sports Revolution: How Texas Changed the Culture of American Athletics* (Austin: University of Texas Press, 2021), 313.

"An awesome," "I know damn well": David Moore, "Cougars' Dream of Stardom for Akeem," *Fort Worth Star-Telegram*, November 2, 1981.

"If Abdul is what": "Abdul & Other Notes," *Fort Worth Star-Telegram*, November 12, 1981.

didn't know if he would ever score: "UH Is Preseason SWC Roundball Favorite," *Galveston Daily News*, November 9, 1981.

bend over: "Olajuwon Still Out as Coogs Play Gauchos," *Houston Chronicle*, December 15, 1981.

fingernail: David Moore, "Williams Confident of Early Return to Cougars," *Fort Worth Star-Telegram*, November 29, 1981.

nervous: Eddie Sefko, "Olajuwon's Play Sparks UH to Title," *Houston Chronicle*, December 30, 1981.

harder than he had anticipated: John Hollis, "Coogs Working, Hoping for Thaw," *Houston Post*, January 14, 1982.

"precious innocence," "The media": Roy S. Johnson, "Olajuwon Charms and Dominates," *New York Times*, March 29, 1983.

"Can you send me a copy?": Ray Buck, "For Akeem, It's a Dream Come True," *Sporting News*, November 28, 1983.

nearly 1.5 billion: "Africa Population," Worldometers, www.worldometers.info/world-population/africa-population.

"a backdrop": Brad Buchholz, "Pinone, Akeem Pit Opposing Styles in Midwest Final," *Austin American-Statesman*, March 27, 1983.

"For too long," "In reality": Dipo Faloyin, *Africa Is Not a Country: Notes on a Bright Continent* (New York: W. W. Norton, 2022), 6–7.

"Watusi": Bud Poliquin, "Big? Who Is the Top Center Playing Out of Houston Today? Hint, He's Not in the NBA," *San Diego Union-Tribune*, December 22, 1983.

"Swatusi": Curry Kirkpatrick, "The Big Brothers of Phi Slamma Jamma," *Sports Illustrated*, March 7, 1983.

"Baskeetbowl," "He may not look": "SWC Review," *Fort Worth Star-Telegram*, February 22, 1982.

"modern-day Goliath": Steve Estes, "Arkansas-Houston Week Produces Media Hysteria," *Tyler Morning Telegraph*, February 24, 1984.

"Olajuwon arrived": "One out of 250 Isn't Bad, When the One Happens to Be Akeem Olajuwon," Associated Press, April 1, 1983.

"He puzzles": Tracy Dodds, "A Tall Story Comes True," *Los Angeles Times*, February 7, 1982.

"[He] speaks in halting English: Gil LeBreton, "Big East's Villanova Aiming to Head West," *Fort Worth Star-Telegram*, March 27, 1983.

"The Dream speaks": Bob Rubin, "Cougars' Hopes for NCAA Title Rest on Dream," *Miami Herald*, March 22, 1983.

struggling to pass: Jim Laise, "Language Barrier," *Fort Worth Star-Telegram*, February 14, 1982.

"The Story": Steve Jacobson, "The Story of Olajuwon: It's Hoops and Scoops," *Newsday*, March 27, 1983.

thirteen scoops: Kirkpatrick, "Big Brothers."

"I know some people": Walter Leavy, "Akeem the Dream," *Ebony*, March 1984.

"Lagos is a big": Curry Kirkpatrick, "The Liege Lord of Noxzema," *Sports Illustrated*, November 28, 1983.

"People didn't believe": Poliquin, "Big?"

Watusi were at least: "Akeem Eager to Join NBA," *Houston Chronicle*, June 17, 1984.

later publicly admitted it: Steve Jacobson, "Akeem Cements His Future," *Newsday*, March 29, 1983.

"manchild": Dave Dorr, "Manchild Leads Houston to Promised Land," *St. Louis Post Dispatch*, March 31, 1983.

copy editor, resigned, threw cups: Robert D. Jacobus, *Houston Cougars in the 1960s: Deep Threats, the Veer Offense, and the Game of the Century* (College Station: Texas A&M University Press, 2015), 3, 19.

first Houston sit-in: Howard Beeth and Cary D. Wintz, eds., *Black Dixie: Afro-Texan History and Culture in Houston* (College Station: Texas A&M University Press, 1992), 214.

shut out or limit the presence: Guridy, *Sports Revolution*, 83–84.

"In this country": George Vecsey, "Changing Planes to the Final Four," *New York Times*, March 26, 1982.

"He's the nicest": Gary Taylor, "'Akeem the Dream' Grows Toward Stardom," United Press International, May 28, 1981.

"He is young": "Lessons from Moses," Associated Press, March 18, 1982.

"Son, tonight": Vecsey, "Changing Planes."

explain the violation: Jacobson, "Story of Olajuwon."

This must be big: Fran Blinebury, "Naismith Basketball Hall of Fame: The Making of a Legend," *Houston Chronicle*, September 5, 2008.

Chapter 7: Slama

wouldn't even throw, "Throw him alley-oops": Clyde Drexler and Kerry Eggers, *Clyde the Glide: My Life in Basketball* (New York: Sports Publishing, 2004), 70.

"basketball's first": Kevin Sherrington, "Cougars' Big Guns Shoot Down Horns," *Houston Post*, February 16, 1983.

"I can go": David Moore, "SMU Flunks Test Against Houston, 105–71," *Fort Worth Star-Telegram*, January 9, 1983.

"How big is the biggest steak": Roy S. Johnson, "Houston Thrives with Inside Game," *New York Times*, March 25, 1983.

red Buick: Thomas Bonk, "Olajuwon Has All the Trappings of an NBA Superstar," *Los Angeles Times*, August 23, 1984.

"As members": Thomas Bonk, "Stuffs to Build Coogs' Dream On," *Houston Post*, January 3, 1983.

"fastest, quickest": Curry Kirkpatrick, "The Liege Lord of Noxzema," *Sports Illustrated*, November 28, 1983.

"I drop a dime": Curry Kirkpatrick, "The Big Brothers of Phi Slamma Jamma," *Sports Illustrated*, March 7, 1983.

pennies, "Keep your head," "mumbled something": Brad Buchholz, "Coogs Indulge Themselves After Revenge in Barnhill," *Austin American-Statesman*, March 5, 1983.

"A star?": Brad Buchholz, "Coogs Grab Midwest Crown," *Austin American-Statesman*, March 28, 1983.

"What's the name": David Moore, "Coogs Hitching a Ride as Olajuwon Spreads Wings," *Fort Worth Star-Telegram*, January 10, 1983.

"We could very well": Bill Lyon, "Olajuwon Now One of Nation's Top Big Men," Knight-Ridder News Service, March 28, 1983.

trouble finding a wife: Ken Denlinger, "Olajuwon Is an All-America—He Just Hasn't Been Named Yet," *Washington Post*, April 2, 1983.

"King Akeem": Fran Blinebury, "King Akeem," *Houston Chronicle*, April 1, 1983.

"Will anybody," "It has been like a dream": Mark Whicker, "Akeem's Dream: 'It Is Like Magic to Me,'" *Philadelphia Daily News*, March 29, 1983.

"he's living something: Steve Jacobson, "Akeem Cements His Future," *Newsday*, March 29, 1983.

"Akeem Abdul": Mike Littwin, "A Dream Is Coming True for Akeem," *Los Angeles Times*, March 11, 1984.

"Guys like that one": "Miller Sticks Foot in Mouth," *Austin American-Statesman*, January 24, 1984.

believed that he was too far, somebody else should have: Kevin Sherrington, "Akeem Found Loss More Than a Dream," *Houston Post*, April 8, 1983.

"I don't want to talk": Michael Madden, "Hesitation, Desperation," *Boston Globe*, April 5, 1983.

they'd discuss academics: Dave Anderson, "Basketball's New Force," *New York Times*, April 4, 1983.

"I want to play": Kevin Sherrington, "Soccer's Loss Is Coogs' Gain," *Houston Post*, March 23, 1983.

if he told his father: Fran Blinebury, "Akeem and the NBA," *Houston Chronicle*, April 20, 1983.

"People ask me": Blinebury, "King Akeem."

"When I didn't play that first year": Olajuwon, as told to Bob McSpadden, "Akeem," *Daily Cougar*, 1984.

Chapter 8: Next

etched in his mind, "There was this Olajuwon": Jonathan Abrams, "Out of Africa," *Grantland*, March 22, 2013.

"Basketball Recruiters": Peter Alfano, "Basketball Recruiters Now Journey to the Bush," *New York Times*, January 7, 1985.

"Now hold on," "say Goran Skoko 10 times fast": Jackie MacMullan, "A New Foreign Policy: Akeem? Uwe? Doron? Who Are These Guys?," *Boston Globe*, December 21, 1982.

Olajuwon's "a Nigerian," "foreigners": John Maher, "What's the Flap over Foreigners?," *Austin American-Statesman*, February 22, 1984.

"taking away": "NBA Scouting Director Likes What He Sees in the Middle," Associated Press, January 15, 1985.

didn't have an American, "Are these our national championships": Peter Alfano, "Foreigners Make Mark in an American Game," *New York Times*, December 9, 1984.

"It's a great game": Alfano, "Foreigners Make Mark."

"Get me a big man": Ed Grisamore, "All-World," *Macon (GA) Telegraph and News*, January 19, 1985.

"like the hula hoop": Peter Alfano, "The Import Impact: Tall Foreigners Invade U.S. College Basketball," *New York Times*, December 10, 1984.

"Well, I can't say": "Sports People; 'Dunk Diplomacy,'" *New York Times*, June 29, 1982.

reggae club, "In Nigeria": Peter King, "Akeem's Dream Is Nightmare of Triple Teaming," *Cincinnati Enquirer*, January 22, 1984.

"We haven't pressed": Remer Tyson, "Akeem: He's Living His Parents' Dream," *Detroit Free Press*, January 2, 1984.

"At the airport": Iyabo Obaleke, "Akeem, a Mother's Dream," *Guardian*, July 1, 1987.

"boyhood hero": Robert L. Miller, "Letter from the Publisher," *Sports Illustrated*, November 28, 1983.

arrested, detained: Michael E. Veal, *Fela: The Life & Times of an African Musical Icon* (Philadelphia: Temple University Press, 2000), 17.

"Akeem, get down here," half-dozen, "I couldn't score": "Olajuwon Guns Down Bird in One-on-One," Associated Press, July 10, 1983.

limousine, McDonald's: Ray Buck, "For Akeem, It's a Dream Come True," *Sporting News*, November 28, 1983.

"My life is not real": Mike Littwin, "A Dream Is Coming True for Akeem," *Los Angeles Times*, March 11, 1984.

wonder if it was really him, "Akeem, big guy," *How did he know*: John Feinstein, "Olajuwon Wants to Be Country's Best Center," *Washington Post*, November 23, 1983.

"[We] want you," "I'm like, 'Dear God!'": Mike Dougherty, "Ewing Gets Hall Call," *Journal News*, April 8, 2008.

Peter Tosh: Peter Alfano, "The Big Men Take Center Stage; Olajuwon Eager to Play," *New York Times*, April 2, 1984.

selfish: Peter Alfano, "Olajuwon Calls Team Selfish," *New York Times*, April 4, 1984.

Chapter 9: Towers

Jimmy Weston's bar: Filip Bondy, *Tip-Off: How the 1984 NBA Draft Changed Basketball Forever* (Philadelphia: Da Capo, 2007), xiii, xiv.

the Rockets were adamant: Mark Heisler, "Thinking Big in Texas," *Los Angeles Times*, October 24, 1984.

did discuss the trade briefly: Bondy, *Tip-Off*, 132.

well lit: Bondy, *Tip-Off*, 165–166.

shocked at the number of cameras: Amina Chaudary, interview with Hakeem Olajuwon for the *Islamic Monthly*, May 27, 2014, held at Olajuwon's home, transcript provided to the author by Chaudary on November 8, 2023.

"Thank God," "This is the best": Bondy, *Tip-Off*, 170.

"It's a completely different league": Roy S. Johnson, "The Union of Akeem and Ralph," *New York Times*, October 21, 1984.

people looked at him differently, blue Mercedes, "I'm still the same": Thomas Bonk, "Olajuwon Has All," *Los Angeles Times*, 1984.

Porsche 944: Fran Blinebury, "Akeem Starts Work with His New Team," *Houston Chronicle*, September 25, 1984.

afraid to approach him: Kevin Simpson, "Akeem-Ralph Formula Working—So Far," *Miami Herald*, October 29, 1984.

couldn't relate: Harry Hurt III, "Towers of Power," *Texas Monthly*, January 1985.

parents' blessing: "Akeem Eager to Join NBA," *Houston Chronicle*, June 17, 1984.

"He is quick-footed": Adekunle Olonoh, "The Dream Is Real: Akeem Olajuwon Is Shooting for Gold in America," *Punch*, September 2, 1984.

"a good ambassador": Banji Ola, "'The Dream' to Dunk for Nigeria If," *Punch*, June 27, 1987.

"he has made Nigeria": Phil Osagie, "Akeem Olajuwon Strikes Again," *Quality*, 1987.

"Akeem is indeed": Ben Edokpayi, "The Million Dollar Dream," *Quality*, July 1987.

"the young millionaires," "I think there's going to be a commandment": Jack McCallum, "Double Trouble, Houston Style," *Sports Illustrated*, November 5, 1984.

"Yes, I am seven feet four": Hurt III, "Towers of Power."

pulled the phone off the hook, a million dollars: David DuPree, "Agonies of Chase Spared Sampson," *Washington Post*, April 12, 1979.

helicopter ride, "Ralph's House": Roland Lazenby, *Sampson: A Life Above the Rim* (Roanoke, VA: Full Court, 1983), 116.

eight plays: "Akeem Learning Ropes," *Houston Post*, September 25, 1984.

***actual* back door:** Charles Leerhsen, John McCormick, and Daniel Shapiro, "Rampaging Rookies," *Newsweek*, November 26, 1984.

miniature doghouse: Jack McCallum, "They Can't Get off the Ground," *Sports Illustrated*, January 19, 1987.

"I want you," handcuffs: David Halberstam, *Playing for Keeps: Michael Jordan and the World He Made* (New York: Random House, 1999), 52.

Ivy League professor: David Halberstam, *The Breaks of the Game* (New York: Hyperion, 2009), 231.

"Footwork," right-footed, "Who taught you," "No one": Bruce Jenkins, *A Good Man: The Pete Newell Story* (Lincoln: University of Nebraska Press, 1999), 266–268.

thirty-five fouls, "The ball": Fran Blinebury, "Rockets Blast Past Mavs," *Houston Chronicle*, October 28, 1984.

Chapter 10: Different

trouble cracking the lineup: Fran Blinebury, "Akeem Not Nervous for Rocket-Jazz Opener Tonight," *Houston Chronicle*, April 19, 1985.

didn't know who Auerbach was: Roy S. Johnson, "The Union of Akeem and Ralph," *New York Times*, October 21, 1984.

"This place is a dump": Thomas Bonk, "Game 3; Garden vs. Forum: It's as Different as East and West," *Los Angeles Times*, June 2, 1985.

"It really doesn't seem real": Peter May, "Hot Rocket," *Hartford Courant*, February 10, 1985.

remind him to bring his coat: Jack McCallum, "Double Trouble, Houston Style," *Sports Illustrated*, November 5, 1984.

100 takes: *Denver Post*, February 7, 1986.

cashmere and linen: Joy Sewing, "Dream Fashion: Olajuwon Hopes to Score with New Clothing Line," *Houston Chronicle*, January 6, 2011.

forty-five tailor-made: Linda Gillan Griffin, "Style: Akeem Olajuwon Fitting in the Dream," *Houston Chronicle*, April 30, 1986.

"a new American hero": Jeff Denberg, "Akeem: Living an NBA Dream," *Atlanta Constitution*, May 29, 1986.

"Once a soccer player": *ABC World News Tonight*, Sunday, November 4, 1984.

"charming media novelty," "a model": Munene Franjo Mwaniki, *The Black Migrant Athlete: Media, Race, and the Diaspora in Sports* (Lincoln: University of Nebraska Press, 2017), 53–54.

Chapter 11: Shake

"putting [the ball] to the moon": Jack McCallum, "Towering Dream in Rocket Country," *Sports Illustrated*, February 10, 1986.

two people could start in the same spot: Michael Murphy, "He's Gazing on a Sunday Afternoon," *Houston Chronicle*, April 7, 1998.

one outfit: Lee Jenkins, "Houston's New Tower of Power: The Post Man Rings Twice," *Sports Illustrated*, October 28, 2013.

"I never really liked being a center": Chris Ballard, "Post Play Is a Lost Art in the NBA: What Happens to Those Who Still Believe in It?," *Sports Illustrated*, January 18, 2023.

"big African kid," 17,505: Jeff Pearlman, *Showtime: Magic, Kareem, Riley, and the Los Angeles Lakers Dynasty of the 1980s* (New York: Gotham, 2014), 281.

"Go to the beach": Pat Riley, *Showtime* (New York: Warner, 1988), 21.

if they had "tried to tie": Jack McCallum, "Big Rocket, Big Blast," *Sports Illustrated*, May 26, 1986.

punched Kersey, "who punched you": Jonathan Abrams, "The Greatest Team That Never Was," *Grantland*, November 8, 2012.

Walton scooped dirt: Dan Shaughnessy, *Wish It Lasted Forever: Life with the Larry Bird Celtics* (New York: Scribner, 2021), 195.

"ashamed": Jack McCallum, "The High and the Mighty," *Sports Illustrated*, June 9, 1986.

heart pounding: Shaughnessy, *Wish It Lasted Forever*, 217.

heart attack: Peter May, *The Last Banner: The Story of the 1985–86 Celtics, the NBA's Greatest Team of All Time* (New York: Simon & Schuster, 1996), 258.

changed his uniform: Larry Bird and Bob Ryan, *Drive: The Story of My Life* (New York: Bantam, 1989), 168.

Chapter 12: Pride

"I have a quick temper": Alan Truex, "Olajuwon Supplies the Punch," *Houston Chronicle*, February 3, 1988.

leading the league in technical fouls: Eddie Sefko, "Mirror Images; O'Neal's Talent, Attitude Resemble the Young Olajuwon," *Houston Chronicle*, January 10, 1994.

"love tap," nineteen violence-related incidents: Dave Anderson, "Sports of the Times: N.B.A. Must Get Tougher," *New York Times*, April 20, 1989.

knocked out cold, personal space: Terry Gross, "Hakeem Olajuwon Discusses," *Fresh Air*, 1996.

"reckless, undisciplined style": Jeff Denberg, "Akeem: Living an NBA Dream," *Atlanta Constitution*, May 29, 1986.

"being violent," "They were labeled": Theresa Runstedtler, *Black Ball: Kareem Abdul-Jabbar, Spencer Haywood, and the Generation That Saved the Soul of the NBA* (New York: Bold Type, 2023), 1, 13.

"Everybody is just out there playing": "Akeem: Rockets Don't Know Roles," *Houston Post*, March 23, 1988.

criticizing the playmaking, wasn't trying to bad-mouth: Richard Hoffer, "H as in Hot," *Sports Illustrated*, April 8, 1991.

"verbally abused": "Akeem Denies Clerk Hit," *Houston Chronicle*, May 2, 1986.

assaulted a TV cameraman, several stitches: Jim Carley, "TV Crew Says Olajuwon Took Tape," *Houston Post*, August 31, 1988.

Chapter 13: Darkness

insist that it was not a matter of trust: Amina Chaudary, interview with Hakeem Olajuwon for the *Islamic Monthly*, May 27, 2014, held at Olajuwon's home, transcript provided to the author by Chaudary on November 8, 2023.

didn't like to be told "no," take them out: Kenny Smith, *Talk of Champions: Stories of the People Who Made Me* (New York: Doubleday, 2023), 208.

misunderstood, slapping, "Do not disrespect me": Smith, *Talk of Champions*, 212.

spat, "Would you stop," locker room: Smith, *Talk of Champions*, 215.

threw a chair, breaking glass, intended to "stab" Olajuwon: Paul Kasabian, "Vernon Maxwell Says He Once Tried to Stab Hakeem Olajuwon During Halftime Fight," *Bleacher Report*, August 3, 2002.

breach of contract: Brenda Sapino, "Olajuwon Seeks to Be Declared Legal Father of Child," *Houston Post*, September 2, 1988.

promised to marry, forcing her to bear, "extreme mental anguish": "Woman's Lawsuit Claims Olajuwon Reneged on Promise to Marry Her," *Houston Post*, August 5, 1988.

a thousand dollars: Robert Falkoff, "Olajuwon Flatly Denies Drug Rumors," *Houston Post*, December 4, 1987.

"Dr. Jekyll": Fran Blinebury, "Dr. Jekyll and Mr. Olajuwon," *Houston Chronicle*, September 3, 1988.

"Akeem Wearing Out": Kenny Hand, "Akeem Wearing Out His Welcome," *Houston Post*, September 3, 1988.

"dark years": Ian O'Connor, "Hakeem Was No Dream," *New York Daily News*, January 25, 1996.

"Now you're an NBA player": "Hakeem Olajuwon Finds Balance of Sports and Religion," *CNN News*, May 17, 1995.

Chapter 14: Found

contemporary, Moroccan: Mike Newlin, "Between Rocket and Hard Place," *Houston Post*, March 31, 1991.

"Pride listens": John Powell, *Happiness Is an Inside Job* (Allen, TX: RCL Benziger, 1989), 21.

"Mr. Olajuwon . . . are you Muslim?": conversation and anecdote from interview with Ibrahim Arch. Olajuwon's memoir, *Living the Dream* (Boston: Little, Brown, 1996), 196–198, also details the encounter and adds further clarity about the exchange.

lost that foundation, didn't know where to find a mosque: Brad Buchholz, "Body and Soul," *Inside Sports*, May 1994.

attended church with friends: Terry Blount, "Dream Come True: Reawakened Olajuwon Comes Full Circle in a Year Likely to End in MVP Honors," *Houston Chronicle*, May 22, 1994.

why he hadn't seen him at the mosque: Amina Chaudary, interview with Hakeem Olajuwon for the *Islamic Monthly*, May 27, 2014, held at Olajuwon's home, transcript provided to the author by Chaudary on November 8, 2023.

hadn't known there was a nearby mosque, sound of the prayers: Olajuwon, *Living the Dream*, 196–198.

what was missing: Olajuwon, *Living the Dream*, 264.

shocked to see him, happiest days, He began to cry: Amina Chaudary, Hakeem Olajuwon interview, *That's Some American Life* podcast, from *Islamic Monthly*, provided to author by Chaudary in April 2023.

didn't have direction: Blount, "Dream Come True"; Terry Blount, "Star in Spirit," *Saudi Aramco*, July/August 1994, 18–19.

hadn't been as grateful: Mike Terry, "More Peaceful Olajuwon, More Formidable Rockets," *Washington Post*, January 13, 1994.

lacked patience: Blount, "Star in Spirit."

better person: Fran Blinebury, "From the Streets of Lagos, Nigeria, to NBA Greatness," *Houston Chronicle*, February 17, 2006.

"We didn't know," handful of Islamic books: Chaudary, *That's Some American Life* podcast.

asking how to handle: Buchholz, "Body and Soul."

Sheikh Mohammed Rashad Khalil, "be true": Chaudary, 2014 Olajuwon interview.

five pillars: Tariq Ramadan, *Introduction to Islam* (New York: Oxford University Press, 2017), 73–86.

never let the sun, most beautiful, beat his alarm: Eddie Sefko, "Olajuwon's Solace Lies in Islamic Faith: Pilgrimage to Mecca Transforms Life," *Houston Chronicle*, October 16, 1991.

work with someone, cassette, *ayat*: Buchholz, "Body and Soul."

memorize the verses, visit the home: Olajuwon, *Living the Dream*, 198.

"Basketball is not just a job now": Hank Hersch, "Stuff of Dreams," *Sports Illustrated*, June 6, 1994.

"I think I can throw," "What is the elbow?": Kenny Smith, *Talk of Champions: Stories of the People Who Made Me* (New York: Doubleday, 2023), 212.

"After this season": Associated Press, February 7, 1990.

Hermes or Chanel, he also realized just how attached: Chaudary, *That's Some American Life* podcast.

"From the artist": Alexander Wolff, "American Dream," *Sports Illustrated*, July 2, 2007.

noticed the city's architecture: Kate Murphy, "A Slam-Dunk in Houston Real Estate," *New York Times*, December 6, 2006.

prayer rugs: Buchholz, "Body and Soul."

"Akeem, if you ever," "you will": Smith, *Talk of Champions*, 211.

fish, most Americans struggled: Smith, *Talk of Champions*, 213.

didn't think the misspelling mattered, she would ask: "Olajuwon: Just Call Me Hakeem," *Chicago Tribune*, March 11, 1991.

"Oh, you who believe": Marc J. Spears, "Being Muslim in the NBA," *Undefeated*, October 17, 2017.

Chapter 15: Perspective

five minutes, heard many other pilgrims, different backgrounds: Hakeem Olajuwon, *Living the Dream* (Boston: Little, Brown, 1996), 208–209.

surprised, sixties, grateful: Eddie Sefko, "Olajuwon's Solace Lies in Islamic Faith: Pilgrimage to Mecca Transforms Life," *Houston Chronicle*, October 16, 1991.

"I began truly to appreciate," "You could almost breathe it": Olajuwon, *Living the Dream*, 210–211.

2:30 in the morning: Brad Buchholz, "Body and Soul," *Inside Sports*, May 1994.

giant wave, inner peace: Sefko, "Olajuwon's Solace."

determined to implement: Olajuwon, *Living the Dream*, 213.

"When he got into": Ed Fowler, "Hakeem's Character Unfailing," *Houston Chronicle*, May 26, 1994.

Vernon Maxwell: Kenny Smith, *Talk of Champions: Stories of the People Who Made Me* (New York: Doubleday, 2023), 217–218.

feel sorry: Olajuwon, *Living the Dream*, 214.

good and evil: Terry Blount, "Star in Spirit," *Saudi Aramco*, July/August 1994, 18–19.

part warrior: Buchholz, "Body and Soul."

"I was in darkness": Terry Blount, "Dream Come True: Reawakened Olajuwon Comes Full Circle in a Year Likely to End in MVP Honors," *Houston Chronicle*, May 22, 1994.

sand, traveling: Rudy Tomjanovich and Robert Falkoff, *A Rocket at Heart: My Life and My Team* (New York: Simon & Schuster, 1997), 72.

"I never knew": Tomjanovich and Falkoff, *Rocket at Heart*, 77.

helper, "I'm not even a first assistant": Tomjanovich and Falkoff, *Rocket at Heart*, 13.

welfare, shoemaker: Tomjanovich and Falkoff, *Rocket at Heart*, 29–30.

garbage, out drinking: John Feinstein, *The Punch: One Night, Two Lives, and the Fight That Changed Basketball Forever* (Boston: Little, Brown, 2002), 125.

If he doesn't win, perspective had shifted, "I want to be remembered": Olajuwon, *Living the Dream*, 216.

"My championship": Buchholz, "Body and Soul."

"Did you give," say he gave his best, if he was destined: Blount, "Dream Come True."

$3,170,000, $7,070,000: Hoops Hype, 1991–92 NBA Player Salaries, https://hoops hype.com/salaries/players/1991–1992.

questioning his integrity: Eddie Sefko, "Olajuwon, Rockets Trade Shots; Club Accuses Star of Feigning Injury," *Houston Chronicle*, March 22, 1992.

A doctor *had* cleared: "Olajuwon Suspended for His Failure to Play," *New York Times*, March 24, 1992.

"coward": "Hakeem Olajuwon: Space City Dream," *Houston Chronicle*, August 5, 2001.

"They said he was greedy": Jackie MacMullan, "Olajuwon Having a Dream Season with Rockets," *Boston Globe*, January 12, 1994.

heart no longer in Houston, asked for a trade: Olajuwon, *Living the Dream*, 229, 221.

Miami Heat was showed: Fran Blinebury, "Heat Is on Miami to Make Offer for Olajuwon," *Houston Chronicle*, June 12, 1992.

Lakers were allegedly: Eddie Sefko, "Spotlight Focuses on Olajuwon," *Houston Chronicle*, June 18, 1992.

Chapter 16: Clutch

four first-place MVP votes: Jack McCallum, "A Dream Come True," *Sports Illustrated*, March 22, 1993.

"I'm not fighting": Harvey Araton, "On Pro Basketball: Olajuwon's Fanciful Vision Is No Longer Merely a Texas-Size Dream," *New York Times*, November 18, 1993.

hugged each other: "Summit Winning Streak Comes to End," *Houston Chronicle*, February 7, 1993.

sit in first class: Robert Falkoff, "An MVP Dream," *Houston Post*, May 24, 1994.

"is a special season": Robert Falkoff, *DreamLand: The Inside Story of the '93–'94 Houston Rockets' Championship Season* (Houston: Gulf, 1994), 38.

posters of chickens, "Dear Rudy T": Falkoff, *DreamLand*, 127–128.

"It's not Choke City," "the Rockets aren't chokers": Rudy Tomjanovich and Robert Falkoff, *A Rocket at Heart: My Life and My Team* (New York: Simon & Schuster, 1997), 215.

"Basketball is a team sport": Falkoff, *DreamLand*, 145.

"grace and elegance": Hank Hersch, "Stuff of Dreams," *Sports Illustrated*, June 6, 1994.

Chapter 17: Ring

"They were never": Chris Herring, *Blood in the Garden* (New York: Atria, 2022), x.

"Patrick is my toughest": Bill Barnard, Associated Press, December 3, 1993.

"He's been a thorn": Mike Dougherty, "Ewing Gets Hall Call," *Journal News*, April 8, 2008.

never seen him play, talked about each player: "Olajuwon's Parents Watch Him Play in NBA Finals for the First Time," *Jet*, June 27, 1994.

discomfort, courtesy of Mason's physical play, pick-and-rolls: Herring, *Blood in the Garden*, 135.

"I've been hearing": Eddie Sefko, "'94 NBA Finals; Mason Laying It on Thick," *Houston Chronicle*, June 14, 1994.

ice chest, "If a team": Rudy Tomjanovich and Robert Falkoff, *A Rocket at Heart: My Life and My Team* (New York: Simon & Schuster, 1997), 221.

"Hakeem the Dream" sandwich: Robert Falkoff, *DreamLand: The Inside Story of the '93–'94 Houston Rockets' Championship Season* (Houston: Gulf, 1994), 169.

feel the pressure: Hakeem Olajuwon, *Living the Dream* (Boston: Little, Brown, 1996), 8.

"I took two dribbles": John Starks and Dan Markowitz, *My Life* (Sports Publishing, 2004), 167.

couldn't sleep, tried to think only positive, plastic: Olajuwon, *Living the Dream*, 10.

"God willing": Olajuwon, *Living the Dream*, 13.

Starks hadn't slept, haunted by the end of Game 6: Herring, *Blood in the Garden*, 143.

"It took such": Fran Blinebury, "Title Can't Slake Hakeem's Desire," *Houston Chronicle*, September 28, 1994.

"Houston": George Vecsey, "Sports of the Times: Houston Finally Has an Edge," *New York Times*, June 23, 1994.

"Dream! . . . I know you don't drink": Amina Chaudary, Hakeem Olajuwon interview, *That's Some American Life* podcast, from *Islamic Monthly*, provided to author by Chaudary in April 2023.

knew the effort: Ian O'Connor, "Ewing Can Reward the Faith of Hakeem," *New York Daily News*, January 18, 1995.

14 karat gold: Frank Isola, "Raising the Banner," *New York Daily News*, November 4, 1994.

"I will miss it": Amina Chaudary, interview with Hakeem Olajuwon for the *Islamic Monthly*, May 27, 2014, held at Olajuwon's home, transcript provided to the author by Chaudary on November 8, 2023.

Five hundred thousand: Mickey Herskowitz, "Ridin' the Title Wave," *Houston Post*, June 24, 1994.

Chapter 18: Discipline

binds the community: Reza Aslan, *No God but God: The Origins, Evolution, and Future of Islam* (New York: Random House, 2006), 148.

"I cannot do it": Eddie Sefko, "Rockets Summary," *Houston Chronicle*, February 27, 1993.

"When you are on the road": Michael Murphy, "Ramadan Inspires Olajuwon," *Houston Chronicle*, January 14, 1997.

camel: "Athlete's Fasting Puts a Spotlight on Islam," Associated Press, February 17, 1996.

"It is a way," discipline, oatmeal: Fran Blinebury, "Devotion to Islamic Laws Taxes Hakeem," *Houston Chronicle*, February 20, 1995.

ten pounds: Phil Taylor, "Try to Stop Him in Taking on Three Pivot Legends in One Week: Orlando's Shaquille O'Neal Rises to the Test," *Sports Illustrated*, March 13, 1995.

"There are 48": Gary Meenaghan, "Ramadan or Not, Hakeem Olajuwon Was a Dominant Force in NBA," *National News*, August 3, 2013.

"He's unsolvable": Michael A. Lutz, "Rockets 102, Bulls 86," Associated Press, January 20, 1997.

"To be able": David Moore, "NBA's Journey of Faith and Discipline," *Dallas Morning News*, January 27, 1997.

"Many people think": Mikal Saahir, "Hakeem Olajuwon on Islam, Fasting, Basketball, and Shoes," *Islamic Horizons*, March/April 1997.

"If only": "Athlete's Fasting."

"I had a burning": Blinebury, "Devotion to Islamic Laws."

fresh date: Shaker Samman, "'Things Are Going to Be Different Now,'" *Sports Illustrated*, September 10, 2021.

hotel bills: Fran Blinebury, "Pistons 96, Rockets 87," *Houston Chronicle*, February 7, 1997.

questions about how thirsty, "Before, you take it for granted": Moore, "NBA's Journey," *Dallas Morning News*, 1997.

"depleted": "Fasting Olajuwon Slows Bulls," Associated Press, January 20, 1997.

"unwillingness to rehydrate": Tim Green and Bob Edwards, "Professional Sport's Hakeem Olajuwon," *NPR Morning Edition*, February 11, 1997.

"When we travel": Samman, "'Things Are Going.'"

"dangerous fanatics": Arun Kundnani, *The Muslims Are Coming! Islamophobia, Extremism, and the Domestic War on Terror* (London: Verso, 2015), 44.

silent-cinema era, *The Sheik*: Fear, Faith and Fair Portrayals of Muslims, NPR, 13:59, www.npr.org/2017/01/26/511840473/fear-faith-and-fair-portrayals-of-muslims.

"Acute anti-Muslim bigotry": Roxanne Dunbar-Ortiz, *Not a Nation of Immigrants: Settler Colonialism, White Supremacy, and a History of Erasure and Exclusion* (Boston: Beacon, 2021), 222.

"Muslim hatred": Edward W. Said, *Covering Islam* (New York: Vintage, 1997), 84.

"Militant Islam": Said, *Covering Islam*, 85.

questioning its compatibility: John L. Esposito, *The Islamic Threat: Myth or Reality?*, 3rd ed. (New York: Oxford University Press, 1999), xvi.

"The Sword of Islam": *Boston Globe*, July 27, 1991.

"The Red Menace Is Gone": Said, *Covering Islam*, xix.

"My role": "Athlete's Fasting."

"When I was playing": Amina Chaudary, "Interview with Hakeem Olajuwon," *Islamic Monthly*, August 23, 2014.

"He wasn't just The Dream": Monis Khan, "Hakeem Olajuwon's Five Most Impressive Ramadan Performances," *Undefeated*, May 24, 2018.

Chapter 19: Heart

Maxwell . . . allegedly punched a fan: "NBA Comes Down Hard on Maxwell for Punching Fan," Associated Press, February 8, 1995.

"All these years": Fran Blinebury, "Title Shortfalls Leave Clyde with Unfinished Business," *Houston Chronicle*, February 17, 1995.

"In my wildest dreams": Eddie Sefko, "The Trade: Clyde Glides Home," *Houston Chronicle*, February 15, 1995.

anti-inflammatory medicine: Moore, "NBA's Journey," *Dallas Morning News*, 1997.

"You must believe": Fran Blinebury, "3–1 Deficit a Test for True Believers," *Houston Chronicle*, May 16, 1995.

"We got them": "Chucky Brown on Jordan, Larry Bird, Olajuwon, Kareem and Much More," podcast, BTM Legends Corner, January 16, 2020.

"Who in the hell": Fran Blinebury, "Truly an MVP for All Seasons," *Houston Chronicle*, May 25, 1995.

"Oh, it's just a move": Michael Murphy, "The Dream Shake: Legendary, Elusive Move Earns Place in History," *Houston Chronicle*, May 28, 1995.

"You don't solve": Jonathan Feigen, "Robinson Learning Olajuwon," *Houston Chronicle*, May 29, 1995.

"I actually thought": Paul Attner, "Double Time," *Sporting News*, 1995.

"unreal": Jim Litke, "Kareem to Shaqeem: Look Out for Hakeem," Associated Press, June 7, 1995.

"I've never seen," grabbed Drexler's arm: Ed Fowler, "Hakeem Displays Uncommon Grace," *Houston Chronicle*, June 2, 1995.

"Where's Hakeem?": Leigh Montville, "The Stuff of Dreams with a Performance for the Ages: Hakeem Olajuwon Lifted His Rockets Back into the Finals," *Sports Illustrated*, June 12, 1995.

snuck in the back: Bob Baum, Associated Press, June 6, 1995.

"Hakeem's the best": Phil Taylor, "Try to Stop Him in Taking on Three Pivot Legends in One Week: Orlando's Shaquille O'Neal Rises to the Test," *Sports Illustrated*, March 13, 1995.

"Happy feet": Phil Taylor, "High and Mighty," *Sports Illustrated*, June 19, 1995.

"Relax," "I thought he was kidding": Johnette Howard, "Sam I Am with Teammates, Foes and Refs," *Sports Illustrated*, November 13, 1995.

"You got one!": Scoop Jackson, "Deuce Is Wild!," *SLAM*, September 1995.

"I have one," "I don't have": Jonathan Feigen, "Two-rrific!: Rockets Win Back-to-Back NBA Crowns, Sweep Magic," *Houston Chronicle*, June 5, 1995.

"torture chamber": Scoop Jackson, "The Next Level," *SLAM*, September 1995.

"That's called paying": Jackie MacMullan, "Icons Club: Shaq and Kobe," podcast, *Ringer*, April 8, 2022.

"I'm not allowed": Jonathan Feigen, "MVP, Again: Olajuwon Shifted into Another Gear for Playoff Joy Ride," *Houston Chronicle*, June 16, 1995.

"I'm happy": Clifton Brown, "1995 N.B.A. Playoffs: Olajuwon Plays Above the Rim, in the Stratosphere," *New York Times*, June 6, 1995.

Chapter 20: Citizen

"We cannot have people": Jere Longman, "Pro Basketball; Olajuwon Ineligible for U.S. in Games," *New York Times*, December 3, 1993.

"It feels more": Fran Blinebury, "Hakeem Has MVP Character 3," *Houston Chronicle*, February 21, 1993.

months of appealing: Eddie Sefko and Fran Blinebury, "Olympic Spot a Dream Come True," *Houston Chronicle*, June 26, 1995.

"There's no place": Eddie Sefko, "Hakeem Becomes U.S. Citizen," *Houston Chronicle*, April 3, 1993.

difficult, even painful: Fran Blinebury, "Atlanta '96; Olympics; Hakeem Olajuwon; American Dream," *Houston Chronicle*, July 14, 1996.

"Drug traffickers," "Being an American," "I have a different," "I hear": Blinebury, "Atlanta '96."

"The decision [to play for Team USA]": Joshua-Akanji, "Hakeem Olajuwon: End of the Dream?," *National Interest*, November 5, 2000.

"The potential": Frank Deford, "A Remarkable Journey," *Real Sports with Bryant Gumbel*, HBO, February 29, 1996.

never apply, chided him: "Atlanta Games," *Atlanta Journal and Constitution*, July 11, 1996.

"There are only," "He is so busy," "My cause is not": Michael Murphy, "Olajuwon Sets Record Straight," *Houston Chronicle*, February 25, 1997.

"Being a good citizen," "I would never deny": Blinebury, "Atlanta '96."

"For Nigerians": Chido Nwangwu, "For Nigerians, Hakeem Is Beyond Basketball," *Houston Chronicle*, June 7, 1995.

ten thousand: Norma Martin, "Pride and Fear; Nigerians Here Say Heroin Cases Wrongly Tarnish Image," *Houston Chronicle*, February 9, 1992.

Mou Zuoyun, "I look forward": Brook Larmer, *Operation Yao Ming* (New York: Gotham, 2005), 111.

a third of NBA teams: Ben Rohrbach, "Luka Doncic, Killian Hayes, Deni Avdija, and the Evolution of the International NBA prospect," Yahoo.com, November 18, 2020.

"Down through," "As I continued": Fran Blinebury, "Olajuwon Opens Up Doors of NBA to World of Talent," *Houston Chronicle*, October 28, 1994.

154 international players, "I've had 15": William C. Rhoden, "Foreign Players, American Courts: A Special Report," *New York Times*, May 28, 1990.

"They approached": Jack McCallum, *Dream Team* (New York: Ballantine, 2013), xxii.

Nelson Mandela: author's interview with Kim Bohuny, as well as Lindsay Krasnoff, "Interview with Kim Bohuny," in *Basketball Diplomacy in Africa: An Oral History, from SEED Project to the Basketball Africa League (BAL)*, May 2020.

sleeping on floors: Bruce Arthur, "The Promised Land," *Toronto Star*, June 15, 2019.

"These are Hakeem's": Phil Taylor, "Dream's Team in His Debut on a U.S. National Squad," *Sports Illustrated*, July 20, 1996.

awestruck grandson: "Atlanta '96; Olympics; Notebook," *Houston Chronicle*, July 24, 1996.

Chapter 21: Business

$200: Gabriel Baumgaertner, "How Hakeem Olajuwon Tried and Failed to Stop the 90s Sneaker Killings," *Guardian*, May 29, 2015.

"How can a poor": "One Basketball Superstar Endorses Real-World Shoes," *Democrat and Chronicle*, November 13, 1995.

traveled to factories, "The big companies": Mikal Saahir, "Hakeem Olajuwon," *Islamic Horizons*, 1997.

never gained mainstream: Baumgaertner, "How Hakeem Olajuwon Tried."

"Where are his cheeseburger," "Madison Avenue": Richard Sandomir, "The Media Business; Advertising; For Houston's Dignified Superstar, It's a Whole New Transition Game," *New York Times*, June 15, 1995.

"After all his years": Fran Blinebury, "Rockets vs. Suns; Calls Sacred, According to Hakeem," *Houston Chronicle*, May 11, 1995.

Visa, "It is my favorite": Fran Blinebury, "Atlanta '96; Olympics; Hakeem Olajuwon; American Dream," *Houston Chronicle*, July 14, 1996.

"You wonder why advertisers": Michael Myerson, "'Dream' as Pitchman," *New York Times*, June 23, 1995.

half a ton, red granite: Jonathan Feigen, *100 Things Rockets Fans Should Know & Do Before They Die* (Chicago: Triumph, 2018), 256.

"flames for a new," "To Muslims who": "Sports Shoe Logo Angers Muslims; Olajuwon Backs Group Seeking Nike Apology," *Houston Chronicle*, April 10, 1997.

Foot Locker, "How do you define": Michael Sokolove and Nita Lelyveld, "A Sneaker Bargain Teens Aren't Buying," *Philadelphia Inquirer*, December 22, 1995.

make as much: Kate Murphy, "A Slam-Dunk in Houston Real Estate," *New York Times*, December 6, 2006.

"I am at": Fran Blinebury, "Olajuwon Quietly Gets the Job Done," *Houston Chronicle*, April 16, 1997.

Jay-Z, *look*, "Every word," footwork: Steve Francis, "I Got a Story to Tell," *Player's Tribune*, March 8, 2018.

relearn running: Fran Blinebury, "Hakeem Takes Some Advice, Runs with It," *Houston Chronicle*, February 13, 1999.

straighter, half a lap, "I don't know": Jonathan Feigen, "Pro Basketball; A Dream Come True: New Training Regimen Puts Olajuwon in Tiptop Condition," *Houston Chronicle*, November 21, 1998.

"Doubt me": Fran Blinebury, "Olajuwon Says He Still Can Provide What Rockets Need," *Houston Chronicle*, August 3, 1998.

"Looking old," "That's 25,000": Jonathan Feigen, "Houston Has Been Dream for Hakeem," *Houston Chronicle*, May 4, 1999.

Wow. That Guy: Pete McEntegart, "4 Toronto Raptors Surrounded by a Young and Deep Supporting Cast, Hakeem Can Dream About Another Shot at a Championship," *Sports Illustrated*, October 29, 2001.

***That is my move*, "I have not lost it":** Michael Murphy, "Dancing Lessons; Olajuwon Labors to Regain Footwork on Signature Moves," *Houston Chronicle*, February 10, 1999.

restricted the flow, "for a while": Michael A. Lutz, "Doctors: Olajuwon Should Stop Playing Basketball 'for a While,'" Associated Press, March 22, 2000.

"I was deep": Fran Blinebury, "Dream Isn't Over for Rockets' Star," *Houston Chronicle*, December 19, 1999.

turned down the deal: Michael A. Lutz, "Raptors Eye Olajuwon but Rockets Say No," Associated Press, June 29, 1999.

learn about by reading, "Common courtesy," "I can't picture," "I guess": Fran Blinebury, "Rockets Let Go of the Trigger," *Houston Chronicle*, June 30, 1999.

blood clot: Michael Graczyk, "Blood Disorder Puts Olajuwon on Sideline: Career May Be Over," Associated Press, March 13, 2001.

"Sometimes [it] was a bit": Dave Anderson, "Namath Is Retiring from Pro Football," *New York Times*, January 25, 1978.

"this has really torn": Michael A. Lutz, "Rockets Owner Says Olajuwon to Be Traded to Toronto Raptors," Associated Press, August 1, 2001.

difficult decision, "Toronto realized": "Decision to Leave Rockets Difficult, Olajuwon Says," *Florida Today*, August 3, 2001.

Chapter 22: Toronto

"Please," "My reaction," "Please, don't put," "I heard the same": Fran Blinebury, "Olajuwon, a Muslim, Appeals to Reason," *Houston Chronicle*, September 17, 2001.

nearly three thousand lives: Corey Kilgannon, "With Bowed Heads, Americans Reflect on 9/11 and Its Aftermath," *New York Times*, September 11, 2021.

Sikh men: Laila Lalami, *Conditional Citizens* (New York: Pantheon, 2020), 14.

27 percent: Federal Bureau of Investigation, "Hate Crime Statistics, 2001."

1,200 Muslims, detained: Deepa Kumar, *Islamophobia and the Politics of Empire: 20 Years After 9/11* (London: Verso, 2021), 153.

"a wide range of signifiers": Nadine Naber, "Look, Muhammed the Terrorist Is Coming!," in *Race and Arab Americans Before and After 9/11*, eds. Amaney Jamal and Nadine Naber (Syracuse, NY: Syracuse University Press, 2008), 278.

"racing religion": Moustafa Bayoumi, "Racing Religion," *New Centennial Review* 6, no. 2 (Fall 2006): 267–293.

"To be sure": Kumar, *Islamophobia*, 7.

firebombed: Kelly Egan, "Muslims Endure Ugly Backlash," *Ottawa Citizen*, September 14, 2001.

Samaj Temple: Fatima Najm, "In the Shadow of Terror," *Eyeopener*, September 19, 2001.

windows shattered: April Lindgren, "Canadian Muslims Suffering Worst Hostility Ever," Southam Newspapers, September 15, 2001.

"Arabic-sounding": Egan, "Muslims Endure."

beaten at a bus stop, "Is tolerance": Lisa Gregoire, "CSIS More Concerned *for* Than Concerned *About* Local Arabs," *Edmonton Journal*, September 21, 2001.

"If I had a gun," "I hope you," worst-ever outbreak, "nowhere": Lindgren, "Canadian Muslims."

"Each one of us," fire-code, "assist": Sutton Eaves, "'The Dream' Guards Against Attacks on Muslims," *Eyeopener*, January 9, 2002.

"Speaking for the Muslim": Lori Ewing, "Olajuwon Adjusting to New Life in Toronto," *CBC Sports*, September 29, 2001.

student lounges, wrote that Friday prayer: Stephanie Cesca, "Basketball Star Backs Bid for Student Prayer Room," *Toronto Star*, December 7, 2001.

"You feel like": Shaker Samman, "'Things Are Going to Be Different Now,'" *Sports Illustrated*, September 10, 2021.

"The demand": Lalami, *Conditional Citizens*, 16.

"We are . . . always": Lalami, *Conditional Citizens*, 47.

needed a mosque: Abdussalam Nakua, a senior executive within the Muslim Association of Canada (MAC), told this anecdote to the author and mentioned that he was recounting information he had been told from those directly involved; he had not yet begun working for MAC.

convinced he could be: Jonathan Feigen, "Dream's Time with Raptors Was Cathartic," *Houston Chronicle*, October 13, 2002.

instrumental in recruiting: Doug Smith, "Carter Helps Woo Teammates," *Toronto Star*, August 1, 2001.

"Coming here": Pete McEntegart, "4 Toronto Raptors Surrounded by a Young and Deep Supporting Cast, Hakeem Can Dream About Another Shot at a Championship," *Sports Illustrated*, October 29, 2001.

"the Olajuwon experiment": Doug Smith, "Dream Fades Out of Raps' Picture," *Toronto Star*, October 1, 2002.

"I don't look": Michael A. Lutz, "Olajuwon Moved by Fans' Celebration of His Retirement," Associated Press, November 10, 2002.

Chapter 23: Ambassador

house in Jordan, "the simplicity," the Call, "My children can," "If you believe," lived to their nineties: all from Amina Chaudary, interview with Hakeem Olajuwon for the *Islamic Monthly*, May 27, 2014, held at Olajuwon's home, transcript provided to the author by Chaudary on November 8, 2023.

background, beliefs: "Hakeem Olajuwon, This Is Your Wife," Associated Press, August 13, 1996.

he knew all the names: Lindsay Krasnoff, "Interview with Amadou Gallo Fall," in *Basketball Diplomacy in Africa: An Oral History, from SEED Project to the Basketball Africa League (BAL)*, May 2020.

sixty-five players: Daniel Eisenberg, "The NBA's Global Game Plan," *Time*, March 9, 2003.

"The Foreign": Dan McGraw, "The Foreign Invasion of the American Game," *Village Voice*, May 27, 2003.

"stop thinking": Chris Ballard, "Giants of Africa: Masai Ujiri's Summer of Going Back and Giving Back," *Sports Illustrated*, September 23, 2019.

satellite views: Kate Murphy, "A Slam-Dunk in Houston Real Estate," *New York Times*, December 6, 2006.

"Islam is about": Alexander Wolff, "American Dream," *Sports Illustrated*, July 2, 2007.

Chapter 24: Mentor

favorite Qur'an verses: Chris Ballard, "Post Play Is a Lost Art in the NBA: What Happens to Those Who Still Believe in It?," *Sports Illustrated*, January 18, 2023.

pivoting on the balls: Fran Blinebury, "Olajuwon to Pass Skills to Big Men in First Camp," *Houston Chronicle*, August 3, 2006.

first fake: Chris Palmer, "Kobe, Howard Learned from Olajuwon," ESPN, March 1, 2011.

"salt in his goatee": Lee Jenkins, "Houston's New Tower of Power: The Post Man Rings Twice," *Sports Illustrated*, October 28, 2013.

"You always have to improve": David DuPree, "Olajuwon: Higher-Powered," *USA Today*, March 7, 1997.

"I was curious": Palmer, "Kobe, Howard."

prank, "Kobe, come on": Jenkins, "Houston's New Tower."

80 percent: Mike Bresnahan, "So Far, Artest Is Not Part of Circus," *Los Angeles Times*, October 1, 2009.

fastest learner: Ballard, "Post Play."

videotapes, four steps, "When I watch": Palmer, "Kobe, Howard."

"Kobe is a genius": Mark Medina, "Inside the Lakers: Hakeem Olajuwon Marvels at Kobe Bryant's Post Moves," *Inside the Lakers*, September 7, 2013.

walked him through: Palmer, "Kobe, Howard."

time off, *maybe one day he could play*: Brook Larmer, *Operation Yao Ming* (New York: Gotham, 2005), 113–114.

aside at half-court: video provided by Jim Petersen.

Epilogue

"I want to be Olajuwon": Jordan Ritter Conn, "Started from Yaoundé, Now He's Here," *Grantland*, June 27, 2014.

"I'm not predicting": Kelli Anderson, "Like a Dream," *Sports Illustrated*, March 24, 2014.

225 million people: "Nigeria Population," Worldometers, www.worldometers.info/world-population/nigeria-population.

median age on the African continent: Declan Walsh, "The World Is Becoming More African," *New York Times*, October 28, 2023.

BIBLIOGRAPHY

Abdul-Rauf, Mahmoud, and Nick Chiles. *In the Blink of an Eye: An Autobiography.* New York: Kaepernick Publishing, 2022.

Achebe, Chinua. *There Was a Country: A Memoir.* New York: Penguin, 2012.

Al-Hakim Al-Mustadrak, *Hadith.* Beirut: Dar Al Kotob Al Ilmiyah, 2012.

Aslan, Reza. *No God but God: The Origins, Evolution, and Future of Islam.* New York: Random House, 2006.

Beeth, Howard, and Cary D. Wintz, eds. *Black Dixie: Afro-Texan History and Culture in Houston.* College Station: Texas A&M University Press, 1992.

Bird, Larry, and Bob Ryan. *Drive.* New York: Bantam, 1989.

Bondy, Filip. *Tip-Off: How the 1984 NBA Draft Changed Basketball Forever.* Philadelphia: Da Capo, 2007.

Campbell, John, and Matthew T. Page. *Nigeria: What Everyone Needs to Know.* Oxford: Oxford University Press, 2018.

Candembo, Silva. *Breve História de Angola nos AFROBASKET's 1980–2005.* Luanda, Angola: Editora Semanário Angolense Luanda, 2007.

Collins, John. *West African Pop Roots.* Philadelphia: Temple University Press, 1992.

Drexler, Clyde, and Kerry Eggers. *Clyde the Glide: My Life in Basketball.* New York: Sports Publishing, 2004.

Dunbar-Ortiz, Roxanne. *Not a Nation of Immigrants: Settler Colonialism, White Supremacy, and a History of Erasure and Exclusion.* Boston: Beacon, 2021.

Esposito, John L. *Islam: The Straight Path,* 5th ed. Oxford: Oxford University Press, 2016.

Esposito, John L. *The Islamic Threat: Myth or Reality?* New York: Oxford University Press, 1999.

Falkoff, Robert. *Dreamland.* Houston: Gulf, 1994.

Faloyin, Dipo. *Africa Is Not a Country: Notes on a Bright Continent.* New York: W. W. Norton, 2022.

Feigen, Jonathan. *100 Things Rockets Fans Should Know & Do Before They Die.* Chicago: Triumph, 2018.

Feinstein, John. *The Punch: One Night, Two Lives, and the Fight That Changed Basketball Forever.* Boston: Little, Brown, 2002.

Guridy, Frank Andre. *The Sports Revolution: How Texas Changed the Culture of American Athletics.* Austin: University of Texas Press, 2021.

Halberstam, David. *The Breaks of the Game.* New York: Alfred A. Knopf, 1981.

Halberstam, David. *Playing for Keeps.* New York: Random House, 1999.

Haleem, Abdel M.A.S. *The Qur'an: A New Translation*. New York: Oxford University Press, 2016.

Herring, Chris. *Blood in the Garden*. New York: Atria, 2022.

Ibn Kathir, Ismail bin Umar al-Damishqi Abu al-Fida. "Comprehensive of the Musnads and Sunnahs, Leading to the Best Practices." In *Hadith* 8540, vol. 7. Beirut: Dar Al Kotob Al Ilmiyah, 2012.

Jacobus, Robert D. *Houston Cougars in the 1960s: Deep Threats, the Veer Offense, and the Game of the Century*. College Station: Texas A&M University Press, 2015.

Jenkins, Bruce. *A Good Man: The Pete Newell Story*. Lincoln: University of Nebraska Press, 1999.

Krasnoff, Lindsay. *Basketball Diplomacy in Africa: An Oral History, from SEED Project to the Basketball Africa League (BAL)*. May 2020.

Kumar, Deepa. *Islamophobia and the Politics of Empire: 20 Years After 9/11*. London: Verso, 2021.

Kundnani, Arun. *The Muslims Are Coming!* London: Verso, 2015.

Lalami, Laila. *Conditional Citizens*. New York: Pantheon, 2020.

Larmer, Brook. *Operation Yao Ming*. New York: Gotham, 2005.

Lazenby, Roland. *Sampson: A Life Above the Rim*. Roanoke, VA: Full Court, 1983.

MacMullan, Jackie, Rafe Bartholomew, and Dan Klores. *Basketball: A Love Story*. New York: Crown Archetype, 2018.

Maier, Karl. *The House Has Fallen: Nigeria in Crisis*. London: Penguin, 2000.

May, Peter. *The Last Banner: The Story of the 1985–86 Celtics, the NBA's Greatest Team of All Time*. New York: Simon & Schuster, 1996.

McCallum, Jack. *Dream Team: How Michael, Magic, Larry, Charles, and the Greatest Team of All Time Conquered the World and Changed the Game of Basketball Forever*. New York: Ballantine, 2013.

McGregor, Jim, and Ron Rapoport. *Called for Traveling*. New York: MacMillan, 1978.

Mwaniki, Munene Franjo. *The Black Migrant Athlete: Media, Race, and the Diaspora in Sports*. Lincoln: University of Nebraska Press, 2017.

Naber, Nadine. "Look, Muhammed the Terrorist Is Coming!" In *Race and Arab Americans Before and After 9/11*, eds. Amaney Jamal and Nadine Naber, 276–303. Syracuse, NY: Syracuse UP, 2008.

Okri, Ben. *A Way of Being Free*. London: Head of Zeus, 2014.

Olajuwon, Hakeem. *Living the Dream*. Boston: Little, Brown, 1996.

Ostler, Scott, and Steve Springer. *Winnin' Times: The Magical Journey of the Los Angeles Lakers*. New York: Macmillan, 1986.

Nance, Marilyn. *Last Day in Lagos*. Ed. Oluremi C. Onabanjo. Johannesburg, South Africa: Fourthwall, 2022.

Pearlman, Jeff. *Showtime: Magic, Kareem, Riley, and the Los Angeles Lakers Dynasty of the 1980s*. New York: Gotham, 2014.

Pokyes, Kavwam. *The Man 80–80 @ Eighty: An Adventurous Life*. Jos, Nigeria: Nyango, 2020.

Powell, John. *Happiness Is an Inside Job*. Allen, TX: RCL Benziger, 1989.

Ramadan, Tariq. *Introduction to Islam*. New York: Oxford University Press, 2017.

Riley, Pat. *Showtime*. New York: Warner, 1988.

Runstedtler, Theresa. *Black Ball: Kareem Abdul-Jabbar, Spencer Haywood, and the Generation That Saved the Soul of the NBA*. New York: Bold Type, 2023.

Russell, Bill. *Go Up for Glory*. New York: Coward-McCann, 1966.

Said, Edward. *Covering Islam*. New York: Vintage, 1997.

Shaughnessy, Dan. *Wish It Lasted Forever: Life with the Larry Bird Celtics*. New York: Scribner, 2021.

Smith, Kenny. *Talk of Champions: Stories of the People Who Made Me*. New York: Doubleday, 2023.

Starks, John, and Dan Markowitz. *My Life*. Champaign, IL: Sports Publishing, 2004.

Tomjanovich, Rudy, and Robert Falkoff. *A Rocket at Heart: My Life and My Team*. New York: Simon & Schuster, 1997.

Veal, Michael E. *Fela: The Life & Times of an African Musical Icon*. Philadelphia: Temple University Press, 2000.

Vecsey, George. *Harlem Globetrotters*. New York: Scholastic, 1970.

Verderame, Sal "Red." *Basketball in Africa*. New York: Pyramid, 1967.

Warner, Barry. *Off the Top of My Bald Head*. Self-published, 2022.

Witherspoon, Kevin B. "'An Outstanding Representative of America': Mal Whitfield and America's Black Sports Ambassadors in Africa." In *Defending the American Way of Life: Sport, Culture, and the Cold War*, eds. Toby C. Rider and Kevin B. Witherspoon, 129–140. Fayetteville: University of Arkansas Press, 2018.

Wolff, Alexander. *Big Game, Small World: A Basketball Adventure*, 20th anniversary ed. Durham, NC: Duke University Press, 2022.

INDEX